TANGWEERA
Life and Adventures among Gentle Savages

UPPER SETTLEMENT, TOONGLA RIVER.

TANGWEERA
Life and Adventures among Gentle Savages

by
C. Napier Bell

Introduction by
Philip A. Dennis

UNIVERSITY OF TEXAS PRESS, AUSTIN

International Standard Book Number
0-292-78066-4 (clothbound); 0-292-78103-2 (paperback)
Library of Congress Catalog Card Number 88-50777
Copyright © 1989 by the University of Texas Press
All rights reserved
Printed in the United States of America

Requests for permission to reproduce material from this work
should be sent to Permissions, University of Texas Press,
Box 7819, Austin, Texas 78713-7819.

This edition of *Tangweera* was printed from the Edward Arnold
1899 first edition.

INTRODUCTION

PHILIP A. DENNIS

IN THE 1980s, the conflicts of eastern Nicaragua's Miskito people with the Sandinista government have received international attention. The underlying dynamic in these conflicts has been an attempt by the Miskito to defend their own cultural autonomy and their land rights, while receiving military support from a U.S. government intent on overthrowing the Sandinista government (see Diskin et al. 1986; CIDCA 1987). However, the basic Miskito antagonism toward Spanish-speaking Nicaraguans has considerable historical depth. Close ties between the Miskito and English-speaking foreigners have existed for several hundred years, and the modern Sandinistas are simply the most recent "Spaniards" to bring their own political aspirations to the Miskito Coast. In understanding current events, the rich ethnohistorical literature on the Miskito is extremely useful. Among the many English-speaking buccaneers, travelers, and traders who visited the coast over the years, several (M. W. 1732; Roberts 1965) left substantial written contributions.

Certainly, one of the best sources for Miskito ethnohistory is this wonderful book by C. Napier Bell, originally published in 1899 and long out of print. Bell was an English boy who grew up on the Miskito Coast among black creole and Miskito people, spoke the Miskito language fluently, and was a careful observer of all he saw and experienced. His writing has a ring of authenticity to anyone who has ever visited the coast. Many details bring back vivid memories from my own fieldwork. For example, even today travel on the coast isn't much easier than it was in the mid 1800s, and Bell's adventures at sea in small boats and his exhausting trips up rivers and along forest trails sound completely modern (see also Nietschmann 1979). Today Miskito women continue to observe menstrual taboos (p. 165); supernaturals, such as the *wari dawanka* and the *wahiwin,* are still feared; and a hysterical condition caused by spirit possession still affects Miskito women (p. 97; Dennis 1981).

Bell lived on the coast at a time of waning British influence. A series of wars between Spain and Britain, in which the Miskito were staunch English allies, had ended in 1786 with the Anglo-Spanish Convention (Floyd 1967). According to the agreement, English settlers would evacuate the coast, leaving the area open to Spanish colonization. The Miskito people, who recognized allegiance to their own kings as well as loyalty to the British, were hostile to Spanish settlement, however, and it was never successful. English traders, including such men as James Stanislaus Bell (C. Napier Bell's father), continued to operate on the coast in the early nineteenth century.

By mid-century, Americans were competing with the British for influence in eastern Nicaragua. After the 1849 gold rush in California, interest in building a transoceanic canal across Nicaragua was intense. The British were seen as adversaries, and a series of confrontations took place along the coast, including an incident in which an American warship bombarded and destroyed Greytown (Dozier 1985). For a brief period an American adventurer named William Walker and his band of frontier riflemen actually took over the government of Nicaragua. Bell witnessed and participated in some of these historical events, which he describes in the book. For example, he accompanied a British military expedition up the Río San Juan in 1848, in a continuation of hostilities with the Spanish; he visited British warships in the harbor at Greytown; he helped sell firewood to the American steamship companies transporting gold seekers up the Río San Juan on their way to California; and he had a personal encounter with William Walker himself.

In 1850 the Clayton-Bulwer Treaty attempted to end the British-American confrontation on the coast by guaranteeing that neither would have exclusive rights to a canal (Dozier 1985). In 1860, Britain signed the treaty of Managua with Nicaragua, guaranteeing a Miskito reservation and ending Britain's territorial pretentions on the coast. The Miskito were left in nominal political control although American commercial interests continued to grow. In 1894 a Nicaraguan army under General Zelaya "re-incorporated" the coast and deposed the last Miskito king, an event that Bell refers to in his Preface by noting "the once happy Indians [are] handed over to their old enemies, the Spaniards."

The Moravian missionaries had just arrived on the coast when Bell was living there. His work serves as a baseline from which we can note the profound changes in Miskito life that the missionaries introduced. For example, in Bell's day, houses of sawed lumber built on posts above the ground—a practical missionary innovation—were not yet common. An interesting practice that, as we learn from Bell, antedates the missionaries is the extreme modesty about exposure of the genital area among both men and women (p. 261), still characteristic of the Miskito. Although this custom undoubtedly gratified the missionaries, they disapproved of and worked hard to change a number of others. They waged war against the native shamans, or *sookia* (*sukia*), whose practices are well described by Bell (pp. 239–241), and today the remaining *sukia* must practice under considerable stigma. The missionaries also inveighed against plural marriages and against the great drinking festivals where gallons of fermented cassava beverage, called *mishla*, were consumed. After living in local communities for many years, the missionaries produced the first grammars and dictionaries of the Miskito language and successfully translated the Bible. With the "Great Awakening" of the 1880s they began to have considerable success in their campaigns to convert the Miskito (Helms 1971). By the 1980s the majority of the Miskito were Moravians, with the remainder divided among other Christian denominations. The conservative influence of the Moravian church extended to the political arena, as twentieth-century Moravian leaders preached against the dangers of Communism, particularly following the Cuban Revolution. Today every Miskito community has a Moravian church headed by a local Miskito lay pastor, or *sasmalkra*. In this broad network of lay pastors and local congregations, the Sandinista government encountered entrenched opponents to their social programs. In his own day, Bell found the Moravian attempts to convert his neighbors in Bluefields amusing (p. 27), little realizing how pervasive the Moravian influence on the coast was to become a century later.

A major theme of Bell's book is ethnic relations on the coast. As today, the Miskito people lived in coastal settlements from Bluefields north to near Black River in Honduras. There were also Miskito communities some distance up the Wanx, or Río Coco. The headwaters of the large rivers were occupied by other groups, including the Twaka, the Toongla, and the Smoos. These people lived in communal longhouses; hunted, fished, and cultivated small plots; and were visited by Bell to recruit mahogany workers. Today, the descendants of these forest Indian groups are generally lumped together as "Sumu," although their languages and ways of life have never been adequately studied. There seem to be two general language groups represented, Miskito and Sumu, with Twaka and Woolwa (Ulwa) being dialects of Sumu, and Toongla a dialect of Miskito. Bell describes Miskito as being widely spoken as a lingua franca in the region. In fact, the Miskito had expanded and prospered at the expense of their neighbors, benefiting from their position as middlemen between the British pirates, traders, and colonists on the coast and the various interior groups (Helms 1971). Bell describes in some detail the interesting trade pattern that existed, in which canoes, jaguar and deer skins, maize and plantains, and other items from the interior were traded for cloth, metal tools and fishhooks, salt, and other trade goods (p. 266). The Miskito king was the nominal ruler over the whole area and the interior groups were forced to pay yearly tribute to him. Prior to the nineteenth century the Miskito had also been slave raiders who traveled far up and down the coast capturing Indian slaves to sell to the Jamaica planters (Helms 1983). Bell describes the fear and apprehension in which the Miskito were held by these interior groups.

The creole, or black English-speaking peoples, were well established in Bell's time, with the largest population around Bluefields and Pearl Lagoon but with individuals up and down the coast. Bell, like Conzemius (1932), mentions a slave ship wrecked near Duckwarra (Dakura), whose survivors had contributed a strong creole admixture to the Miskito population between Dakura and Cape Gracias a Dios. Bell's racist comments about the "childish, simple-minded, faithful, affectionate" nature of blacks (p. 20 and elsewhere throughout the book), must be understood in a nineteenth-century context, a period when theories of biological determinism were widely accepted. In a similar vein Bell comments on the innocent simplicity of his Indian friends and even mentions that they are far inferior to whites in mental abilities (p. 307).

However, more important than Bell's racism, which was practically universal among nineteenth-century Europeans, was his liberal attitude in defending ways of life that he saw under attack by the European colonial system. Bell argues that the Indian cultures he knew were happier, more in tune with nature, and less crime ridden and violent than were "civilized" ones. In this romantic attitude toward native peoples, Bell also followed a strong current of thought in Europe, dating at least from the time of Rousseau. Bell's unique contribution was that his defense of native cultures was not based on the theoretical, secondhand understanding of them of Rousseau or of Engels and Marx. To the contrary, he knew the Miskito and the Sumu firsthand, from having lived among them and having shared their way of life for a significant part of his life. About native peoples in general, he argues that one has only to learn their language and live among them to understand that, in fact, they are as human as ourselves (p. 308). Bell, a nineteenth-century British colonial, thus seems to paraphrase Bronislaw Malinowski, the father of modern fieldwork in anthropology.

Bell was a remarkable ethnographer. His father had been named the guardian of the young Miskito king and his sisters in Bluefields, and the king became Bell's closest friend and playmate. Bell grew up speaking Miskito as well as he did English. He was a keen observer, curious about the people and the natural world around him, and at an early age he began taking notes and making sketches. He tells us that this book was written late in his life, after he had lived in many other parts of the world. It is interesting to compare it with a much earlier, more scientific article published not long after Bell left the coast (1862). In writing *Tangweera*, Bell tells us that his youthful sketches provided the details of natural history and ethnography and that it took him some ten years to organize them and to write the complete narrative. He sometimes slips into the present tense

(p. 267), as if he were re-creating a forty-year-old scene from his notes and memory.

Bell's attention to detail is remarkable. For instance, he provides the text of a Miskito love song and funeral dirge (p. 312), as recorded verbatim in his youth. Bell seems to have been a natural ethnographer whose curiosity provoked him to seek out interesting aspects of native culture. He went to a creole wake, where whites were not allowed, underneath the skirts of a woman he called Ma Patience (p. 30). He observed the *seecro* (*sikro*), or feast for the dead, of the Miskito (pp. 90–95), and he witnessed the whipping of the young people in Dakura for their "misbehavior" by the king's *quatmus* (pp. 278–282). Like Malinowski, Bell also lived long enough with local people to appreciate the difficulty of translating from one cultural world to another. He tells us that "the music produced cannot be described. To a European it would have no meaning until he is accustomed to it and has entered into the spirit of the whole performance, and then it acts on him as it does on the natives, filling them with a thrill of excitement and superstitious awe" (pp. 93–94). Because of its wealth of ethnographic data, observed and recorded at an early date by a person fluent in the language, the book is invaluable to those interested in contemporary Miskito culture.

As a young man, Bell worked with his father cutting mahogany, a job that required him to spend months in the interior forests with the Indian laborers he himself had recruited. Because he was the foreman, Bell's job was to rouse the Indian workers early and to visit each work party during the day to make sure there was no shirking, until the conch shell was blown at the end of the day (pp. 188–190). The laborers were not used to these plantation-style work habits, and Bell tells us it was a constant job to keep them at work. We see here the contrast between work in a subsistence economy and work in a wage-labor system. By the mid nineteenth century, the Miskito were already involved as wage earners in the world capitalist economy. In fact, many of the villages were periodically deserted during periods when all the able men left to work in some European enterprise. This paralleled a traditional pattern in which women, children, and old people were left behind in the coastal villages during the annual turtle fishing expeditions. Mahogany cutting in the nineteenth century was to be followed by gold mining, lumbering in the pine forests, banana raising, lobstering, and turtle fishing as economic enterprises run by outside capitalists in which the Miskito would contribute their wage labor. We see in Bell's book the beginning of the boom-and-bust economic cycles that would characterize the coast for the next 120 years. As Helms (1971) points out, the Miskito would feel rich when good wages were available and poor when the companies left and subsistence activities again became the only way to make a living. In the process, the coast's natural resources were exploited and often depleted, while most of the profits went to outsiders. Control over their own natural resources is in fact one of the major demands of the Miskito and the other *costeños* in their current negotiations with the Sandinista government.

Bell describes an idyllic coastal life of hunting, fishing, and trading, recounting adventures with jaguars and alligators and trips made with Indian companions. He provides us with detailed descriptions of mahogany cutting, turtle fishing, and other activities in which he participated. Throughout the book, he devotes great attention to the natural environment: the animal and plant life, the rainy and dry seasons, the rivers and forests. He obviously loved the Miskito Coast, and his descriptions of tropical rain storms, invasions of army ants, the habits of man-o'-war birds and coatis, and many other natural phenomena are quite simply superb. Bell's interest in the classification and habits of the animal life paralleled that of his Miskito companions, whose detailed knowledge of their environment continues to interest scholars (Nietschmann 1973; Dennis 1988). His descriptions of nature reflect a world seen not only through the eyes of a European naturalist but also through the eyes of a person who partially shared the Indian culture of his companions. These lyrical descriptions alone make the book worth reading today.

This book is, as its title suggests, a nostalgic reminiscence of a happy boyhood spent among "gentle savages." It will delight its modern readers, and the University of Texas Press is to be congratulated for making it available in this new facsimile edition.

JUNE 1988

REFERENCES CITED

BELL, CHARLES NAPIER
 1862 "Remarks on the Mosquito Territory, Its Climate, People, Productions, etc., etc., with a Map." *Journal of the Royal Geographical Society* 32:242–268.

CIDCA (Centro de Investigación y Documentación de la Costa Atlántica)
 1987 *Ethnic Groups and the Nation State: The Case of the Atlantic Coast of Nicaragua*. Stockholm: Department of Social Anthropology, University of Stockholm.

CONZEMIUS, EDUARD
 1932 *Ethnographical Survey of the Miskito and Sumu Indians of Honduras and Nicaragua*. Bureau of American Ethnology Bulletin, no. 106. Washington, D.C.: U.S. Government Printing Office.

DENNIS, PHILIP A.
 1981 "Grisi Siknis among the Miskito." *Medical Anthropology* 5(4):445–505.

1988   "Herbal Medicine among the Miskito of Eastern Nicaragua."
        Economic Botany 42(1): 16–28.

DISKIN, MARTIN, and THOMAS BOSSERT, SALOMÓN NAHMAD S.,
STÉFANO VARESE

1986   *Peace and Autonomy on the Atlantic Coast of Nicaragua: A Report
        of the LASA Task Force on Human Rights and Academic Freedom.*
        Pittsburgh: Latin American Studies Association.

DOZIER, CRAIG L.

1985   *Nicaragua's Mosquito Shore: The Years of British and American
        Presence.* University, Ala.: University of Alabama Press.

FLOYD, TROY S.

1967   *The Anglo-Spanish Struggle for Mosquitia.* Albuquerque: Uni-
        versity of New Mexico Press.

HELMS, MARY W.

1971   *Asang: Adaptations to Culture Contact in a Miskito Community.*
        Gainesville: University of Florida Press.

1983   "Miskito Slaving and Culture Contact: Ethnicity and Oppor-
        tunity in an Expanding Population." *Journal of Anthropological
        Research* 39(2): 179–197.

NIETSCHMANN, BERNARD

1973   *Between Land and Water: The Subsistence Ecology of the Miskito
        Indians, Eastern Nicaragua.* New York: Seminar Press.

1979   *Caribbean Edge: The Coming of Modern Times to Isolated People
        and Wildlife.* Indianapolis: Bobbs-Merrill Co.

ROBERTS, ORLANDO W.

1965   *Narrative of Voyages and Excursions on the East Coast and Inte-
        rior of Central America.* Gainesville: University of Florida
        Press. [Originally published 1827.]

W., M.

1732   "The Mosqueto Indian and His Golden River: Being a Famil-
        iar Description of the Mosqueto Kingdom of America." In *A
        Collection of Voyages and Travels*, ed. Awnsham Churchill,
        6: 285–298. London: J. Walthoe.

PREFACE

THIS book was written in my old age; but it is a record of my youth, passed among the gentle savages of Central America, amid the gorgeous scenery of the tropics—an ideal life for a boy, and such as not one boy in a million has ever enjoyed.

I may be allowed to say for myself that it is not every boy who could enjoy the wild and free life of the bush in the way I did; for it is in my experience that not every boy has such a love of nature, such a reverent awe of the great untrodden forests, or takes such an interest in the birds, beasts, insects and plants, as I did at that time of my life.

If I had written this book while I was a boy, it would have been a book for boys; but it will be perceived by readers that it partakes of the nature of both a boy's and a grown man's book, which is due to the way in which it has been written.

While I was a boy living in Central America, I incessantly wrote down what I saw and heard, so that when I left the country I had a great mass of notes, memoranda, and sketches. These lay untouched during a busy life of thirty years devoted to my profession of a Civil Engineer. At last, during a short period of leisure, I commenced to write out my notes, and to arrange them in book form; and during the last ten years, whenever I could steal an interval, I kept writing them out until I finished.

Now, whatever readers may think of this story of a boy's life among the savages—whether they condemn it as too tame and silly, or too pretentious and improbable—I can assure them that all is true and nothing exaggerated or invented.

I have never returned to that beautiful country, but I hear that the lovely scenery, and the peaceful, happy life of the Indians, is now disturbed and upturned by political and commercial changes. The silence, the sweet holy calm of those lovely rivers, is now outraged by the busy river-steamboat; the beautiful forest along their banks is felled and cleared to make room for plantations of bananas for the American market ; the once happy Indians, handed over to their old enemies, the Spaniards, are now worried to frenzy by taxes, and Catholic priests dispensing the dubious blessings of civilization, accompanied, as usual, by disease, demoralization and death.

C. NAPIER BELL, M.Inst.C.E.

Wellington, N.Z.

CONTENTS

INTRODUCTION.

CHAPTER I.

CHAPTER II.

CHAPTER III.

CHAPTER IV.

CHAPTER V.

CHAPTER VI.

CHAPTER VII.

LIST OF ILLUSTRATIONS

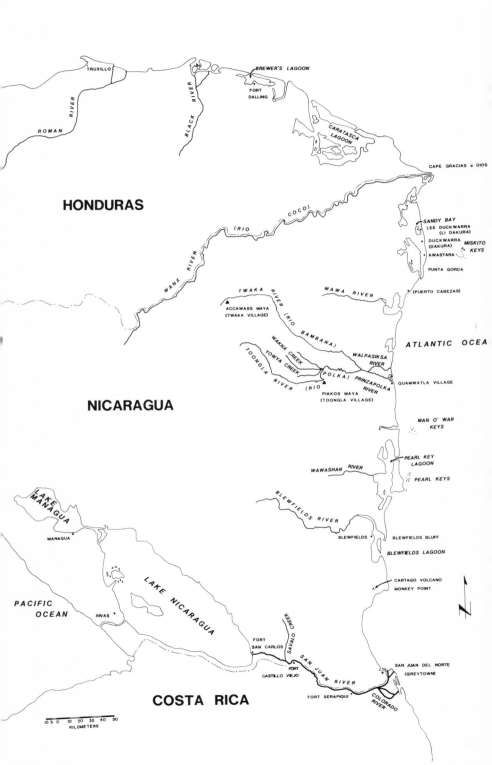

TRUXILLO

BREWER'S LAGOON

FORT
DALLING

ROMAN
RIVER

BLACK RIVER

CARATASCA
LAGOON

CAPE GRACIAS a DIOS

HONDURAS

(RIO COCO)

SANDY BAY
LEE DUCKWARRA
(LI DAKURA)

DUCKWARRA
(DAKURA)   MISKITO
                  KEYS
AWASTARA

PUNTA GORDA

WANX RIVER

TWAKA RIVER (RIO BAMBANA)

WAWA RIVER

(PUERTO CABEZAS)

ACCAWASS MAYA
(TWAKA VILLAGE)

ATLANTIC OCEA

NICARAGUA

WAKNA CREEK

YOWYA CREEK

TOONGLA RIVER

(RIO POLKA)

PIAKOS MAYA
(TOONGLA VILLAGE)

WALPASIKSA
RIVER

PRINZAPOLKA
RIVER

QUAMWATLA VILLAGE

MAN O' WAR
KEYS

PEARL KEY
LAGOON

WAWASHAN RIVER

PEARL KEYS

LAKE
MANAGUA

BLEWFIELDS RIVER

MANAGUA

BLEWFIELDS

BLEWFIELDS BLUFF

BLEWFIELDS LAGOON

LAKE NICARAGUA

CARTAGO VOLCANO

MONKEY POINT

PACIFIC
OCEAN

RIVAS

N

FORT
SAN CARLOS

SAVALO CREEK

SAN JUAN RIVER

SAN JUAN DEL NORTE
(GREYTOWN)

FORT
CASTILLO VIEJO

FORT SERAPIQUI

COLORADO
RIVER

COSTA RICA

10 5 0   10 20 30 40 50
        KILOMETERS

TANGWEERA
Life and Adventures among Gentle Savages

TANGWEERA

INTRODUCTION.

The tribes—Arrival of negroes—Mortality among the aborigines—An abandoned dependency of Britain—Clayton-Bulwer Treaty—Mosquito Shore a bone of contention—Two hundred years' history of a brave people—Report of Don Carlos Marenco—Recommends great warlike preparations—Treaty misunderstood by Ministers—Mosquito Shore a British colony—Mosquito men volunteer to join Nelson—Fort Dalling abandoned—Colonists appeal for help to Mosquito men—Disastrous evacuation of the colony—Mosquito Indians maintain dominion—Superintendent of Honduras crowns a Mosquito King—British officials appointed.

THE country known as the Mosquito Coast lies on the western shores of the Caribbean Sea, between 11° and 15° north latitude. Almost the whole of it is level alluvial land, flat near the sea, but rising gradually, and becoming more and more hilly inland, with ranges of mountains at the back from 100 to 150 miles from the coast, which ranges come down to the sea at Monkey Point, near Greytown, and at the extreme north near Black River. The coast lies, as sailors say, in the 'eye of the north-east trade winds'—that is, in the latitudes where the trades are most constant. In the rainy season the back ranges receive the excessive rain, which flows down in innumerable rivers to the coast.

The Mosquito country was formerly definable as the region under the sway of the Mosquito Indians, and used

I

to extend from the Black River, 100 miles west of Gracias à
Dios, to the river San Juan del Norte, which flows into the
Caribbean Sea at the port of Greytown, where the Nicaragua
Canal is to commence.   It is well known, however, that the
sway of the Mosquito Indian Kings extended some hundred
or more miles to the south of Greytown.   The Mosquito
Indians gave their names to many places south of Greytown,
even as far as Chagres, and these Mosquito names, as God
Buppan (God's Harbour), King Buppan (King's Harbour),
are in everyday use.   They also made regular expeditions
every year in well-armed canoes to collect tribute from the
different Indian tribes along the southern coast, and continued to do so until 1846, when the British Consul put a
stop to all claims of sovereignty by the Mosquito King south
of Greytown.

The Mosquito Indians are a maritime race, who from
their instincts are incapable of living far from the sea, and
have never done so.   They are an offshoot or ancient colony
of the formidable Caribs of the West Indies.   Except in
their copper-coloured skin and black hair, they differ
materially from the other Indian tribes of Central America.
They are tall, slim, bony, and muscular, with thin noses and
sharp features.   In character they are bold, daring, adventurous, quarrelsome, and self-assertive, frank and outspoken
to each other or to strangers, fond of the sea and of ships,
and not particularly clever in the bush.   They differ in these
particulars from all the other Indians of Central America,
who are generally short, plump, and thick-set, with broad
noses and high cheek-bones, while in character they are
reserved, silent, phlegmatic, not fond of travel or adventure,
awkward at sea, but masters of the bush, peaceable, plodding,
and industrious.

The ancient Mosquito territory was inhabited by five
tribes of Indians, besides the Mosquito men.   These were
all subject to the Mosquito King, but they served no other

purpose than to pay tribute or taxes, never joining in the wars or expeditions of their masters. These tribes all spoke languages of their own not understood by the others.

From Blewfields Lagoon to Lake Nicaragua and Grey-town River the country is inhabited by the Rama tribe, a fine, stalwart, fair race of Indians, now much reduced in numbers, except in the mountains of Costa Rica, where they are still numerous and extremely hostile.

From Blewfields River to the Wanx, or river of Cape Gracias à Dios, the interior is inhabited by Woolwas or Smoos, a sturdy, thick-set, taciturn race, a cross between whom and the Mosquitoes has produced the Toonglas, now constituting a tribe by themselves, and living on the Toongla River, a branch of the Prinzawala River.

The Twakas are a handsome and peculiarly fair race, hard-working and industrious, living on the Twaka River, the north branch of the Prinzawala River ; and another part of the same tribe lives on the Black River, west of Cape Gracias à Dios.

The Payas live in the interior of the Black River, and inland from Caratasca Lagoon.

The Prinzoos formerly lived in the interior between Pearl Key Lagoon and the Prinzawala River. ('Awala' means river in Mosquito.) But they have become extinct, because they waged a constant war with the Mosquitoes, who raided, enslaved, and finally exterminated them.

In the beginning of the eighteenth century a large Dutch ship full of slaves was wrecked on the Mosquito Coast, near Duckwarra. As a result of this, the inhabitants from Cape Gracias à Dios to Awastara and Duckwarra are now what are called Sambos—that is, a mixture of African and Indian blood ; but in my day this race had not spread any farther.

Towards the end of the eighteenth century the British Government deported all the Caribs of the island of St. Vincent to the northern part of the Mosquito territory, where they are now settled on the stretch of coast from Caratasca Lagoon to near the confines of British Honduras. These are Caribs in name only, as they are nearly pure African in blood, speak an African dialect, and their every motion and expression is African.

The Indians call themselves Tangweeras (Straight-hair), to distinguish them from the half-breed Sambos, who speak the same language.

The Mosquito Indians were once very numerous, but they are greatly fallen off in numbers. The reason of this decline is very difficult to account for. Generally, savages die off in presence of civilized races because of change of life and habits induced or imposed on them by the superior race; but it is not evidently so in this case, because the Mosquito Indians have never changed their habits. This decline in numbers affects all the Indian tribes of the country.

The life of a savage people is peculiarly tender. Though strong, robust, and sound in constitution, they are especially liable to be infested by the germs of diseases generated by large communities. Thus, small-pox, measles, whooping-cough, cholera, common catarrhs, are very destructive to them. But even periodical visits of these diseases cannot account for a steady decline in numbers extending over more than a century. If the people were fecund they would soon make good the losses. The root of the trouble is the great infant mortality and a small birth-rate. All the American Indians, from Canada to Cape Horn, have suffered from this blight, with the exception of the Mexican, Peruvian, and Central American Indians of the Pacific shores. These had attained an indigenous form of civilization, and though not proof against our diseases, their fertility secured them from extinction.

The causes of the dying out of savages in presence of a civilized people have been totally misunderstood and wrongly diagnosed by Europeans. When the American Indians, the

South Sea Islanders, the Fijians, and Maoris were constantly at war and devouring each other as cannibals, they were happy, prosperous, and most numerous; but as soon as they abandoned tribal wars and attempted to live the life prescribed to them by civilized people, they were stricken by the hand of death. They are told by a race whom they respect for its superior arts and knowledge that if they leave off fighting, have only one wife, till the soil, and live an industrious life, all will be well with them. They try it, and invariably find that the whites are blind guides leading the blind, and that if they change their old way of living there is only one option left to them, and that is the grave. This has been the invariable result of 400 years' messing and meddling by Europeans with the habits and lives of savage people.

Before venturing to submit to my readers an account of my pleasant and interesting adventures on the Mosquito Shore, it will be as well to give a short account of the history, so far as this can be gathered from data in my possession, of the Mosquito Indians, who for 200 years lived under the protection of Great Britain, but who through the shifts and turns of politics were cast off just when the long 'Pax Britannica' had totally unfitted them for taking the stand they formerly took on their unconquered soil, and handed over to their hereditary foes, the Spaniards of Nicaragua.

This was in 1856, when a treaty was made between Great Britain and the United States, whereby the former agreed to relinquish the protectorate of the Mosquito Shore. The territory was handed over to the republics of Honduras and Nicaragua, with the exception of a part, which was to be a reserve for the Indians, and in which they were to be left to themselves, while the Spaniards of the two republics were to respect their personal and territorial rights, and not to interfere with or molest them. About 1862 an amendment was made to this treaty, by which the Mosquito reserve was virtually handed over to Nicaragua, with certain stipulations, soon to be disregarded, that the republic was not to interfere with the Indians in any way.

By the treaty of 1856, called the Clayton-Bulwer Treaty, the territory to be reserved for the Indians, under the name of the Mosquito Reserve, extends from Monkey Point, 30 miles north of Greytown, to Cape Gracios à Dios, a distance of about 210 miles, and inland to the range of mountains about 100 miles from the coast. It was in 1856 that the Mosquito territory, after remaining for the last three or four generations almost unknown, except to the small traders who plied their trade along the coast, suddenly blazed up into notoriety, and threatened to become a bone of contention between Great Britain and the United States.

The Americans, just as ignorant as the English regarding the country and its history, could not be made to believe that the connection they all at once discovered between it and Great Britain was not a pretence contrived on the spur of the moment to obstruct the American Transit Company's newly-opened route through Greytown and Lake Nicaragua to the Pacific. In point of fact, the association of England with the Mosquito territory was quite respectably remote. For though little had been written, or even known, about the Mosquito country since its discovery in 1502, except from the vague accounts of buccaneers, yet a legitimate connection with the country commenced in the reign of Charles I., when the Earl of Warwick, by letters of reprisal against Spain, made himself master of the island of Old Providence, lying off the Mosquito Coast. The island was granted by Charles I. to the Earl and his family, and was formally ceded by Spain to Great Britain by the treaty of 1670.

The Earl proceeded to open trade and communication with the adjacent Mosquito Coast; gained the confidence of the Mosquito King and his people; left his relative, Colonel

Morris, as a hostage, and took the King's son with him to England as a commencement of friendly intercourse. The Prince remained three years in England, and he and the Indians of the coast were so favourably impressed with the conduct of the Earl and his trading agents that, upon the Prince succeeding his father, the Mosquito Indians petitioned to be taken under the protection of the British Crown.

This is the first official connection between England and the Mosquito men; but the annals of the buccaneers show that they were always on cordial terms with the Indians, who often joined in their expeditions and always extended to them hospitality and protection from pursuit. Captain Blewfields was a buccaneer of the early part of the seventeenth century, who established his headquarters in the Blewfields Lagoon, which afforded good shelter, and plenty of places where he could conceal his ships. Captain Wallace was another famous buccaneer who established himself at Belize, or Ballis, as they called it after him. He built a castle or stronghold near Belize from which he supplied the Mosquito Indians with arms and ammunition, and with them he made many desperate attacks on the Spanish towns to the north of Belize. It was the stout defence made by the buccaneers and Indians together that led to the founding of the colony of British Honduras. The English would have been compelled to abandon their logwood-cutting and been driven away from the country had it not been for the war-like Mosquito men, who dearly loved to be led to battle by the English, and constantly solicited the whites to come on and have another go at the Spaniards.

It does not appear that Charles I. took any action upon the request of the Mosquito King and people to be taken under British protection. But in the reign of Charles II. the King and chiefs of Mosquito again tendered allegiance to the British Crown through the Governor of Jamaica, who accepted it in the name of his Sovereign, and promised them protection. The same formalities occurred in the reign of James II., when the Mosquito King repaired to Jamaica with a large retinue of chiefs, renewed the tender of fealty through the Duke of Albemarle, and received assurances of protection. Of this occurrence a record was made by Sir Hans Sloane, who was present. This renewal of allegiance was made by the Kings and chiefs of the Mosquito Coast to every succeeding Governor of Jamaica, and by him accepted. Nor was this an empty ceremony. The Mosquito men for about 150 years fought sword in hand side by side with the English. Dampier testified that the Mosquito Indian was an expert swordsman and dangerous to encounter. By the 'American Treaty,' signed at Madrid, June, 1670, the sovereignty of Mosquito was assigned to 'Great Britain for ever,' as included in the possessions she then held in America.

As British subjects began to form settlements on the Mosquito Shore, the Governors of Jamaica appointed justices of the peace to reside there for the maintenance of order among them. In 1720 the inhabitants of Jamaica had great difficulty in suppressing the revolt of the negroes. So the Governor, on June 25, made a convention with Jeremy, King of Mosquito, for the transmission of a body of Indians to aid in the Maroon War, which by their aid was soon terminated.

On February 1, 1731, Don Carlos Marenco, Mayor of Porto Bello, makes a report to General Don Lopez Pintado, on the subject of the Mosquito Indians, their territory, and the best means of conquering it.*

He says the coast is held by the Mosquitoes, and the interior by 'Wild Caribs, who unite with the Mosquitoes and pilot them through the forests to the attacks on the Spanish settlements; that the King resides at Cape Gracias à Dios,

* _Government Gazette of Costa Rica_, June 5, 1852, from State Archives.

where are 7,000 persons well armed and munitioned with supplies from Jamaica ; that the place is fortified with trenches, ditches, terraces, and stockades; that the buccaneers find refuge among the Mosquito men, and that lately a party of pirates had crossed from the South Sea through Segovia, plundering on their way, and in one battle our people had with them more than 400 of our men fell; that they made their way to the coast by the river Segovia ' (Blewfields River).

Don Carlos then makes a long report of the means he would advise for reducing the Indians and driving out their English allies, which was, however, never attempted. He recommends forces and equipments on a scale almost sufficient for a war with Great Britain, to subdue these aborigines who 'have usurped this portion of the patrimony of His Catholic Majesty, whom God preserve.'

But a war with Great Britain was probably expected, for after dilating on the injuries suffered by the provinces of Nicaragua, Honduras, and Costa Rica from the incursions of the Mosquito Sambos and their allies, the English and the pirates who had associated with them, Marenco states that 'these people combine readily for any exploit by land or sea, finding themselves well supplied with arms and munitions of war by the English of Jamaica, and holding the King of England as their King.'

But it was the capture, by Spanish men-of-war, of British vessels on the Mosquito Coast and Bay of Honduras that caused the declaration of war in 1739, and in 1741 the British Government established troops on the Mosquito Coast under the authority of a Superintendent, and after that appointed magistrates and courts of quarter sessions.

In the Treaty of Paris, concluded in 1763, Article XVII. says: ' His Britannic Majesty shall cause to be demolished all fortifications which his subjects have erected in the Bay of Honduras and other parts of the territory of Spain.'

Nothing is said about the Mosquito Coast, which is not in the Bay of Honduras, nor part of the territory of Spain. But the Ministry of the day, misunderstanding the locality, and disregarding the treaty of 1670, destroyed the fortifications on the Mosquito Coast, and withdrew the troops. They, however, soon saw the absurd blunder they had made, and approved of the conduct of Superintendent Otway, who had refused the Spaniards admission into the country. The sovereignty of the British Crown over the Mosquito country, therefore, continued to be maintained, and in 1775 a more effective system of administration was put in force.

By Minutes of Council of Jamaica, in a report to the British Board of Trade, it was stated that the British inhabitants of the Mosquito Coast in 1770 numbered 300 whites, 200 of mixed race, and 900 slaves. The Mosquito Indians, formerly numerous, had been greatly reduced by small-pox, and numbered 7,000 to 10,000. The Mosquito Shore had, indeed, to all intents and purposes become a British colony. But the administration of the country betrayed such laxity that the Spaniards appear to have presumed on the indifference of the British Ministry, for in April, 1776, they captured a British vessel on the Black River. The Council of Government and the Superintendent of the Mosquito Shore reported this and other outrages to the British Government, and requested that a blockhouse be built, arms and munition furnished, and that some of the cannon formerly taken away be sent back, with a force of 100 or even 50 men, to preserve the negroes and defend the roadstead. But Lord George Germaine, instead of weighing the matter and looking over the treaties, sent a despatch to Jamaica, severely rebuking the Superintendent of the Mosquito Shore for the request he had made, as being in contravention of Article XVII. of the Treaty of Paris, and advised him instead to apply himself to promote the prosperity of the settlements, to improve their commercial advantages, and cultivate a stricter union with the Indians.

After this snubbing of the Mosquito Superintendent, and refusal of the paltry support asked for, it is startling to find the Governor of Jamaica in 1780 directing the same Superintendent to join the expedition of Captain Horatio Nelson with all the force at his command. He and his people did so promptly. The Mosquito Indians also volunteered in great numbers, and, largely by their clever assistance, the expedition up the San Juan River was successful. The strong castle of Castillo Viejo was captured, Nelson returned to Jamaica, and sent more than half his force, sick with fever, to recruit at Blewfields, then considered the sanatorium of Jamaica.

But this expedition was disastrous to the colonists. While the Superintendent and all the free people were away with Nelson at Greytown River, the chief settlement at Black River was left defenceless. The Spaniards of Truxillo made a foray on the settlement, burnt it, and destroyed the sugar plantations and provision-grounds; while the slaves, left to themselves, rose in revolt, and declared they would be free. They were suppressed by three English officers from the settlement on the island of Ruatan, who crossed over to Black River with a party of settlers.

In 1782 another invasion of Spaniards was made with 1,350 foot, 100 horse, and 350 Indian allies as guides. These descended from the south by the Black River, and appeared before the settlement on March 15. On the 29th there arrived 1,000 more foot from Truxillo by way of the coast, and on the 30th a line-of-battle ship and a frigate anchored off Fort Dalling, and, under shelter of a cannonade, landed 500 men. Thus a force sufficient to conquer the whole country was concentrated round the devoted settlement, the metropolis of the colony. There were twenty-one soldiers to defend Fort Dalling, under the command of the

Superintendent, with a few hundred settlers, negroes, and Indians, hastily assembled, but ill-armed, and without ammunition or provisions.

All that could be done was to spike the guns and retreat upon the settlement at Cape Gracias à Dios, upwards of 100 miles off, across pathless forests and savannas, and many rivers, creeks, and lagoons. The women and children suffered severely in this forlorn retreat, which was accomplished with many losses.

In April, 1782, Admiral Rodney's victory put renewed heart into the Mosquito colonists, and on August 7 an expedition was despatched from Jamaica for their relief, consisting of 150 of the Royal American Rangers, with arms and ammunition, provisions and presents for the Indians. The colonial forces to the number of 1,000, of whom 80 were regulars, advanced against Black River settlement. The Spaniards opened a conference, ending in a capitulation, by which the place was surrendered on August 31, with 715 officers and soldiers as prisoners of war.

In those turbulent times the colonists of the Mosquito Shore and those of British Honduras were always wide awake, as an old Belize paper shows, to the value of the assistance they received from the Mosquito Indians.

In January, 1783, a definitive treaty was concluded with Spain, which specifies that His Britannic Majesty's subjects shall evacuate all parts on the Spanish continent, or any of the islands dependent on the same, except such parts as shall by the treaty remain in the possession of Great Britain. But two years after this the discussion of British and Spanish claims was renewed, and after a debate of ten months a convention was made, signed in London in 1786, under which the British Government ordered the evacuation of the Mosquito territory by all British subjects. The plea put forth by the English Ministry was the compensating concession made by Spain of some further privileges for the

British settlement of Honduras, thus seeking to propitiate a nation hereditarily inimical (and soon after this actively hostile) by ruining one colony for the partial benefit of another, and abandoning to their enemies those Indian allies who had faithfully adhered to the English through every trouble which the country had ever sustained.

Loud complaints and strong reclamations were made by the cruelly-wronged colonists. The affair caused a great outcry in England, and a threat was made in the House of Lords of impeaching the Ministry. But through the fierce factions in England at that time, and the lowering aspect of the Revolution then threatening in France, the Mosquito troubles were soon forgotten. Most of the colonists, filled with indignation, removed with most of their slaves to British Honduras, where they introduced the cutting of mahogany, which has since been the principal export of that colony. But some settlers disregarded the orders for evacuation, and remained at their plantations on the coast.

As for Spain, she was too much pressed elsewhere to attempt the conquest and occupation of the Mosquito Shore. She made an attempt on the Black River, but this the Mosquito Indians repelled, and she made no other attempt during that century. Then came the independence of the Spanish colonies. Meanwhile the Mosquito Indians maintained the dominion of the whole coast as if nothing had happened, imposing tribute on the subject Indians as far south as King Buppan, not far from Porto Bello, and also imposing tribute on the Spaniards themselves for permission to trade at Greytown and Salt Creek, or Moyn.

The British Government received favourably the renewed advances of the Mosquito Indians at Jamaica and Belize, and from that time till 1856 the Mosquito Kings were educated and then crowned at Jamaica or at Belize. English settlers in smaller numbers returned to the coast with their slaves, and engaged in trade and mahogany-cutting, the West Indian world seeming to have quite forgotten the pranks of the British Foreign Office.

Thus we see the queer anomaly that although the English had been ordered in 1787 to evacuate the country, yet the protectorate over the Mosquito Shore was officially retained by Great Britain. In April, 1806, Captain John Bligh, of H.B.M.S. *Surveillant*, captured the island of St. Andrews, and drove out the Spanish Governor and his troops, as the island was considered to be a dependency of the Mosquito Shore.

On January 14, 1816, Sir George Arthur, Superintendent of British Honduras, addresses a despatch to Prince George as follows: 'Your request to be crowned in the settlement in presence of your chieftains and such of your people as are assembled here, I shall most cheerfully comply with, and I sincerely trust that you will not be disappointed in the advantage you expect to derive by its being understood by your subjects that you are in a particular manner under the protection of the British Government. . . .'

Again, in 1840 the British Commissioners for the Mosquito Shore appointed Messrs. Samuel and Peter Shepherd as Sheriffs and Commandants of the southern half of the kingdom from Little Snook Creek to King Buppan Bluff. The Messrs. Shepherd reply to the British Commissioners, accepting the appointment offered, but they observe that the port of San Juan (Greytown) must be exempted from the liability to pay duties, the use of the harbour having been granted to the State of Nicaragua for a fixed sum to be paid annually to the Mosquito King.

In 1841 King Robert died, and by his will left his son and three daughters, then very young, in charge of James Stanislaus Bell, whom at the same time he appointed Sheriff and Commandant of the kingdom and its dependencies.

In 1846 the British Government appointed Patrick Walker Consul-General and Superintendent of the Mosquito Shore. In 1846 the young King George was crowned at Belize. He died about 1862, leaving no children, and the son of his sister Victoria succeeded as King of the Mosquito Indians, who had fallen on evil times.

CHAPTER I.

Inhabitants—Habits—Creole language and character—Mixed breeds—
Early recollections—' Ma Presence '—' Ta Tom '—' Ma Presence ' a
praying soul—Christmas at Blewfields—' Wakes.'

THE village or town of Blewfields is situated on several low
hillocks or ridges which project into the lagoon, with creeks
between each ridge. The town is surrounded by primeval
forest that has never felt the edge of the axe or been scorched
by fire. The town in my day was inhabited by 500 or 600
blacks and mulattoes, and by two or three whites. The
settlement was surrounded by a small extent of clearing,
covered by grass and bushes, over which grazed pigs, goats,
and fowls. The houses were mostly wattled, but three or
four, our own among them, were of a better style, the floor
elevated on posts 6 feet above the ground; walls, floor and
partitions of American lumber; roof thatched with palm
leaves; tables, chairs, beds, etc., all good furniture; but the
kitchen here also a detached building.

The lagoon is a beautiful sheet of water, 16 or 18 miles long
by about 5 wide, dotted with wooded hilly islands, enclosed
from the sea by a strip of low land a mile wide, densely
covered by forest, with an opening opposite the town under
Blewfields Bluff, a hill 260 feet high, and another opening at
the far south end, opposite some pretty islands inhabited by
Rama Indians. The Blewfields River enters the north end
of the lagoon by an extensive low delta, through which it

discharges in many mouths, like the Sunderbunds of the
Ganges. The mouths are so many, and so intersected by
cross-creeks, that not everyone can find his way through
them into the main river, three-quarters of a mile wide at
the head of the delta. In these deep, narrow, gloomy creeks
of the delta the old buccaneers used to hide their vessels
from the Spaniards, and on Blewfields Bluff they had a
blockhouse mounted with guns, and kept a look-out. Where
the many mouths of the delta discharge into the lagoon
there is about 12,000 acres of shallow water, the bottom
sandy and muddy, the shoals covered with water-grass, the
haunt of countless flocks of ducks, teal, coots, and every
kind of water-bird. The water varies in depth from a foot
or two to 6 and 8 feet, and swarms with fish, among them
sting-rays and sharks, with a few manatees, and an alligator
here and there. The rest of the lagoon is deep enough for
schooners to sail over, and in the rainy season, when the
trades blow up it, it is very rough. The islands in the
lagoon are little hills of basalt, with rich soil, and densely
covered with forest—the home of the migratory pigeons,
which roost there in thousands. They shelter also countless
shags and a few pelicans, with yellow-tails and parrots in
great numbers. These birds know well the value of islands,
where opossums, raccoons, bush-dogs, tiger-cats and snakes
cannot molest them.

The coloured people call themselves Creoles, as ' nigger '
is a term of opprobrium, and ' mulatto ' is of doubtful
significance. Their plantations are placed far from the
village to avoid the necessity of fencing out the pigs. At
the Bluff, and on the many ridges that jut into the lagoon
along its western shore, they fell the forest and cultivate in
small patches plantains, cassava, rice, yams, breadfruit,
eddos, Indian corn and the edible arum root, with oranges,
sapodillas, guavas, mammees, papaws, star-apple, pineapples, sour-sops, custard-apple, sugar-cane and mangoes.

2

Except a small settlement of Rama Indians on the islands
at the south end of the lagoon, there are no Indians at
Blewfields; yet there are evidences of their having formerly
lived there in great numbers. In the middle of the town are
two gigantic mounds of oyster and cockle shells, and in
various places along the western shores are several similar
mounds overgrown by forest. The mounds in the town
have long been used to 'metal' the roads, and innumerable
objects of antiquity are found all through them, such as flint
spear-heads 6 inches long, and arrow-heads generally 2
inches long; broken pottery in vast quantities, generally
ornamented with patterns, showing traces of colour; children's
toys or idols, whichever they are, made of baked clay, some like
a parrot's head with a loose ball in the mouth, others rude
little figures of men with hideous faces; discs of clay with
a hole in the centre for inserting a spindle to spin cotton
yarn; stone axes and charred bones of every animal in the
country. The lagoon still abounds with cockles and oysters,
but it must have taken centuries to accumulate such heaps
of shells; and as the mounds are 30 feet high, an arbitrary
custom must have compelled the women to climb to the top
to deposit the little basketful of shells, the product of the
day's consumption.

No one can tell when the Indians lived in such numbers
on the shores of Blewfields Lagoon; neither can anyone say
when the Mosquito Indians first settled on the coast. In
Dampier's time the Mosquito men were perpetually at war
with the interior tribes, and I have no doubt that the course
of affairs was similar to what happened in New Zealand;
that is, that the Mosquito Indians living on the coast were
the first to get hold of European weapons, and with them
they at once overpowered the interior tribes and drove them
from the coast to the creeks and rivers inland. Dreadful
times these must have been; yet, strange to say, these were
the times when the Indians were the most numerous and

prosperous, and, like the New Zealanders, the more they fought and devoured each other, the happier they were.

The negroes, mulattoes and quadroons composing the population of Blewfields in my day, though somewhat kept up to the mark by Europeans trading and living among them, yet were slowly relapsing into the superstitious, gloomy, half-savage state into which the blacks, left to themselves, always sink back. They were divided into cliques which hated each other, and practised *obeah* and wakes in the regular African fashion. Wife-beating was fearfully common, and quarrelling was carried out systematically. In the still nights we used to listen with horror to the yells and screams of beaten women, while one or more old women for an hour at a time would make the woods echo with abuse and curses, as from a distance they defied their enemies, who took no notice of the volleys of imprecations till next night, when their own old woman would take her turn at it. I remember going with my sister to a woman's house about some washing ; a girl was sitting at the door, whom my sister asked : ' Pennyluppy, (Penelope), where is your mother ?' ' Him gone da Ole Benk gone quarrel ' (She is gone to Old Bank to quarrel) ; and sure enough we could hear her far off uttering a shrill and ceaseless torrent of abuse.

I shall speak* of the Mosquito language, with its defined grammar and well-observed rules ; but who can describe the language spoken by the Creoles of Blewfields ? It was a jargon of English which, left to itself, would soon have become a distinct language. As a boy I learned it in no time, and for years after my sister had a hard task in bring-ing me back to pure English. Let me give a sample of it. Every year, about February, the men used to depart for the hawksbill turtle fishery, returning in May ; and as soon as a returning canoe entered the lagoon, the crew in turns blew a conch shell until close to the landing-place. These turtle-

* See Appendix A.

fishers always went to the southward for their fishing, and
were therefore called 'southward men.' One day I heard
the shell blowing, and ran into the house calling out:
'Sudderd man day com.' My sister asked, 'How do you
know?' I replied: 'Bin a mid day yerry de coong shell bin
day blow.' It is not easy to discover that this meant:
'Because I hear the conch shell blowing.'

An old negro used to tell us astonishing stories of duppies
he had seen in the Bush, and if we doubted him he would
exclaim: 'Fo tooroo a wish him tonda pillit a me na lacka-
tone!' which means 'For true (if not) I wish thunder may
split me like a rockstone.'

Everybody knows that the negroes are, compared with
ourselves, a childish, simple-minded, faithful, affectionate
people, easily led or imposed on, credulous and superstitious,
easily worked up to religious fervour, or even frenzy, yet
incapable of understanding anything of religion but its out-
ward observance ; fond of children, yet bad mothers because
of ignorance or thoughtlessness ; inveterate thieves, cunning
and sly, yet at the same time open-hearted, generous, and
capable of the strongest friendship and personal attachment ;
brave enough to make good soldiers, yet by no means
truthful ; hard-working, yet fond of ease and idleness ; frugal
and simple in habits and desires ; more temperate in drink
than the whites, but less so than the Chinese or Indians ;
great lovers and very prolific.

Our negroes at Blewfields were partakers in all the above
rare traits, and were as amiable and odd a people as one
could find anywhere. But we had all shades of colour
besides the negroes — brown mulattoes, coffee - and - milk
coloured quadroons, and a few nearly as white as myself.
Generations of ship captains had come and gone, leaving
families at all the Creole settlements. Each captain as he
succeeded the last added some more white blood, till the
result in my day was that at Blewfields, Pearl Key Lagoon,

Boca del Toro, Corn Island, St. Andrews, Old Providence, which are the other principal settlements of the Creoles, there were some families nearly white, with coffee-and-milk mothers, brown grandmothers, and black great-grandmothers. One family I knew had all these alive.

Some captains seem to have had a preponderating influence on the population. Wherever you went you would not fail to find Shepperds or Hodgsons; others were more rare, such as the Quins and Haleys. Those on whom captains had not smiled generally dispensed with surnames. Crusoe's father, for instance, might be either Robinson or Crusoe; I never ascertained which. Humphrey's father was Ta Tom, *ta* being a pet name for uncle. John Thompson's father was only known by the name of Black Tiger, because he was unusually black.

Our women and girls had good names, but much transfigured. Rooty (Ruth) was a fine bouncing mulatto girl; Pennyluppy, a handsome black; Joody (Judith), a lively quadroon; Joney and Minta (Joannah and Araminta), a pair of tall, well-made twins as black as sloes. But the old ladies rejoiced in stately names, such as Ma Prudence, Ma Patience, Ma Presence, Ma Fidelia, *ma* being mother.

My earliest recollections of Blewfields are those of bathing and sailing toy boats in the lagoon, and it seems to me now that a considerable part of my young days was spent in the water. My companions were the Mosquito King and coloured boys in great numbers. In the early part of the day they had to cut and split firewood, fetch water, grate cocoanuts, and mind the baby. I and the King had to do our lessons, but when we had had our dinner at one o'clock we would rush off to the lagoon, tear off our clothes, and plunge in. Then we would produce our toy boats, which were hidden in the bushes, and trimming the sails to the fresh trade wind, we launched them in batches to race, following after with shouts and yells. This was done every day during the dry season. The King and I were inseparable companions, but were not distinguished from the rest. As we grew older, the King developed the great fondness for boating which is inherent in the Mosquito Indians. Some of his relations from the Cape brought him a little canoe in the rough. It was about 10 feet long, with beam just enough to fit our little posteriors. We got it beautifully trimmed—that is, dressed down to proper shape and thickness—provided a shoulder-of-mutton sail, and sailed about the lagoon, he and I.

I cannot help thinking Heaven had a special care of me, when I think of all the risks I ran, sailing about for years in that little tub of a thing. Every day we capsized, sometimes many times a day. The lagoon was full of sharks and alligators, and my white skin made the risk much greater to me than to the King. Many times when capsized and swimming about we have smelt the strong musk smell of the alligator, or the oily, fishy smell of the shark, said to be caused by its vomiting the scales and bones of fish it has eaten. We would then swim to the canoe, scramble in, bale out, and feel very frightened, till in a short time we forgot all about it. Sometimes we idled about at the islands, not noticing that the sea-breeze had come down very strong. We would put up sail to return across the lagoon, but as soon as we cleared the shelter of the land we got into very rough water, and upset forthwith. Then we found that we could not get in again, because the waves swamped the canoe as fast as we baled out, so we had to put up the sail and hang on to the gunwale till the wind and waves carried us across the lagoon. This proceeding was doubly dangerous, first on account of sharks, next because if by accident we should let go the gunwale, the canoe might sail away, and we might not be able to catch it again. Poor Crusoe, whose name is mentioned above, was drowned in this manner.

Sometimes we ventured right out to sea, and choosing a day when the breakers rolled in, we would run the breakers in our little canoe. This was so great a pleasure that we required company to enjoy it, and we used to get other boys in other canoes to join in the fun. We all approached in a line as near the breakers as we dared; then, letting all the big ones pass, we would give the signal for a little one, paddle towards the shore as hard as we could till the breaker overtook us, then steer the canoe as it rushed through the water with the breaker roaring beside us. Those who exerted the most strength and skill reached the beach safely; the 'duffers' were slewed round broadside on, and rolled over and over. However, we had a timely accident, which so alarmed us that we abandoned a sport which for young boys was far too risky. On this occasion we had taken our breaker in fine style, and were shouting with exultation as we rushed at 15 miles an hour through the water, when suddenly the canoe seemed to stand up on end. The bow must have stuck in the sand, for the canoe was flung over end for end with great violence, and both of us were hurt.

One great source of amusement was to shoot a fish called mootroos. For this purpose the water must be calm, and early morning, before the sea-breeze set in, was the proper time. For the sport we provided ourselves with little bows 2 feet 6 inches long, made from split 'wild cane,' and a few arrows made from the midrib of the cocoanut, and wading in water knee-deep we sought our prey. The mootroos is a fish without scales, from 2 to 4 inches long, striped and dappled silvery white and dark brown, with prominent eyes, and hard sharp teeth like a parrot's bill; it is found in great numbers swimming in shallow water. When pierced with the little arrow, it immediately blew itself up like a ball, in which condition its skin, previously smooth, became rough and prickly. We used to draw it off the arrow, and fling it violently on the water, which caused the skin to burst with a loud pop. This was great delight, and if we reflected on the cruelty of it, we justified ourselves by the great annoyance the mootroos caused in fishing by taking off the bait.

There was an old African woman named Ma Presence. She had been a slave all her life, and, being now blind, had been discarded by her master and thrown upon her own resources for many years before we knew her.

Her little hut stood not far from our house. It was, like all the houses of the common people at Blewfields, built of hardwood posts, rafters, and ridge-pole, the sides and ends wattled with split papta palm; it was thatched with the leaves of the silico palm, and divided by a wattled partition into a bed and a sitting room, with a back and front door, and at the back there was a separate shed for a kitchen. The sitting-room was furnished with a rough table and two benches. The bed in its room was a framework of sticks, supported on forked posts stuck into the ground. On the sticks was a wide sheet of thick bark as hard and stiff as a board. On this was a thick soft mat made from midribs of the plantain leaf, bound closely side by side with twine. A gay patchwork coverlet was all the bedclothes necessary in this hot climate. A large pillow stuffed with down of the silk-cotton and covered with a clean pillow-case completed the bedclothes.

Ma Presence had lived by charity before we knew her. My sisters practised charity towards her, with the inevitable result that very soon the cost of her living was thrown entirely upon us, and we fed and supported her for about fifteen years.

To me Ma Presence was a source of mystery and wonder. She told me long stories of Africa, to which I was never tired of listening. She was a Mandingo, probably from the head-waters of the Niger, and her tribe were Mohammedans. She remembered that when she was a little girl she lived in a village of huts surrounded by a high strong fence. At night the gates were shut, and the jackals and hyenas howled round about, whose cries she imitated until my blood ran cold. Sometimes on dark nights she heard the crashing and tramping of *ahsoonoo*, which I understood to be elephants. Her tribe must have been warlike, for she described with pride the gallant appearance of the warriors who went away to battle and returned with trophies and spoil. The clearing in which her village stood was surrounded by forest, and a beautiful river flowed over a rocky bed in the valley below, where the children bathed all through the hot day. One day, while they were bathing, they heard a dreadful screaming and the sound of guns up at the village, and presently saw flames rising from the huts. They rushed up the bank to see what was wrong, when a warrior seized our little girl by the arm, and dragged her away to the bush.

She seemed to have a very indistinct recollection of her journey in company with all the captives from her village, and others who formed the slave caravan, but when she saw 'the great black sea' she covered her mouth with her hand, and was lost in astonishment and fear. In short, she crossed the sea, and was sold to a planter in Jamaica, by whom, when she grew up, she had a child which died young. Then she was sold and brought to Blewfields, where she worked till she was old and blind, in which condition she was thrown on the world as we found her.

Under our protection, Ma Presence was held to be in good circumstances by other needy and greedy old negro women, who, when they visited my sister, would throw out hints that there were other women quite as deserving of attention as Ma Presence. Nor was it the old women only who envied Ma Presence her comfortable circumstances; the old men also had their eye on her. An old African negro named Ta Tom (or Taam, as they pronounce it) came courting Ma Presence. My sister was astonished, when Ma Patience came to visit and beg, at her 'sucking her teeth'—a gesticulation of great contempt among the negroes—and saying, 'Tcho! some old woman him too papisho foo tooroo, him no had no shame,' sucking her teeth again. On my sister asking what she meant, she said: 'May be you no bin yerry Ma Presence an Ta Taam gwine hab.' The word *papisho* means puppet-show, and is used by the negroes to express a silly, foolish person or action. Also, as there was then no proper marriage among the negroes, *gwine hab* means that they were going to be married in their fashion.

Thus it happened that old Ta Taam sneaked into the household of Ma Presence in order to enjoy some of the comforts that we dispensed to the old woman. In return he cultivated her little garden, which had previously been a waste of bushes, and Ma Presence was thus able to make us little presents from time to time of a basket of okros, a plateful of gungo peas, a yam, or a few eggs.

Ta Tom was a tall, powerful old negro. He often got drunk, and was violent in his cups; and many times, at all hours of the night, we would be alarmed by the shrieks and yells of Ma Presence being beaten by her husband. On the arrival of myself and sister he would desist and go to bed, leaving us to bathe her bruises with vinegar and brown paper. Negro women are used to being beaten, and it makes no difference in their attachment to their husbands. But one night he beat her too much altogether. So the magistrates, who were two negroes and a white man, had Ta Tom tied to a guava-tree and well whipped with a manatee strap, and then he was told to go away, and not return to Ma Presence's house.

About a week after this Ta Tom quarrelled with a powerful negro who had run away from his master at the Island of St. Andrews to enjoy the freedom which then prevailed at Blewfields, and poor old Tom was brought in with his ribs stove in, unconscious and dying, and laid on Ma Presence's bed. As became a decent wife, she howled and wailed properly.

So Ma Presence was again a lonely widow. She used to poke with her stick, and find her way to our house several times a week. She was a cheery, humorous old soul, and could tell stories of scenes in her life and all sorts of gossip with such vivacity and spirit that I never tired of listening to her. No people in the world can tell stories like the negroes, and she was among the best of the kind, and withal her simplicity was almost childish. In course of time some Moravian missionaries settled in Blewfields, and all the people forthwith took up religion and praying.

It was not long before this fervour attacked Ma Presence. The chief missionary's name was the Rev. Mr. Pfeiffer, and for a while she became his devoted disciple. One day she groped her way to our house, and said to my sister : ' Miss Bell, please gie me pair a old silpas. Maas Pfeiffer say me mus turn pryin soul ; but how me foo turn pryin soul when me no hab no silpas ?' So having been provided with a pair of old slippers, she duly attended at church, and became a praying soul.

Christmas at Blewfields was something worth seeing. Everyone who possibly could came home for the festivity, and a week or so before it all the men went hunting to provide meat for the occasion. For although a few pigs, fowls, and goats were kept, nine-tenths of the meat of the people was procured from the sea or the bush. Thus, at Christmas every properly-provided house had much store of barbecued monkeys, warree (a large species of peccary), deer, tapir, curassow ; also salted fish, live hiccatee (river tortoise), and iguanas ; also plantains, green or made into foofoo—that is, cut up, put into large baskets, and buried in the earth till partially rotten, then dried in the sun, and made into flour. Yams and rice are also laid into store, and much sugar-cane, and if anyone has a pig or goat to spare, it feels the knife on this joyous occasion. The girls, among those who can afford to buy flour, make great piles of plantain tarts, which I used to think the most delicious sweetmeat in the world. It is made by taking ripe plantains, boiling them, and beating them into a thick paste, then flavouring with pimento, ginger, grated lemon-peel, and a little black pepper. Then make a light dough of flour, eggs, and a little fresh lard ; make portions of the dough into little boats, fill the cavity with ripe plantain paste, pinch up the dough till the little boat is closed round it, and bake in a Dutch oven.

For a week previous to Christmas you will see women and boys laboriously squeezing sugar-cane in the odd-looking African mill. This is a stout post fixed in the ground, into which a flat slab, like a little table, is mortised and wedged up tight. Above the slab is a round hole in the post, into which a stout bar of wood fits loosely. Then a large calabash is placed on the ground below the little table, a lad inserts the long bar in the hole, and lifts the end high enough for a woman to slip the sugar-cane between the bar and the table. The boy then presses down the bar, the cane is crushed, and the woman slips it forward till it is all crushed ; then she twists it like a rope, and wrings the last drop of juice into the calabash. A great pot is on the fire, into which every calabash as it fills is poured. An old woman, skilled in the art, presides over the pot with her implements, which are a cocoanut shell fixed to a long stick, and a large branch of sea-fan. With the latter she gathers the scum from the boiling juice, and with the former she ladles and tests its thickness, and bangs the woolly heads of urchins who are watching around to steal a calabashful. When the juice is boiled to a clear thick syrup it is stored in demijohns for use, to sweeten coffee and chocolate, and make lemonade.

Now all is ready for the feast, and Christmas Eve is announced by firing guns. A good deal of rum is being drunk, and much fighting is going on among men and boys ; but it is taken in good part, and bunged-up eyes, bleeding noses, and cut lips are soon forgotten in the general merriment. Soon as the evening shades prevail the drum takes up its wondrous tale, and together with the fiddle inspires the mad capers of the jig, the carabini, the punta, or the country dance; while the horse's jaw-bone, the teeth rattled with a stick, and two other sticks beating time on a bench, with the drum and the wild snatches of song by the women, provide the stimulus for the weird and mystic African dances, at which the younger men and the young women of the period look askance, as savouring too much of African slavery.

It will hardly be believed that dancing is carried on almost continuously till a week after New Year. On Christmas Day and Boxing Day, on New Year's Day and next day, the dancing is carried on day and night, the rest of the time at night only. The dancers and musicians go from house to house without asking leave, for no one dreams of refusing admission to the merrymakers, except in our house, where they never intrude. Those who are tired out lie down and sleep in the beds of the houses they happen to be in, or on the floor or on the benches. The musicians give their instruments up to others and sleep wherever they like, and still the mad frolic goes on. Crowds surround the house where dancing is going on, and follow the dancers to the next house, going inside and joining the dance when they like. Guns are fired continually. Many pairs of men are fighting with the fist, for they are expert boxers, and admiring crowds surround them and see fair play. The contagion of fighting extends to the boys, until the general mêlée becomes too serious, when the women rush in and restore harmony, which is easily done, for it seems a point of honour not to harbour anger at Christmas time.

The weather at Christmas is generally fine, and numbers

of women may be seen in all their finery sleeping on the
grass in the shade of the trees.   From time to time one or
more wake up, wash their faces in a calabash of water, and
hasten off to join the dancers.   Of course the children don't
dance, but they are sailing boats in the lagoon, or practising
with straightened sticks for spears on cocoanut husks for a
target ; or they gather quantities of green limes or the fruit
of a species of solanum called ' cock up bubby,' and forming
themselves into opposing armies, each with a leader, pelt
each other till one side gives way.

The little girls are generally burdened with a naked baby
sitting astride on the hip, but they manage to amuse themselves, sometimes at the cost of the babies, which they have
left sprawling and crying on the grass, till the mothers, being
warned of the state of affairs, rush from the dance, pick up
the babies, and pursue the delinquents into the bush.

There are other diversions for those who are tired of
dancing; for sailing races on the lagoon, and cock-fighting,
have each their votaries at Christmas-time.

Before the Moravian missionaries arrived we were very
heathen at Blewfields.   There was no marriage, no christen-
ing, no church, and even when the missionaries introduced
marriage the people did not take to it much : they preferred
their own looser tie.

The first thing the missionaries did was to abolish ' wakes,'
as being too heathen.   The old *obeah* men who conducted
the wakes would not have white people at them ; but on one
occasion Ma Patience concealed me beneath her dress, so
that I saw something of it.   It is so long ago, and I was so
frightened, that I have a very dim recollection of the ceremony.   The dead body was in an adjoining room, and the
room where the wake was held was lighted with pitch-pine
torches stuck into the ground.   An old African *obeah* man
sat on the ground, and with hideous faces and ghastly rolling
of his eyeballs muttered some dreadful words, while he mixed

something in a calabash and went round the room offering it to various persons. The *obeah* man all the time was chanting and grunting in unknown words. Some of the people drank from the calabash, some did not. Then those who had drunk got up and walked round the room, singing some strange refrain, while those seated, among whom were a few old women, clapped their hands and chanted a sort of response.

I only remember one of these. The *obeah* man called out some strange words, when immediately those who were walking round sang the refrain :

> 'Ah quaqua hanancy doo,
> Aha tonda rake am.'

The women and those sitting clapped their hands and followed up this song, but all in different tones, till the air seemed alive with the refrain in every imaginable key, but all answering each other in exact time.

No one knows what the first sentence means. 'Tonda rake am' is English, and means, 'May thunder rake (or strike) him.' Then the *obeah* man talked some more words, and this started the others in another weird song.

After this an old African told *hanancy* stories. *Hanancy* is some African name for a spider, which is usually the hero of these strange animal stories, for which the Africans are famous and unequalled. I regret that I do not remember any of these stories, which this old man would never repeat except at a wake. I asked him once to tell me one of his wake stories, but he turned a horrid eye on me, and said, 'Go way, Backra buay, you too papisho.'

CHAPTER II.

Danger from tigers—Danger from alligators—Joys and sadness of Blewfields—Eboes in season—Gathering shell-fish—Manatee—Bowman
caters for us—The King and I disport ourselves—Turtle—The rainy
season—Crickey-jeen and butterflies—Thunder, rain and storms—
Winged ants and their consumers.

WE were surrounded by forest in Blewfields, and to my
young imagination this forest was interminable and mysterious. Our house was close to its edge. We had a garden
of 8 or 10 acres, and the bush was at the back of it. At
night we would listen to strange and unknown cries and
noises in the forest, which filled us with mysterious dread.
Our house was built on posts, the floor being 5 feet above
the ground, and our goats and pigs slept in the dry dust
under the floor. Once or twice, on dark, stormy nights, we
heard the goats and pigs rush out from under the house, and
in the morning we found the tracks of a tiger in our yard,
from which the pigs, smelling it, had fled in dismay.

Once, on a dark rainy night, my sister and I were awakened
by a headlong rush of the goats under the house, and the
shrill squealing of a pig. While we were discussing what
was to be done, the squeals ceased and all was still. Next
morning we found a lot of blood and hair under the house,
and our goats and pigs would not come near the place, as
they smelt the tiger's scent.

Soon a number of men and dogs proceeded to track the

THE AUTHOR'S HOME AT BLEWFIELDS.

beast through the bush. Presently the dogs were heard barking a long way off, and on coming up we found they had driven a large puma into a tree, on which it lay crouching flat against a sloping branch. In this position it was difficult to hit it, and several shots were fired before one took effect. The puma snarled horribly, and, turning round to get to the trunk of the tree, received three more shots. This made it squat again, and several more shots were fired. At last it started to its feet and made a move to get to the trunk, but in doing so fell to the ground. Twenty dogs at once attacked it, and a terrible scrimmage took place. The puma fought furiously with the dogs, several of which were so torn that they died. The men could not fire at the struggling animals, and no one dared go near them, but in a few minutes the puma was dying, the dogs were driven off, and it was shot dead. It was skinned on the spot, and a quantity of the meat was carried home by the men to eat. We then searched round, and found the half-eaten carcase of our largest boar, which must have weighed 200 pounds.

Subsequently we fenced in the lower part of our house so as to exclude the goats and pigs, and had a large open shed built, in which was kept firewood, with odds and ends of every kind, and the goats and pigs slept there. One dark night my sister woke me, saying a tiger was killing one of our goats. I got up and heard a piteous bleating in the woodshed. We lighted the lantern and fired off my gun, but still the cries continued, so my sister and I sallied out to the rescue. She held the lantern while I walked in front with my double-barrelled gun cocked. We walked cautiously over the 40 yards of grass and stopped at the shed, afraid to enter its dark shadow; but the piteous cries of the goat still continued, and we were surprised to see the pigs lying in the dust quite unconcerned, and all the goats with their green eyes glittering in the light of the lantern, composedly chewing their cuds. We were certain from this evidence that there was no tiger about, and we searched all round to see where the cries came from. At last my sister saw the horns sticking out of an upright barrel of tar. The head had been opened and a gallon or so of tar taken out to tar a canoe, and the head replaced loosely. The goat, like all goats, loving high places, had jumped upon the top of the barrel, and the head giving way, it was plunged up to the neck in tar. So I mounted on top of the barrel with my feet on the rims, and laying hold of the horns, I hoisted the goat out of the tar and tumbled it on to the ground, and then we laughed and went to bed. Next morning the poor goat was covered with cocoanut-oil, washed with hot water and soap, and made as clean as possible, but all its hair dropped off, and it was a long time before it grew again.

On another occasion an Indian named Bowman, who slept in a part of our large kitchen, heard the pigs and goats rush wildly away, and then a short, sharp squeal from a pig. He opened the door, shouted, and threw firebrands out, then got his gun and fired two or three shots. We all woke and called out to Bowman to know what was the matter, but he did not know. All the dogs round about began barking, and daylight was close at hand. In the morning we went to feed the pigs with cocoanuts as usual, but to our astonishment, when they came near us, they gave a bark and rushed away in great alarm. We discovered the cause of this in the tracks of a tiger, and soon Bowman called to us to come and see what he had found, which was one of our largest pigs lying dead among the wood-pile, with its jaws broken and skull fractured. This had been done by a slap from the paw of a tiger, which had then been frightened and left its prey.

We had a large boathouse close to the edge of the lagoon, where our own and other people's canoes were kept. There was also a work-bench in it, and lots of shavings about, and many goats and pigs slept in this boathouse. They were continually disturbed in the night by the alligators, but as they were natives they were too wary to be caught. We had a large English pig of a whity-yellow colour, with large hanging ears, which was the admiration of the people, whose own pigs were black, long-legged, and with pointed up-standing ears. This pig usually slept in the boathouse, and one night we were wakened by a frightful screaming, but before we got to the boathouse the alligator had already reached the water with the pig.

On another occasion some Woolwa Indians had come down from the interior and slept in the canoes in the boat-house. In the middle of the night one of them heard a noise, and shouted out, when the alligator lashed out with its tail and split the canoe he was in from end to end.

But what pen can tell the joys of Blewfields to us boys? Every season had its own special pleasures.

About January most of the men went away down south for the hawksbill-turtle fishing, and the women and boys were left at home. Then followed the dry season, bright, joyous, beautiful. When at nine in the morning the land-wind died away, a squall or two and some showers followed; then down came the fresh sea-breeze, roaring among the trees, and lashing the lagoon into white waves—a cool, delicious, invigorating wind that never failed, steady at north-east. It made one long to bestir one's self and be off to the great world to take one's part in everything that is going on. You look up at the driving clouds and long to see what they are passing over, and go where they are going, and so one understands the longing of the migratory birds, and even of the butterflies and fish, which wander to distant parts, impelled by the seasons.

A district extending from the north of Pearl Key Lagoon to about Monkey Point is the exclusive home of the eboe, which is found nowhere else in this country. This is a gigantic tree, with immense trunk and spurs, like the

buttresses of a church. The wood is like rosewood, and so
hard that the best axes cannot cut one down. In February
it is covered with lovely pink blossoms, with a scent like
bitter almonds, and about April the nuts are ripe, and fall to
the ground in thousands. These are 3½ inches long, about
the thickness of one's thumb, round, but flattened at two
sides. On the outside is a grayish skin, inside of which is
an olive-green pulp a quarter of an inch thick; beneath that
a hard shell, which nothing but the powerful beak of the
macaw can crack, and inside is the eboe nut, 2¾ inches long,
and as thick as one's little finger.

Soon the bush is filled with women and children gathering
eboes. We suck the mawkish sweet pulp till we are sick of
it, but the nuts are gathered in calabashes and carried home
in great bag-like baskets made of withes and called *oosnoos.*
Then the piles of nuts are thrown on the ground, and pigs
and goats have a surfeit of the sweet pulp. When thoroughly
dry, the women set to work to crack the nuts, and make the
boys and girls help. To do this, you must get a good-sized
stone, and with a cold chisel cut a socket in it; then take
the cut-off end of a gun-barrel, place the nut in the socket
and strike it with the gun-barrel, and it cracks open.

Then for a while everyone is eating eboes, which are excellent in every form. They are, however, chiefly reserved for
boiling, when a quantity of very fine oil floats on the water.
This is skimmed off and bottled for use or sale. It is chiefly
used as hair-oil, and commands a price of five shillings a
bottle in Jamaica.

Our chief diet in the dry season was cockles and oysters,
of which great quantities exist in the lagoon. Gathering
cockles was a delightful occupation. They are found in the
muddy sand round the shores, but not in any great depth of
water. On an appointed day, women, boys and girls wade
into the shallow water and feel in the mud for the cockles;
but standing and stooping is tiresome, and the sun roasts

your back, so very soon all are lying prone on their faces in the water, each with a calabash in one hand, which is filled with cockles by the other. Chatting, laughing, and playing, this agreeable work is carried on for hours, till great piles of cockles are accumulated on the shore. The water, being at a temperature of above 80°, is even warmer than the air, so one does not get cold by being in the water for many hours.

Oysters exist where currents keep the rocky bottom clear of mud round about the islands, and in many isolated beds in the lagoon. Girls and boys are employed to gather them, which is done by anchoring the canoe on the bed in 4 to 8 feet of water. The boys and girls then slip into the water, holding on by the gunwale of the canoe, from which they dive to the bottom and fill a basket with the oysters. Often they are alarmed by the musky smell of an alligator, or the rank fishy smell of the shark. In such cases they scramble into the canoe and make much noise by beating the sides with their hands; but, strange to say, none were ever injured. I often joined in oyster-gathering parties, but I always had an instinctive feeling that my white skin was not safe.

It was more exciting to go with the men spearing fish. This pursuit is carried on in calm weather, generally before the sea-breeze comes down, and the immense shoals at the mouth of the Blewfields River are the most favourable place for it. In the lagoon are great numbers of calapever, which is a gigantic mullet, when full grown nearly 5 feet long, and the same shape as the common tropical mullet. There are also numbers of a still larger fish called snook, which is the Dutch name of the European pike. It is something like a pike, and equally voracious. The tarpum is a large fish with scales $2\frac{1}{2}$ inches in diameter, glittering like plates of silver.

The fishermen, two in each canoe, are provided with a light spear 9 feet long. At one end is fixed a fish harpoon,

generally made out of an old file, in which several barbs are
cut. A light strong line of silk grass, 50 feet long, is fastened
to the harpoon, and wound round a large wheel of very light
wood, which is stuck on the end of the spear. Paddling
gently along, the man in the bow sees the ripple made by a
fish swimming near the surface. At the distance of 60 or
70 feet the man aims his spear, and throws it into the air in
such a way that it descends on the fish almost vertically.
One has only to try to see how difficult it is to hit an object
in this manner, but the boys practise on cocoanut husks
from their earliest youth, and practice will make perfect
even in so difficult an exercise as this. When the fish is
struck the harpoon comes out of the end of the staff, and
the fish makes off, dragging the reel after it, by aid of
which it is pursued and captured.

A more exciting game is the capture of the manatee,
which is effected with the same weapons; but this is a
powerful animal, and only after chasing for a long time and
repeated harpooning can it be secured. This curious animal
belongs to a race nearly extinct. One species lives in the
sea, and is found in West Australia and New Guinea. It is
there called dugong, and is the animal from which the
fable of mermaids originated. Another species is found in
Africa, and one species is only found on the east side of
America and within the tropics.

The manatee is about 8 feet long, nearly 3 feet in diameter
in the thick part of the body, and weighs 500 or 600 pounds.
The female has breasts like a woman, and carries its young
under its flippers. The manatee has a mouth just like a
cow, and has no teeth in front, only hard gums. It has fore-
flippers, but no hind ones. The body contracts towards the
hind-part into a tail like a spatula. It loves fresh and
brackish water, and will venture into the sea, but does not
care for salt water. It never leaves the water, but I have
seen it half out of water munching the cutch grass that

grows on the banks of the rivers. It is covered with a thick slate-coloured hide, on which are a few scattered hairs, relics of the time, millions of years ago, when it lived on land and had legs, for hairs have no possible meaning in water. It has no ears, though its hearing is very keen, and its eyes are very small. The flesh is the most delicate and delicious, perhaps, in the world. It is pale like veal, and is all streaked with fat—a most delicate fat—like that of a sucking pig. Two hundred years ago, according to Dampier and others, the manatee was very plentiful, but it is getting rare now. One of the most important uses to which the manatee is put is to make straps from its thick hide to whip wives and other delinquents.

I have mentioned the Indian named Bowman who lived with us. He was sent to Blewfields from Cape Gracias à Dios by the Mosquito Queen to hunt and fish for her children. He was a great fisherman, but not much of a hunter, though sometimes he brought us an agouti, a monkey, or a curassow. His fishing was chiefly done with the bow and arrows, and most of the fish he killed were tooba, a deep, short fish like a perch, of a bluish-purple colour. In fishing he would softly paddle along under the steep banks, or glide along round snags, whistling all the time in a plaintive tone. Seated kneeling on the bow, bow and arrow in hand, he waited with the patience of a cat at a mouse-hole till the fish came near the surface, when he very seldom missed his mark. All day long he would idle about in this way with stolid patience, never uttering a word, but constantly whistling to the fish.

The King and I used to make frequent excursions in our canoe, hunting and fishing all day among the creeks and over the great shoals of the lagoon. Often we took the King's sisters with us, at which they were as delighted and as eager as English school-girls are to go to a picnic. Old Bowman would shoot fish for their amusement, or we would put him ashore in the bush while we went out on the vast shoals, where we taught the girls the art of spearing a large species of crab called ratee, which may be seen swimming along the bottom in 4 or 5 feet of water. Then we would paddle into the creek, and gather bunches of the fruit of the keesoo palm, which bears large bunches of large purple nuts, inside of which there is a white pulp, deliciously acid and sweet, while inside the pulp is a hard white nut. At times we were fortunate enough to find a few bunches of the 'hone' or oil palm, the same as that of Africa. It grows close to the water, within the tidal limits, with a thick short stem and very long fronds. The fruit is in bunches of 60 to 80 pounds' weight, bearing several hundred bright yellow nuts the size of a walnut.

The girls always took care to provide themselves with some plantains or a few roots of cassava, and at mid-day we would land in the bush, make a fire, and set the girls to roast the plantains or cassava and such game as we had, which was either fish, or crabs, or one or two ishilly lizards. Then towards evening we would go and pick up Bowman, and, getting into the open lagoon, put up sail and make for home, five or six miles off. Generally at this time the sea-breeze is very fresh, and as the canoe tore through the water, plunging over the waves and heeling over at the gusts till the water poured in over the lee gunwale, the girls screamed and yelled with fright, at which we were highly delighted. The girls could swim as well as we could, but girls love to scream, and do not like to get wet.

In May the turtle have arrived on the coast, and our food for two months or so is turtle meat and turtle eggs. At one time Gunter of London set up here an establishment to tin the turtle fat for the gourmands of London. He had great kraals made, in which there were hundreds of turtle confined, and as the people of the town could not consume a quarter of the meat he daily killed, it and all the offal was

thrown into the lagoon. The consequence was that sharks
and alligators swarmed to an incredible extent, and all our
bathing and games in the water were put a stop to. I was
told that the convict authorities in Tasmania took similar
means to prevent the escape of convicts from the peninsula
by swimming across the Eaglehawk inlet. All the offal of
Port Arthur and Hobart Town was taken to the inlet, and
there thrown into the water, with the result that it became
alive with sharks.

I have said above that in May the turtle arrive on the
coast. They stay till August, and then depart, no one
knows where, but it is probable they go to Florida and the
Bahamas. If the instinct of a carrier pigeon to find its way
home is wonderful, how much more so is the migration of
the turtle? They cannot see under water more than 20
yards or so, and even when they lift their heads out of water
to breathe, they can only see a very short distance, yet they
wander thousands of miles away, and every year return to
the Mosquito banks and keys, and know their own sandy
bays to lay their eggs in.

The valuable hawksbill turtles do not come to the great
coral banks and keys of the north, but frequent the southern
coast from about Monkey Point as far as Chagres, and
perhaps still farther south, in which parts the esculent green
turtle is rare. The green turtles also periodically visit
Ascension and St. Helena, but it would be rash to say that
they come from the Mosquito Coast, though this is the
principal centre which the green turtles frequent, and almost
all the turtles used in Europe come from the Mosquito
Shore. Besides the green and hawksbill, there is the
loggerhead turtle, but no one eats it, and it is never killed.

A full-grown turtle is proof against the bite of a shark,
but these wolves of the sea often bite the flippers off, and
we often got turtle so mutilated. Chicken turtle are either
crushed in the shark's jaws or swallowed whole, for I have

taken pounds of turtleshell out of a shark's maw. The eggs are so well concealed in the sand that they are seldom disturbed except by man. The young turtle, when they are hatched, are about twice the size of a penny, and as they struggle out of the sand no end of enemies devour them. When the survivors reach the water, the barracouta, dog-fish, and other fishes devour them, and when they grow to be chicken turtle, say the size of the top of a lady's bandbox, the sharks attack them, and as the turtle are not fast swimmers, only such can escape as are not noticed.

Towards the middle of May there are signs of the approach of the great rainy season, which is so remarkable a phenomenon in these latitudes. The crickey-jeen, a large cicada, then sounds its note, and the air is filled with its shrill ringing song, a dreamy, sleepy sound that promotes reveries and poetic fancies. The opening of certain flowers, the song of certain birds and of this cricket, each in its season, are the almanac of the Indians, the only marks they have to tell the periods of the year, and I have seen an Indian boy with tears in his eyes on hearing the song of the crickey-jeen, which reminded him of his home on the Wanx River, hundreds of miles away. This cicada is called katy-did in North America. I have also heard it in Brazil, but its song was different there, and failed to recall the dear associations which ours did.

About the end of May a butterfly of a greenish-blue, with golden-green stripes and long tails to its wings, passes over the country on its way to the south. At first they appear singly and at intervals, but soon in a continuous stream over the whole country and for miles out to sea. Day after day the air is filled with them, till about the middle of June, when they have all passed south. The Indians say they only fly along the coast, although I have seen them in the savannas and flying across the rivers. It is, however, possible that they prefer to fly low, which, on account of the lofty forests, they can only do by keeping along the coast. At sea they fly close to the water, and often alight on the surface to rest. In calm weather the stream of them extends many miles to sea, and over the shore to the edge of the forest. In heavy weather they are blown over the top of the forest towards the interior, but return to the coast when the land-wind blows. On some days they are in dense flocks; on other days there are only a few here and there. Thousands fall into the sea, of which most rise again, but many are drowned. If it becomes stormy or wet, the stream of butterflies ceases until the weather moderates.

Now the steady trade winds of the dry season become baffling and uncertain; frequent calms occur, and every day towards evening a dense dark bank of clouds hangs over the west, and the growling of distant thunder is heard. This thunder, the first of the year, is the warning signal for all eggs to hatch. If they fail to obey it, floods will drown the young creatures. Alligators, iguanas, tortoises, and sea-turtle, all hasten out of the egg at the warning of Alwaney, the great spirit of thunder, in whom we find the only conception of a god which the Indians of this coast acknowledge. Alwaney created the world, and governs it by appointing the seasons, but no one dreams of praying to him; he cannot be approached by man.

In June heavy squalls are frequent. They are like the tornados of the African coast. Their appearance is dreadfully ominous. Always coming from the east, they rise over the horizon black as night, or rather a ghastly bluish-black. Often waterspouts precede them. As they approach, the sky is overcast, the strong trade wind dies away, the wind comes off the land blowing towards the approaching squall, which is seen coming over the lagoon, lashing the waters furiously, and shrouded with a thick curtain of falling rain. First come scattered drops and flying puffs; then the squall breaks wildly over the land, accompanied with torrents as if the clouds had burst. Leaves and branches torn from the trees fill the air. Everyone rushes inside and closes his door, for if the wind gets into the house the roof will be hurled into the bush. The crash of falling trees is heard far and near in the woods. As the squall progresses the wind veers, showing that it is a rotary storm. Then after a quarter of an hour it is gone; a calm succeeds for a short while, then down comes the trade wind again, which in the rainy season is very strong, blowing east, and sometimes from the south of east. These squalls pass by one after another, sometimes five or six in the twenty-four hours.

But the great feature of the rainy season is the stupendous rain and thunderstorms which from time to time pass over us. The whole eastern horizon becomes a dense black mass, out of which the thunder growls incessantly. The east wind freshens up, and soon the sky is covered with such a thick mass of clouds that one can scarcely see to read inside the house. The rain comes down with a roaring sound on the leaves of the forest, like the sound of a great waterfall, or if you are at sea it makes a hissing noise on the surface of the water which is deafening. The lightning and thunder are terrific. I have been since those days over a great part of the world, and never heard thunder to compare with that on the Mosquito Coast. Some claps roar as if a world had burst; the noise is appalling, and totally unnerves one. Other claps tear through the air as if a demon were rending some gigantic cloth; others sound as if a million tin pans had fallen on the floor. For hours this may go on, then subside, and then commence again. The quantity of electricity to supply these thunderstorms is marvellous. I was once wakeful in bed, and witnessed a distant thunderstorm in the mountains to the south. There was a pendulum clock in the hall which ticked seconds, and for more than two hours there was a flash of lightning at intervals of never more than five seconds, and hundreds at intervals of one and two seconds. I fell asleep, and left this magnificent display still going on.

Usually there is a week or so of this weather. The rain generally comes up in the morning with the incoming sea-breeze, and pours in torrents until about four in the evening; then the rain subsides, but a dull slate-blue bank of clouds covers the sky. Then every drenched and hungry living thing comes out to snatch a hasty meal; the air is filled with millions of winged ants of different species, but the winged white ants (termites) in much the greater numbers. These fly to great heights, but vast numbers fall or alight on the ground, where they immediately raise the tail end, with which they dislodge their wings, and so become a crawling, soft and helpless insect. The floor, the table, the beds, and out of doors all the ground, are covered with shed wings, while the insects crawl about seeking concealment.

The winged males and females of the weewee, or leaf-carrying ant, are also on the wing. These are stout, heavy insects, with a round abdominal part as large as a pea. They also after a short flight come to the ground, knock their wings off, and immediately commence to burrow underground. One must suppose that ninety-nine and nine-tenths per cent. of them are destroyed, because the great underground nests of the leaf-carrying ant are permanent communities, and newly-established nests are rare. In Brazil the women and children gather the flying females of the leaf-carrying ants, wring off the abdominal part, and when a basketful is collected, roast them like peas in a frying-pan and eat them. I have often eaten them, and they taste like shrimps, but richer and fatter. In Blewfields we did not know of this delicacy.

But one should see the delight of the birds when the flying ants are out. Swallows dart about in thousands; great mysterious birds, which except on such occasions are never

seen, called rain-birds, hunt on the wing at an immense
height, far out of reach of the gun, and I never met anyone who had seen this bird to examine it.   Eager for the
occasion, and forgetful of their nocturnal habits, bats and
goat-suckers mingle in the festivities.   The fly-catchers are,
of course, masters of their art ; but now with astonishment
one sees birds totally unaccustomed to fly-catching timidly
and awkwardly trying their hand at it.   The toad, rare
visitor in the daytime, is now on the scene ; he sits on the
grass like a fat alderman in an armchair, motionless except
his goggle eye, which rolls in its socket as it follows the
course of a creeping white ant, and looks as if he were a
stage villain meditating some dark atrocity.   Suddenly he
jumps round in his armchair attitude—the creeping thing is
gone, and the toad smacking his lips.

The lizards of every kind are at the festive board on this
joyous occasion ; the little house-lizard—the male dark horn
colour, with saffron head and shoulders, and his wife ashen
gray, with little dark spots—one is glad to see getting a good
tuck in, for he is our friend in the house, and works hard for
a living, stalking flies on the walls and ceiling.   But the wild
lizards of the bush are there also.   A beautiful pale-blue
slender one is particularly active, and does a roaring trade
at picking up the crawling female white ants.   Also a large
bulky lizard, beautifully coloured, which rarely leaves the
shelter of the forest for fear of hawks, cannot now resist the
opportunity of having a good feed of fat white ants.   He
ventures into the open with much misgiving.   Turning his
head in all directions, he keeps an anxious lookout while he
furtively snatches up the choice food.   This is a true table
in the wilderness, spread by the Lord for His humblest
creatures.   The hen clucks to her chickens, and carefully
shows them that these crawling things are very good.   The
cock and his hens are as busy as can be ; the poor sitting
hen, hungry and patient, has at last discovered the state ot

affairs, and rushes with spread wings and loud cackling to the welcome feast. But one scene of horrid cruelty mars this joyful occasion. The resentful and wicked fire-ants are abroad in regiments and battalions. Their advance guard and skirmishers swarm over the ground, and everywhere is seen the poor soft, harmless white ant, writhing and struggling in agony between the cruel mandibles of its foe.

CHAPTER III.

'Marching army' ants—'Sheep's head' fishing—Close of the rainy season
—Migratory birds—Wees—Pigeons—Other visitors—Ducks, teal
and coots—Resident birds—Fly-catchers, etc.

AFTER a week or so of daily torrents, the weather clears up
for a few days or a week, the sun shines intensely, and the
ground steams. This is the time for the inroads of the
'marching army' ants, the Huns and Vandals of the insect
world. Everything falls before these invaders; old and
young are delivered over to their ruthless mandibles, and
they leave nothing but ruin behind them.

I have never found where these ants lie concealed when
not engaged in foraging; but two or three times in the year,
just before or after heavy rain, they come out of the forest
in millions, advancing in a solid column, which may cover
an acre of ground. Sometimes the column may separate in
divisions, one going in one direction, one in another. Each
travels in a fixed direction, in which it is directed by the
guards, distinguished by enormous heads and threatening
mandibles, who march ahead of the main body as if to
reconnoitre the ground. The army follows after its officers,
and rummages everything as it advances. Some swarm up
the trees to considerable heights, searching in all the cracks
of the bark, or among the parasitical plants; every fallen or
hollow log, and every stone, is carefully inspected. They
destroy as if a fire had passed over the ground. Snails,

beetles, butterflies, slugs, spiders, caterpillars, scorpions, centipedes, everything is devoured; wasps' nests are rifled of the grubs; birds are driven from their nests, and the young ones eaten up. Fortunately, few birds lay in the rainy season, but occasionally incursions of the army take place before the rains, when the birds are rearing their young. I have seen lizards 8 inches long writhing, lashing the tail, rolling over and over, covered with ants which have the horrid instinct to attack the eye first, distracting the unfortunate victim. Full-grown snakes are not molested, but I have seen the skeletons of small ones which had been devoured.

Twice in the middle of the night we have been roused by such invasions of the 'marching army' ants, and had to rush out of the house and wait outside till the foray was over. But we were consoled by their leaving us a clean house, for the ants search the thatch through and through, plunder the wasps' nests which line our eaves, and drag from hiding every lizard, cockroach, and spider. The greatest trouble we had on such occasions was to protect our hens and young chickens, and sometimes we saw the shocking sight of a poor chicken rolling on the ground covered with ants, its eyes eaten out, and cheeping pitifully.

Sometimes foraging parties from different nests meet, and dreadful battles take place, in which the armies are mixed in a confused mass, struggling, biting, tugging, and rolling over each other. The fight may last for twenty minutes, when the survivors draw off and go their way, leaving the ground covered with the dead and maimed. Sometimes an ant will lift up and carry away a wounded companion, but with what intention I could not ascertain.

But the dreadful rainy season, when, as the Indians say, 'no man goes out of doors,' has also its delights for us. A few days after a heavy burst of rain we perceive that the lagoon is brown with mud, and trees and rafts of driftwood

4

are floating all over it. Now is the time for 'sheep's-head' fishing. With all convenient speed we gather some calabash-fuls of cockles, and soon rows of canoes with women, girls, and boys are seen anchored about half a mile from the shore busily fishing for this delicious fish. Sometimes it rains in torrents, but that does not signify ; drenched to the skin, we eagerly pursue our sport. After a good flood the fish are abundant, and soon everyone in the town is eating fried 'sheep's-head.'

This fish is another of our mysteries. It is migratory, like so many living things in Mosquito-land. In fact, I often think that there are more migratory animals in this country than in any other part of the world. The 'sheep's-head' is over 12 inches long, about 8 inches deep, and 3 inches thick, striped black and white like a zebra. It appears at the first floods in June, and stays till about August, then disappears. It is found in the rivers of Florida and other parts of the Gulf of Mexico, but whether it migrates from here no one knows.

I used to be greatly puzzled by finding occasionally a stone in the brain of this fish. This is generally an angular fragment, clear as glass, but sometimes cloudy white. How it gets into the brain, or what purpose it serves, I have never heard explained.

July and August are dreadful months ; rain, thunderstorms, and squalls are constant, but towards the end of August it begins to clear up. The trade wind, which for three-quarters of the year is constant at north-east, becomes fitful and variable, and shifts to south-east, and occasionally there are a few days of south-west wind. When this happens, a wonderful change takes place in the atmosphere : the air becomes dry and cool, and the sky is deep blue—so different from the pale blue of ordinary weather. In June, July, and August the rainy season passes over us, taking two and a half months to do so.

From August to November migratory birds arrive, one species after another.

The wees yoola, or 'pet of the wees' (*Euphonia affioni*), arrive about the end of August, and depart at the end of December. They go in flocks of eight or ten. Their cry, 'wees-wee, wees-wee,' the Indians say, is meant to call the wees, and let them know the season is ready for them. When the sun is shedding his evening rays, a flock of wees yoola may be seen on some low tree, warming their breasts in the sun, and giving out their sweet plaintive notes. Then, night coming on, they ascend to the high trees to sleep.

The wees then begin to arrive, at first in small numbers, presently followed by immense flocks. On first arriving, feeling strange, they keep to the highest trees, and in the night their cries are heard as flock after flock passes overhead to the south. Soon the whole country swarms with them. At first they are very lean, but before long they are so fat as to be scarcely eatable, although the fat is white and palatable, and the bird is the most delicate morsel in the country.

As soon as they are perceived, the little black boys announce the fact by shouting joyously, 'Wees, day come.' Soon every favourite tree is crowded with hungry birds, while others, unable to obtain foothold, flutter round, or vainly try to settle on the backs of those that are perched. Others crowd the neighbouring trees, patiently waiting for their turn to feed. Should the weather be wet on their arrival, they resume their flight southward, and on a rainy day they sulk in the high trees, coming down to feed in the calm, still evenings.

Soon the wees have increased in numbers, and venture to descend on the wild sage, and before long they are in tens of thousands, and swarm in large flocks on every bush and tree. Every available weapon is now brought to bear on them—blunt-headed arrows, stones, sticks, and guns. They are so fat that they often burst in falling. Again the Lord has spread a table in the wilderness, and for weeks and weeks we all eat fat wees. In whatever way prepared, they are delicate, rich, and delicious. The poor birds are the victims of sparrow-hawks, which now appear in unusual numbers, and are very successful in killing them.

After staying with us for about six weeks, the wees diminish in numbers, and then disappear till next year.

The Indians know that autumn has come by the cries of this bird, heard as they pass at night, 'wees, wees, wee, wee,' and they call the autumn *weestara* (great wees).

P. H. Gosse, in his 'Birds of Jamaica,' says the wees arrive there in April, but if they go from here to Jamaica, or come from there here, they are long about it, as they leave here in October. They arrive in the islands of St. Andrews and Old Providence in October, in so exhausted a condition as to be unable to fly.

Soon after the wees the bootkoo pigeon makes its appearance. Some of these pigeons stay with us all the year, but about November their numbers are greatly increased by migration from somewhere else, probably from Mexico. Our pigeons time their arrival for the ripening of several fruits, such as that of the trumpet-tree, on which they very frequently meet their death. Their arrival is welcome, and they are saluted with volleys all over the bush, against which they protest with their 'bootookoo,' now heard in every tree. Pigeons are, like the English, very fond of islands. All over the world this is noticeable, and if it were not for their numbers, I believe they would live nowhere else. On an island in Blewfields Lagoon, they crowd in vast numbers, and there prefer to live and build their nests. They also, in the migratory season, frequent the keys and islands off the coast, much to the annoyance of the resident pigeons, who live on those islands and nowhere else.

The bald-pate pigeon lives on the keys and islands, and never ventures to the mainland, although some of the keys are only 12 miles off. It is probable that it does not like the risk of living where it must be continually on the watch for hawks, monkeys, toucans, snakes, quashes, and opossums. All species of our pigeons build their nests in trees, and I know of no rock pigeons in America.

In September and October the migratory butterflies mentioned above begin to return from the far south, and great streams of them cover the country and the sea, making for the north.

About this time some rare and beautiful birds pay us a short visit. The most striking of these is the redbird (*Pyranga æstiva*), called by the Indians awas yoola, or 'the pet of the pine-tree,' *awas* being the pitch-pine, and *yoola* a pet animal of any kind. This beautiful bird is rare, and only a few are to be seen, perched on low trees and flying from bush to bush. Its slim figure and crimson plumage make it the most elegant and most remarkable of all our birds. Nature, having given it a beautiful dress, has seen fit to withhold any other gifts, and except its little chirp it has no voice. I have seen this bird in the savannas of the north at other seasons than that at which it visits us, so that its migrations probably extend no farther than the northern parts of this coast.

Another visitor at this time is the bluebird. I have seen this bird in Brazil, and it is common all over South and Central America. With us it is certainly a migratory bird, but it is difficult to determine where it comes from or goes to. The small migratory birds seem to keep together in little flocks, so that when they arrive they are easily noticed. The hen birds are usually different in colour, and even in figure, from the cocks. The Creoles, and even the Indians, do not always know this fact, and one is apt to be deceived as to the number of species that arrive. Both the awas yoola and this bird are slim and elegant, and active fliers. This bird arrives in November, and departs in July.

The sickla is so punctual in its arrival that the Indians

call the month of August by the name of the bird, or *vice versâ*. This bird, the upper parts of which are olive-green, and the under parts bright yellow, loves the savannas and all open places. Alighting on an orange or mango tree, they immediately begin an inspection of the branches, hopping to the outermost tips in search of insects and snails. Even spiders' webs are robbed of the captured flies, and several times I have seen the bird caught in the powerful web of the hanancy spider, where it must have suffered a lingering death, for it is very doubtful whether the spider would attack it. After a day of rain, in the dull, still evening the little flocks of sicklas swarm over every bush, chirping sweetly and brightening the scene with their brisk action and lovely colours.

The migratory greenbird, which has the head of a dark slate colour, shaded into olive-green on the back and shoulders, is a brisk and lively bird, with a pleasant chirp. It only remains with us six weeks, and during that time it is very busy among the bushes, and even hunting its prey among the grass.

The redhead blackbird is a small dumpy bird, jet black, with thighs and parts under the wings light yellow, while the head is bright scarlet, fading into white at the edge of the black. This bird is slow and heavy in flight, quiet and solitary, with no voice worth listening to. It always seems uneasy, and anxious to be off, wherever that may be to, for it only stays with us a few weeks.

The blackhead greenbird has the entire plumage a fine bluish-green, with metallic lustre; the crown of the head being black in the males only. This bird is of a solitary habit, going alone or at most in pairs. On a bright sunny morning, however, I once saw a flock of them disporting themselves on one of those vast leafy curtains which shroud the banks of the rivers, hanging from the tops of lofty branches to the edge of the water and matted throughout, composed of convolvulus and other flowering vines. To the face of this curtain the birds were clinging, diving through its apertures into the recesses of the foliage.

One of the most important migrations is that of the ducks, teal, and coots. These, flying before the advancing winter of North America, now seek our genial latitudes.

I have mentioned the enormous expanse of shoal water at the mouth of the Blewfields River, which is overgrown with water-grasses and other weeds. Here the migratory water-fowl settle in vast flocks, which are dotted about over the shoals, and on still nights their quacking and the noise they make on the water can be heard miles off. The ducks and teal mix together, but the coots keep by themselves in great flocks. Among them are a few of the beautiful whistling ducks of Florida; but these are very restless, not having completed their migration; and every night we hear their shrill cheery whistle as they fly farther south.

Now for many months the vast invading hordes of ducks, teal and coots stay with us, feeding on our ample water pastures. At first men as well as boys go out shooting them, but before long they become extremely wary, and then the men leave the sport to the boys, who follow it up with energy and skill.

On a duck-hunt we would leave home at four in the morning, so as to arrive before daylight along the mangroves of the river mouth, hidden by which we decided on our mode of working the ducks according as we found the flocks distributed. If they were close by and in shallow water, one of us would slip out of the canoe and lie flat on the bottom, the head out of water, crowned with a tuft of leaves; and holding the gun above the water, we would advance by burying the big toe in the mud and pushing the body forward. If, as usual, the ducks were a quarter of a mile off, we would make a most exhausting journey, and be ready to sink under water before we got within range. The ducks also would be suspicious of the peculiar object on the water, and would keep edging off, till we could endure no longer, when rising on our feet suddenly, while the ducks did the same on their wings, we would discharge both barrels into the crowd of birds, and generally kill or wound fifteen or twenty. Then the canoe would come up, getting into which we joined in the pursuit of the wounded birds.

This sport was not without some risk. On one occasion, a boy in getting out trod on a large stingray, which pierced his heel with the barbed bone it carries over the tail, inflicting a wound which took months to heal. On another occasion I was just preparing to get into the water, which was about 4 feet deep, when I noticed what I took to be a large log on the bottom. One of the boys poked it with the sail-sprit, when it whisked round, nearly upsetting the canoe, and made off, appearing on the surface at a distance—an unmistakable alligator. Another time one of us was preparing to get out of the canoe, when a large shark came cruising by. Our Indian, Bowman, buried an arrow in its back, and we had the satisfaction of seeing the end of the arrow flying through the water till it disappeared in the distance.

When the ducks, by dint of much hunting, got very shy, our last ruse was to dress up the canoe in mangrove bushes, make a great circuit, get to windward of them, and let the canoe drift with the wind towards the flocks ; then by twos and threes the more suspicious would take wing, till at last, with a roar like a gale of wind, the whole would rise, and our only chance was to fire among them, however far off they were. Finally they became so shy that there was no getting near them, and they were then left in peace.

We must not forget our resident birds which stay with us all the year ; and of these the most conspicuous are the fly-catchers, a very dominant tribe all over America.

The kiskidee, or tyrant fly-catcher, is a bird that is not to be passed unnoticed. He takes good care to be seen and heard on all occasions. It is a spirited and powerful bird, much given to attacking and pursuing other birds. I have often been amused at the perplexity and distress of a great John-crow vulture pursued by a pair of these birds, which fly faster than the John-crow. Rising over it, they swoop down and dig into its back with their bills. The vulture tosses and dives, and tries to ward off its pursuers with its wings, but the little tyrants never leave it till they think it is far enough from their nest, to which they return with triumphant screams.

He is cheerful and bold, and enlivens the country with his loud cries, resembling ' kiskidee, kiskidee,' uttered from the highest trees all round, from which he makes constant excursions to capture passing insects. In the cold foggy mornings, just about daybreak, they warble a most peculiar loud and musical note, resembling, as the negroes say, ' Fiddledee, fiddledee to maree.'

Another species, called by the Indians keeooroo, and by the Creoles Rise-up-hair, is a pensive and melancholy bird. He plies his trade busily in the cool of the morning and evening; but in the heat of the day he seeks a shady retreat, where he pensively calls to his mate ' lewee,' which the negro boys say his mate answers with ' wide awake,' but this is a poetic fancy of theirs. But among the many sleepy sounds which pervade the air in the drowsy heat of mid-day, the plaintive inquiry of ' lewee ' is always heard.

A bird called by the Indians peeweeo, but known in books as the clapper lark, is noticeable in the woods by his loud cracking noise. These birds go in little flocks of six or eight, with one cock bird to each flock. The male has the singular habit of amusing his females by perching sideways on an upright twig and darting to another in the same position, or to the ground. This is done very rapidly and frequently, and each time he makes a loud cracking noise, followed by the cry ' peeweeo '; thus, crack, ' peeweeo,' crack, 'peeweeo,' in rapid succession, pronounced in an excited tone like the crow of a cock. On one making his crack, all the others within hearing do the same, till all round it is as if fifty men with guns were snapping percussion caps. I have often enticed the birds by breaking a dry twig, on hearing which they would at once begin to dance and crack. If I kept up the game, they would, as if provoked, fly round me looking for their rivals. The hens, meanwhile, listen with approval to the brave noise of their cock, giving him encouraging glances, but going on with their search for insects, which they perform by turning over leaves and sticks on the ground, or swarming up a mossy trunk, searching round and round it with great diligence. I often thought the cock bird would starve because he devotes so much time to dancing and cracking; but no doubt he has his time for feeding also. In the male the crown is black, the neck, throat and upper part of the back white, so that the bird looks as if it had a tippet on. In the female all upper parts and the throat are dark olive-green.

A little bird of the sparrow tribe is the most constant and most pleasant songster we have. It is remarkable for its diminutive size and its thick, heavy bill. The male is black, the female olive-green. In the morning it trills a little set song, which is heard everywhere, from the number of birds which are singing together, while the little hens are dumb as mice. This bird is very fond of wild-sage berries, the seeds of which he cracks with his powerful little bill. Leaving the hens to feed, the cock perches on a dry twig where he can see and be seen, and then whistles with spirit. Occasionally he stops to listen intently to the notes of another of his kind, then tosses up his head and shows what he can do. After a while he has enough of this, and dives down among the bushes to feed, and silence reigns till he is satisfied.

English writers of travels often remark that tropical, or rather foreign birds have no song, and it is difficult to convince them that they are entirely wrong. Thus, Brazilian and Australian writers pronounce the English birds a fraud in song; and the truth is that appreciation of the songs of birds is entirely founded on association and sentiment. It is as impossible that the songs of English birds should arouse any admiration in a New Zealander as it is that the lovely notes of the New Zealand birds should be admired by an Englishman.

CHAPTER IV.

Early adventures—Perilous voyage—On the island—Voyage resumed—
The *Nile*—Across the bar—Attack on Fort Serapiqui—Make a
' prize '—Filibuster Walker—Adventures.

I OFTEN wonder how it was I escaped with my life from the
innumerable risks I ran in my youth among the Creoles and
the Indians of the Mosquito Shore, in bathing and voyages
in the rivers and lagoons, in capsizing at sea, or among the
breakers of the beach or the river's mouth.

Once I had occasion to go from Blewfields to Greytown,
a distance of 60 miles. We made the voyage in a small
cranky canoe, in which were two mulatto boys of sixteen and
nineteen years of age, and myself. In the canoe were an
axe, a machete, an iron pot full of boiled turtle meat, a bunch
of plantains, and a small demi-john of water, all securely
lashed to the thwarts.

We sailed out of the lagoon with the early land-wind, and
arriving at the bluff, we noticed that the sea was rough and
there were occasional heavy breakers on the bar. We
dodged them and got out to sea. The sea-breeze soon came
down strong from the south, and we discussed the prudence
of going back into the lagoon, but resolved to go on. As the
wind was southerly and our course due south, we made a tack
to sea until we were out of sight of land, but the wind and
sea kept rising and the sky looked very bad to the south-east.
We then tacked again, but by this time the wind was fresh

and squally and the sea very rough. The canoe went tearing through the waves, and we sat on the weather gunwale when the puffs came, and suddenly dropped back into our seats as the puffs passed, luffing up to the wind when the canoe heeled over too much, and keeping away when possible. But these are ticklish manœuvres, and before long the canoe went bows under and upset. We soon righted her, baled out, and proceeded on our voyage; but the wind and sea were too much, so we took the sprit out of the sail, thus making a shoulder-of-mutton sail of it. Thus shortened of sail, the canoe would not keep up to the wind, and we saw that we could not make a course for Greytown.

Presently we saw through the clouds the mountains of Monkey Point, and we made for the shelter of the island which lies off it. In coming round between the point and the island, we found a rough and breaking sea. One breaker took the canoe in the stern, buried the bow under water, and rolled us over and over. One after another the breakers rolled the canoe over and nearly drowned us, as we had to dive to avoid each breaker. At last we were washed through this tide-race into smooth water in the lee of the island, and gladly got into the canoe, baled out, and paddled to shore on the island. By this time it was blowing hard with squalls of rain, and dense clouds rolled over the mountains to the west of Monkey Point. Shivering with cold and drenched till our skin was wrinkled and white like soaked sheepskin, we took out the shot-bag, and to our delight found that the horn tinder-box was quite dry. Our axe and machete were safe, but the pot of meat had broken loose and was at the bottom of the sea, and our demi-john of water was gone. We soon had a good fire of driftwood and roasted our plantains, while the boys went round the rocks to see what was to be had, returning to the fire with hats full of large whelks, crabs, and mussels, which, roasted, made a good dinner with our plantains.

Taking advantage of the little daylight that remained, we cleared away the stones, hauled up the canoe, turned it bottom up, and lay naked in its shelter till our clothes were dry. Then we gathered round the fire to smoke, but finding that smoke increased our thirst, we had to give up that comfort. We slept well under our canoe, soothed by the roar of the breakers on the windward side of the island and the rustling of the wind among the trees. Towards morning the sea-breeze subsided, and the cold land-wind came off, but with it came millions of sandflies, which soon put us in a fever of irritation, and compelled us to rise and make up our fire to get into the smoke. These sandflies are the size of particles of very fine dust—that is, they are only just visible—and it is a mystery how such a minute fly can have a bill long enough to penetrate through the coarse skin of a man or a horse, and reach the bloodvessels below. They destroy all the pleasures of the seaside in the tropics, but fortunately they do not spread inland.

As soon as it was daylight, we went to look for water, and soon found enough in the little trickling gullies that descend from the higher parts of the island. Then we ascended a tree and had a good look out on the sea. The east looked windy, and the sea was rough, though better than yesterday. We made a hasty breakfast on roasted plantains, and set off with the land-wind—a beautiful fresh wind, laden with the sweet smell of flowers. For an hour or two the sky in the west cleared, and we had a glorious view of the rough, densely-wooded mountains, and to our astonishment we saw in the clear sky, above all the clouds, the vast summit of the volcano of Cartago, with a wisp of smoke rising out of it. This volcano is 12,000 feet high, and in the rainy atmosphere of this coast is rarely seen. We also saw on Monkey Point a straight path cleared in the woods from the water edge till lost in the mountains of the interior. This path, half a mile wide, was evidently the work of a waterspout.

The coast from Monkey Point to Greytown forms a deep bay, and our course being straight across it, we were soon out of sight of land. About 8 a.m. the land-wind died away and left us becalmed under a roasting sun, and with no water to drink. We could see from the sky that the sea-breeze was not far off, so we did not care to heat our blood by paddling, but, pouring water over our heads, waited on Providence, assisting with much whistling to bring the wind. Here we were unnecessarily alarmed by an enormous jew-fish, a thing which none of us had ever seen before. It seemed to be 20 feet long and quite as broad, and kept at the surface, flapping its great wing-like sides, and causing waves in the sea which broke on its back as if it were a rock. Not knowing the character or functions of such a monster, we made haste to get away from it.

At last the hot, glassy sea was marked with the ruffling of coming gusts, and after a few of these had passed, with intervals of calm, the sea-breeze came down in earnest. The breeze was well to the north and behind us, so we carried on in great style, and tore through the water.

About two o'clock we saw a large ship at anchor right ahead, and the dim outline of the coast behind her. The nearer we got, the larger the ship appeared, and we wondered exceedingly. By this time the wind was very fresh, the sea running high, and we had all we could do to manage the wild career of our canoe, flying over the waves and threatening every moment to upset. As we came near we were lost in wonder and admiration. The ship was like a floating mountain. We had never seen anything like it. There were three decks of guns ; the masts were like the largest trees in the forest, and at the stern were verandas and windows. The vessel was anchored 2 miles outside of Greytown bar ; she was pitching heavily, and the seas were flying over her bows.

We sailed close by her, and numbers of people were looking

at us.   As we came near the bar of the harbour, we noticed
with uneasiness the waves breaking heavily here and there,
and before we knew what we were about, a green sea toppled
up, roaring, and in an instant broke over us, upsetting the
canoe and rolling it over.   One of the boys jerked the mast
out of the thwart, while we swam round to pick up our
paddles ; then one got in and baled out with a paddle as
hard as he could, while we hung on to the gunwales.   While
in this position we heard a shrill whistle from the three-
decker, and saw them lowering a boat in all haste, and soon
they were pulling towards us to help us in our perilous position, for there is no harbour in the world so dangerous for
sharks as Greytown.   By the time the man-o'-war boat was
within 300 yards of us we had baled out, put up sail, and
sailed in over the bar without accident.

Inside the harbour were two English frigates and one
American.   The English, if I remember rightly, were the
Spartan and *Cossack*, and the ship outside was the *Nile*, line-
of-battle ship, commanded by Commodore Erskine.   At this
time the American Transit Company was running steamers
from Greytown up to Lake Nicaragua, to the Pacific port of
Rivas, where the Californian steamers met them.   The company had a large settlement on the landspit which enclosed
Greytown Harbour from the sea, and there I landed and put
up at the house of one of the steamboat captains.

One day I was at dinner at Consul Green's, and the officers
of the *Nile* were there also.   They were talking about the
gale, and one of them mentioned that the evening before it,
while a heavy sea was running, a little canoe with a white
boy and two Creole boys had passed close to them, and upset
not far off ; but before they could get to them in the boat,
they had righted the canoe, put up sail, and were off.   They
were much astonished when I told them I was the white boy,
and after that they took me on board the *Nile*, and were very
kind to me.

My father had a large contract to supply firewood to the steamers, and being backwards and forwards in Greytown for a long time, I soon knew all the men-of-war officers, and especially the midshipmen, whom I used to pilot about the various creeks in their eager pursuit after alligators and the most voracious sharks in the world.

In the year 1848 Consul-General Patrick Walker took possession of San Juan del Norte as belonging to the Mosquito kingdom, and renamed it Greytown. Soon after the Nicaraguan Spaniards came down the river, and captured two or three officials who had been appointed by Consul Walker to administer the affairs of the port. The result was that two frigates and the steam-corvette *Vixen* called at Blewfields to take in Consul Walker, and I begged Captain Ryder of the *Vixen*, with whom I was a great pet, to take me along, which he did.

We were soon all anchored at Greytown, and about twenty boats, with sailors and marines, were got ready. The paddle-box boats of the *Vixen*, and two large boats from each frigate, with howitzers in the bow, set off up the river a few hours after our arrival, with captured guides to show us the way through the many-branching creeks which form the delta. I was in Captain Ryder's gig, Consul Walker in Captain Loch's gig, and my brother-in-law, G. F. von Tempsky— afterwards killed in the Maori War—in another boat.

We pulled up the river till late at night, when all the boats anchored in the middle of the river, three miles below the Spanish fort of Serapiqui. Here Consul Walker fell overboard and was drowned, no one knows how.

At daylight the boats were all pulling up the river against a strong current. As we neared the fort we kept close under the bamboos on the far side of it, and many shots were fired at us out of the bush, which the marines returned with volleys.

Turning round a point, we saw the fort on the opposite

side. It was placed on a sloping bluff, all the forest of which had been lately felled, the hillside being covered with a tangled mass of trees and branches blackened by fire. The fort was formed of two heavy stockades, one close to the water, the other higher up. The walls were made of large logs laid lengthways one above the other, secured by heavy posts stuck in the ground. Embrasures were made for the guns, and the line of walls was zigzagged in and out to allow the defenders to fire along the outside of the walls. The fallen trees had been dragged and piled up along the landing-place, and to this day I do not know how the sailors and marines got through them. Many houses were built above and outside the fort, and within it were two or three large buildings containing stores and arms. Both stockades were armed with carronades, but how many I do not know.

As soon as we appeared, round shot was fired at us, which mostly crashed through the trees on our side, among which their own men were firing at us. I was nearly at my wits' end with terror at the whistling of bullets and the noise of the cannon-balls; but I was sufficiently in possession of my senses to hear the mode of attack talked over by Captains Loch and Ryder. The former said: 'We will pull up till we get above, then drop down and make a dash at them.'

So all the boats pulled along under the branches until some distance above the fort; then they turned round and 'gave way'; but the nearest boats grounded on a shoal in the middle of the river, and then there was a pretty mess, which under less cool and able leaders than Captains Loch and Ryder would have resulted in disaster.

I was so excited and alarmed that I cannot give an account of what was done. I can only relate incidents. The captain's gig, in which I was, pulled round in and among the boats, giving orders. The gun-boats were firing shell on the fort. Some of the sailors were up to the armpits in the river, pushing the boats off. The cracking of musketry, the explosions of cannon, the 'ping' of bullets, the roaring of cannon-balls, shouting, cheers, cries of all kinds, passed all description. I heard the sailors say that the fort was firing grape-shot at us, and one or two went through our gig.

One gunboat grappled hold of our gig to keep it steady; the mouth of its cannon was between me and the coxswain, and in this position it let drive at the fort. The explosion knocked me down in the bottom of the boat, and nearly burst my ears; the smoke curling round choked me. The next explosion nearly finished me, but Captain Ryder, who was as cool as possible, seeing my agony, ordered the gunboat to let go and clear out. The boy in the bow of our gig was shot through the neck, and the coxswain next me was wounded in the leg. At last—I knew it must come—something, said to be a splinter, struck me on the forehead and temple, and I remember no more, although I was told Captain Ryder threw a cloak over me, thinking I was dead.

I suppose it was the intolerable heat which made me come to. I threw off the cloak and sat up. All the boats were at the shore, and soldiers were guarding them; but a fearful noise was going on up at the fort—shots, cries, yells, roars, cheers. It was awful!

Seeing a big paddle-box boat close by, I went to it and saw a middy, a great friend of mine, badly wounded and soaked in blood, and a sailor in the same plight at the bow. The middy was in agonies and apparently dying, and I never forget that he could give a thought to others. When I looked down at him he said: 'Good God, Bell! what a face you have! Where are you hit?' In fact, I did not notice till then that the whole side of my face was black and blue and swelled, so that it was like a mass of blubber.

He said: 'Oh, if I could get an orange!' So I went off up to the fort to see if I could get anything for him. By this time the firing was quite fitful, carried on away up the hill near the standing forest.

When I got inside the stockade I noticed dead bodies lying all about, and wounded men creeping and crawling to get into shelter. One cannon near the gate I entered was upset, several dead men lying beside it, and some wounded groaning and crying at the foot of the stockade. A large dog was lying on the ground with a bullet through its body.

Seeing soldiers and sailors bustling about in the great storehouse, I went in, when a corporal of marines from our ship, the *Vixen*, said : ' Come on, youngster, quick, and get something.' With the butt of his musket he knocked off the lid of a large trunk, and pulled out piles of ladies' clothing. In a box was a lot of jewellery, of which he gave me a beautiful coral rosary with a heavy gold cross. A sailor gave me a fine double-barrelled fowling-piece. The sailors were tossing out of the windows into the yard below sacks of oranges, barrels of flour, bunches of plantains and bananas, bales of jerked beef, bags of sugar, and no end of boxes of people's luggage.

I now remembered my poor middy, so I filled my shirt-bosom and my hat with oranges, and hastened to the landing-place. As I was feeding him and the sailor, a volley was fired at the boats, some of the bullets striking our boat. In the twinkling of an eye I jumped into the boat, and lay trembling at the bottom.

The boat guard hid themselves behind the boats, and blew a bugle, when in no time a party of marines came down and drove the enemy from the thicket of sung-sung trees on a projecting point a few hundred yards off.

I then returned to the fort, and met Captain Ryder, who said : ' My dear child, I thought you were dead ! But what a face you have got ! Come with me and look round.' He had a guard of sailors, and we walked all over both forts.

I saw the dead being placed side by side, and the wounded lifted on to stretchers and carried down the steep bank to the landing. We came to where the men were lifting a handsome young officer and placing him on a plank; his leg was shattered below the knee. We followed as they carried him carefully down the bank. In doing so his leg slipped off the plank, and it looked so horrible that I turned away, deadly sick.

About two in the afternoon the boats drew off to the middle of the river, and there anchored to have dinner. Before long we noticed a number of women at the landing waving a cloth at the end of a stick, and Captain Loch ordered a well-armed boat to go and see what they wanted, telling the officer of it to be careful and not be surprised. He came back, and said there were about thirty women, some only half dressed, and they begged to have their clothes given to them, which they must have assumed the sailors had plundered. So all were made to give up what they had, and the boat was sent back to the women, who were asked if they wished to be taken to Greytown; but they said their friends were in the bush, and they would stay with them.

At night several boats were despatched back to Greytown with the wounded, and I was sent in one of them. Next day, while we were pulling down the river under a terribly hot sun, we saw a large river cargo-boat, called a *bongo*, drifting along with the current. We pulled alongside of it, and found it to be loaded with cochineal and indigo. I told the midshipman in charge that the cargo was immensely valuable, and he resolved to make a prize of it. The sailors got into it, and pulled it into a little creek out of sight of the main river, and there they tied it up.

We soon reached Greytown, and I went to live in the *Vixen* till Captain Ryder returned from the expedition, which had proceeded up the river to Lake Nicaragua to rescue the captured Mosquito officials. Next day an old

Spanish merchant came on board the *Vixen* in a furious rage. The officers could not understand his Spanish, and I was summoned to interpret. I was struck with confusion when I saw him stamping on the deck and calling out, with wild waving of his arms :

'Quadrillas de ladrones han robado mi bongo.' (A parcel of thieves have stolen my *bongo*.)

'What does he say ?' asked the First Lieutenant.

'He says they have stolen his *bongo*.'

'Ask him who stole it.'

'Algun ladron de ustedes.' (Some of you thieves.)

I was now on the horns of a dilemma. I was among the thieves, and I did not like to betray the middy who had thought it was lawful prize of war.

The Lieutenant asked angrily :

'What does he say ?'

In my perplexity I blurted out :

'Some of you thieves.'

'Some of us thieves! What the devil does he mean? Tell him if he uses such words to a British officer I will have him tied up and flogged.'

Matters had now come to what the French call an *impasse*, so I explained to the officer what we had done. He looked very angry, but I could see a smile behind his frowns.

'The damned little jackass! Where is he ?'

'Gone ashore, sir,' said a midshipman.

'Send and bring him off.'

After awhile I was summoned again, and had to interpret the apology which my friend was made to give to the irate Spaniard. To our astonishment, the benevolent old man had completely changed, and instead of receiving apologies he poured them on our heads. Then a sailor was sent to show him where his *bongo* was hidden, and all was peace.

Eight years after this I had another adventure on the Greytown River. My father had large contracts with the

SAVALO CREEK, GREY TOWN RIVER.

American Transit Company to supply firewood to the steamers, and on this occasion we had about forty Mosquito and Toongla Indians cutting firewood at the mouth of the Savalo, a tributary of the Greytown River.

At this time Walker, the filibuster, had possession of Nicaragua with a small army of Kentucky riflemen and other adventurers; but all the Central American States had combined to drive him out, and they sent a circular paper to everyone on the river warning them to leave, otherwise the Central American States would not be responsible for their lives or property.

I was alone with my Indians, my father and Von Tempsky being at Blewfields, and I was pushing our men to the utmost to get our contract completed, so that we might leave before catastrophes occurred; but I could not get down the river without a pass from General Walker, as his troops held the forts of Castillo Viejo and Serapiqui.

The wood-station at Savalo had an extensive clearing, on which the Company had many head of cattle. In my camp I had ten barrels of flour, several of salt beef, a hogshead of molasses, several barrels of biscuits, and many bunches of plantains.

On Sunday the Indians went hunting, and returned with half a dozen monkeys and several of a small species of alligator about 6 feet long, which is edible. This meat was all barbecued and hung up. Early on Monday the Indians came to me in great alarm, saying several steamers crowded with men were coming down the river. I tried to reassure them, but the Indians liked Americans as little as they did Spaniards, and they fled into the bush.

With much misgiving I stood my ground, while the steamers landed 700 men at the station. It was soon evident that they were hungry, for they killed the Company's cattle and ate up everything I had, including the monkeys and the crocodiles. When I told them what kind of meat it was, they swore promiscuously, but did not seem to mind it.

After awhile I approached General Walker, who was seated upon a rug on the grass, surrounded by officers. He was a little strip of a man, about 5 feet 3 inches high, and I wondered to see him in command of these stalwart Kentuckians and tall Germans.

I asked Walker for a pass to get out of the river. He asked me what countryman I was. I said I was an Englishman. He replied: 'This is no place for an Englishman; give him a rifle, and send him on board.'

I thought this was very unkind, seeing that Walker was my own countryman; but I was not allowed to argue, and all I could do was to write to the British Consul and to the agent of the Transit Company, telling him that the Indians would leave, and that there would be no more wood at the station.

Walker and his army went down the river to strengthen the forts, and I went by a return steamer to Rivas, on Lake Nicaragua. On our way we dismantled the fort of San Carlos at the entrance of the lake, spiked the guns and threw them into the water, burned the buildings, and cut down the stockade, for all the forts were made of logs except Castillo Viejo, which is an old Spanish fort of stone. Lake Nicaragua must be the most beautiful lake in the world. Over the blue water the soft north-east trade wind constantly cools the tropical heat, and lashes the water into bright, flashing waves. Wooded islands, partly cultivated, dot its southern side, and at its western end two volcanoes rise out of the water to a height of 7,000 feet. To the south-east are the lofty ranges of Costa Rica, with the Volcan de Cartago, 12,000 feet high. Among these mountains rises the Rio Frio, where to this day a remnant of the Rama Indians defy the white man, and allow no one to enter their country. To the north are the distant savannas of Chontales, with the faint outline of the mountains to the east of them, interesting to me because they are the mysterious mountains where all our rivers of the Mosquito Coast rise. Among them the first thunder of the year utters its warning growl, and from them come our dreadful floods of the rainy season. West of them are dry weather and grassy country; east of them, rainy weather and dense forests.

At Rivas no one seemed to be in charge of me, and I soon made friends with the rough but frank Americans in the camp. I used to sit at their fires and tell them of my adventures among the Indians, and perhaps the information I gave them may have been useful, for shortly after I left there was a dreadful battle in which the Americans were defeated. They were shot wherever they were found, and the only ones that escaped were those who reached the Chontales Sierras and descended the rivers to the Mosquito Coast.

Before long General Walker returned and gave me a pass to get out of the river, and the agent of the company directed me to fill up the woodshed and come to Greytown before the Spaniards cut off my retreat.

CHAPTER V.

DURING the past three years we had been cutting and rafting mahogany on the Toongla River, and having spent a short holiday at Blewfields, it was necessary to return to that river and finish our work. So one evening, in the month of November, 1856, we loaded the little canoe, which had served us in many an expedition by sea and river, with our luggage and a few provisions, anchored it out in the lagoon to be safe from prowling dogs and pigs, and retired to our beds. At three in the morning our crew of two Indians, who had slept in the boatshed at the waterside, roused my brother-in-law and myself, and after partaking of a cup of hot coffee, we set out.

All was still and dark as we embarked; the trees hung their tops over the village and seemed to slumber with it. Cocks were crowing fast, and fish splashing in the still lagoon, as is their habit just before daylight. The moon had long set; the great morning star shed a path of silvery light across the water, driven into ripples by the fresh land-wind; the vast Milky Way brightened up the south-east sky as if daylight was coming from that quarter, and the stars kept watch over the sleeping earth.

Just as we shoved off we remembered that we had no fresh water, so the Indians jumped out, groped their way to a stream which issued from the forest beside our house, filled the demi-john, and got back into the canoe, when we set sail. Then, lighting our pipes, we composed ourselves to wait for daylight. By degrees talking subsided, the pipes were laid down, vain efforts were made to keep awake, but one after another we leaned our heads on the luggage and yielded to the overcoming influence of 'before-day sleep,' except the man in the stern steering with his paddle.

We were wakened by the tossing of the canoe, and looking up, found we had passed out of the lagoon and were at sea. Streaks of pale reddish light showed that daylight was coming, but a dark bank of clouds on the eastern horizon and the high sea rolling in foretold a stormy day when the sea-breeze should come.

As there was a good stiff land-breeze blowing, we steered far out to sea, so as to have a good offing when the sea-breeze came. We washed the sleep out of our eyes with a drop of fresh water, then breakfasted on roast turtle-meat and boiled plantains served in a calabash, then lighted our pipes and waited patiently to see what the sea-breeze would do for us. Presently the sun rose with the splendour of the tropics, but was not welcomed by us, who had to endure his pitiless rays in a cramped canoe on the open sea. The fresh, cool land-wind soon felt his influence, and retreated back to the forests where it lives ; great masses of white cloud in the east, with mares' tails above them, showed a windy sky ; an interval of calm and stifling heat passed over us, then the sea-breeze came down in gusts and showers. At first it was north-east, and we could scarcely make the canoe lie her course along the coast ; but while we were debating as to the necessity of returning for shelter to Blewfields Lagoon, the wind shifted to the east, and then to the south-east, and came on to blow with a high sea running. We struggled on

with all sail, and got swamped once or twice, as the canoe
was heavily loaded ; but by constant baling and sitting on the
weather gunwale during the gusts, we kept her from capsizing.
We were continually drenched with the spray, and the wind
blowing on our backs made us shiver with cold. We tried
hard to procure the comfort of a pipe by sitting together with
our backs to the spray, but we were afraid of wetting our
tinder-horn, in which case we should have nothing to eat
until we reached the next settlement ; so we had to suck at
the empty pipes as a relief from the salt spray.

In the afternoon the sky looked very black to windward,
and presently down came a heavy squall and torrents of rain.
The little craft could not stand it, so we took the sprit out
of the sail and tied down the peak, and with this reduced
sail we went flying and tearing over the water, yawing from
side to side like a runaway horse. Sometimes her stern rose
high on a wave, and her bow was buried with a wall of water
standing up on each side of it ; then again she rushed along,
balanced on the crest of a wave, and sinking down into the
rolling troughs. The spray and rain were so thick that we
could not see fifty yards off, but steered our course by the
direction of the waves.

Finding the weather too rough to keep at sea, we steered
for a little cove called False Blewfields. The sea was breaking heavily at the entrance to the bay, but we got through
the surf and found ourselves in a quiet little bay with a high
bluff to windward, and, best of all, there was a small deserted
hut at the foot of the bluff. We were delighted at the prospect
of shelter from the cold wind and rain, as we were blue with
cold, and shivering so as to be hardly able to speak. But
we found this delightful-looking place swarming with sand-
flies, which put us into a fever of irritation as we stood on
the beach. So we walked round the bay in search of firewood, and also gathered a number of green cocoanuts, and
had a refreshing drink of the milk. Having lighted a great

fire in the hut, we were relieved of the flies ; we then cooked our dinner of salt pork and plantains, served up on a papta or fan-palm leaf, and finished up with a pipe. Then we wrung out our clothes and put them on again, and, crouching round the fire, went to sleep regardless of the storm of wind, rain and thunder that raged around.

We rose before daylight to find the land-wind gently blowing, but the sea still high. However, we embarked, got through the surf safely, and sailed along the coast. When the sun rose we steered close along the edge of the breakers thundering on the beach, and had one or two narrow escapes through careless steering, when a wave larger than usual came rolling in with its top showing a bottle-green colour, and, after heaving us violently over its back, broke with a roar just after leaving us. I amused myself watching the deer and agouti that every here and there issued from the bush. The latter gambolled on the sand, or galloped along with that odd throw of the hind-quarters that distinguishes the gait of all rodents, and from time to time squatted on their haunches to nibble the seed held in their fore-feet. The deer stalked along cropping the wild convolvulus vines that grew over the sand, lifting their heads and gazing all round every minute; they never perceived us until we got to windward of them, when they sniffed us at once and bounded into the bush.

In places there are groves of cocoanut-trees miles in length. Sometimes the groves extend for some hundreds of feet in from the beach; at other places the trees are in single rows. As no one ever planted these trees, it is singular that they only grow in groves at very long intervals ; and why the whole beach from end to end is not covered with cocoanuts is not evident. Another beach palm is the wow, or beach cabbage-palm. This has a stout stem and grows 60 or 80 feet high ; but it requires good soil, while the cocoanut grows best on sand soaked with salt water.

The sea-beach in this part of the country has a beautiful appearance on a bright sunny morning ; the bush grows to high-water mark, and the brilliant green, relieved by dark shady recesses, sets off the pure white of the breakers against the long line of yellow sand. In the distance great black stumps of trees, sticking out of the sand, look like people wandering about ; the crests of the waves, as they curl over and rush forward, are blown back by the land-wind, forming an endless vista of elegant wreaths of spray.

Towards evening we arrived at the Pearl Keys. These bright islands are surrounded by reefs of the most beautiful corals, in every variety of shape and colour. Some grow in great circular patches with broad thick leaves of a delicate orange-yellow, some in sprigs of pale brownish-red. The brain coral grows in large pudding-shaped masses with grooves all over the surface, and coloured reddish-purple. Here and there are large sea-fans growing from the coral in a beautiful purple fan 4 feet high. Other corals appear as pulpy masses of bluish jelly. As we sail over these beautiful colours, acres of sand are seen enclosed by walls of coral, the sand overgrown with green sea-grass on which the turtle feed. The bright sunlight and the trembling, rippling water give a dazzling unreality to the wonderful display of colour, over which the boat passes without allowing time to distinguish anything distinctly. Occasionally shoals of fish are seen passing over the coral ; some, with colours as bright as its own, hide among it or graze on the seaweed growing from the dead coral. Often the dark form of a ground-shark is seen moving slowly about, just touching the grassy bottom with his belly, and rising over the coral masses.

It is not safe to walk over the coral even where the water is shallow, as the living coral is soft and pulpy, and very soon gives an intense irritation to the bare feet (everyone here goes bare-footed). There are also numerous sea-eggs with long brittle spikes, which cause very troublesome wounds.

The keys are composed of broken heaps of coral with shelly and coral sand piled up by the waves, and carrying 9 or 10 inches of black vegetable soil formed from rotten leaves and the decay of stranded trees. The keys are in all stages of formation, from those a few inches above water to others just beginning to bear a few bushes and straggling mangrove-trees. The larger ones are covered with fine trees of beech, grape, button-wood, and santa maria, and abound in land-crabs, bald-pate pigeons, iguanas, and ishilly, which is a large green lizard with a high comb on its head and neck, and very good to eat.

On one of these islands we beached our canoe and made a roaring fire. Then we waded round the dead coral at low-water, and gathered a dinner consisting of whelks as big as a man's fist, conches, and a lobster or two. These we roasted and ate with roast plantains. As night came on we walked through the grape-trees to the windward side of the island, to inspect the surf and the appearance of the eastern horizon; for all weather comes from the east in the tropics. We then tied up our provisions to the branches to save them from those troublesome pests, the soldier or hermit crabs; and having propped our canoe on its edge, and spread the sail over it, we lay in the soft coral sand under its shelter, with our feet towards the fire, and chatted and smoked till, lulled by the monotonous roar of the surf upon the reefs, we fell asleep. As usual on these keys, we enjoyed a very disturbed sleep; the hermit-crabs were continually nipping us on the toes, fingers, and ears, and walking all over us without ceremony.

The blue land-crab is very plentiful in the above islands, and is found in many of the keys, but is unknown on the mainland. The Creole inhabitants of the islands account for its annual migrations from the interior to the shore by saying

that the crabs want a drink of salt water after their diet of
bush stuff; but it is known that they are impelled by nature
to lay their eggs in the sea, and when they have provided
for the welfare of their young in the sea, they toddle back
again to the mountains.

The beech-grape is a short gnarled tree with smooth white
bark and hard, dry, glossy leaves. It bears great quantities
of round grapes about 1 inch in diameter, of a purplish-
blue colour, or often varied by reddish-yellow. The fruit is
sweet, slightly acid, and refreshing after one has suffered the
parching heat of the sun on the sea ; but somehow one soon
tires of this food. So it is not entirely satisfactory, although
there is nothing else to be had on the keys, where even
cocoanuts are scarce.

These coral islands, or keys, are situated 20 miles from
the coast, and extend from the Pearl Keys northwards for
about 30 miles, in groups called King's Keys, Man of War
Keys, and Maroon Keys. The sea round about them is
shallow, the bottom being coral reefs and sand covered with
sea-grass ; and on these banks the green and hawksbill
turtle feed in great numbers.

We woke before daylight, anxiously expecting the land-
wind ; but it failed, as the sea-breeze blew all night. We
had a fair wind to start with, and as we sailed over several
'turtle banks' we saw numbers of turtle coming to the
surface to blow, and others quietly basking in the sun. As
we had no harpoons, the Indians stifled their regrets in
sighs and exclamations. In the afternoon the wind hauled
ahead, so we had to paddle to sea on one tack, and sail
towards the coast on the other all night. Towards morning,
overcome with sleep, we moored the canoe by means of a
large stone for an anchor close to the edge of the breakers,
and placing the thwarts and paddles on the bottom of the
boat, lay down on them, and, roughly rocked by the rolling
and tumbling of the canoe, we were lulled to sleep by the

singing of hundreds of fish on the bottom of the sea. The 'singing' of fish at night, so peculiar to the tropics, has always been a mystery to me, as they have neither breath nor lungs wherewith to make a noise. Nevertheless, these strange sounds are heard even by those sleeping in the cabin of a ship. They are commonly attributed to the catfish, but there must be other fishes which sing, as catfish are only found in rivers or brackish harbours. The sound is exactly like the striking of the string of a harp, and varies from high to low notes.

We woke before sunrise, feeling very sore from the rocking of the canoe, and shivering with cold. The wind being ahead, we poled the canoe along just outside the breakers, until we reached the Quamwatla Creek, which is one of the mouths of the Prinzawala River. Poling a boat at sea seems a strange sort of navigation, but it is commonly practised by the Indians with a head-wind or in calm weather, when the edge of the breakers is not too far out for the pole to reach bottom.

From the entrance of the creek to the lagoon and village of Quamwatla (house of the bird called quam) is a distance of 19 miles through a narrow, winding, salt-water creek, the banks covered with the ordinary air-root mangrove, the black mangrove — a tall straight tree — fan palms and stunted bamboos. The mangroves are covered with orchids and parasites of every kind, and the air, particularly at night, is laden with rich, heavy perfume, especially from one orchid, which bears a white flower, and liberates its powerful aromatic smell only at night. The water of this creek is of an inky black, said to be caused by the mangrove roots, but really by the infusion of decaying leaves and branches. Nevertheless, the water is quite wholesome, and swarms with fish. It is perhaps peculiar to the Mosquito Coast that mangrove swamps there are not unhealthy, and there are many villages quite surrounded by them where both Indians and white people enjoy good health.

6

We paddled for several hours under a broiling sun, with scarcely a breath of air, and finally emerged into a small lagoon, at the opposite side of which was the village of Quamwatla. The whole village turned out to receive us, eager to hear news from the King and the outer world. Among the rest came the headman, whose name was Sookoo, and invited us to stay at his house, to which we agreed.

We reposed for a while in hammocks, and presently a large mahogany bowl containing boiled turtle and cassava, and also cocoanut-shells containing a sauce made of lime-juice, chili peppers, and salt, were placed before us on the ground, while two little girls were stationed beside us, to drive away the dogs and hens. Then we had a calabash of our own coffee, sweetened with wild honey. While we ate our dinner, the house was filled with men sitting on benches, while the women and children blocked up the door-way, and peeped through the wattling of the walls ; but they never question visitors while eating, as that would be bad manners.

I hastened my dinner in order to satisfy the impatience of the people, and proceeded to set out in great detail the move-ments of the King—Court gossip being always interesting to the Indians—the latest trials and delinquencies, foreign news, and the price of turtles and turtle-shells. Everything was repeated at great length among themselves. The old chief explained the policy of various actions, and drew wise lessons and examples for the edification of his children, as he calls the people of his village. All this time a pipe was being passed round and smoked in turn. Finally, all retired to their respective houses, our host's children lay down on pieces of bark on the earthen floor, while he and his wives retired to a room of their own, which is an unusual luxury in Indian houses. Von Tempsky and I had our hammocks slung over and among the sleeping children, and we talked

MOSQUITO INDIAN.—SOOKOO, CHIEF OF QUAMWALTA.

by the flickering light of the pitch-pine burning on the hearth, until sleep, which had been attending to others, came to wait on us.

By daylight the women were up, and had our coffee ready for us when we woke at six. We first washed off the lethargy of sleep by a swim in the lagoon, taking great care to keep clear of the jelly-fish, which are in great numbers, and the sting from whose feelers is very painful. After breakfast we paid off the men who had come with us, and hired four others to go up the Twaka River. I then strolled about the village, talking to old friends, among whom were many I had known from childhood.

The village of Quamwatla is situated on the banks of a lagoon two miles long and broad. It was a considerable settlement before the cholera in 1855 swept off the best part of its people.

The lagoon is separated from the sea by a belt of mangroves and bush a mile wide, through which there is a road, and the people live alternately at the lagoon or on the beach. Along the beach for miles is a succession of plantations of cassava, yams, and sugar-cane, and there are extensive groves of cocoanut-trees, the nuts of which are sold by the Indians, or offered in payment of the King's tribute. The lagoon and the creeks which connect it with the sea on one side and the Prinzawala River on the other swarm with fish, such as snook, resembling an enormous pike; kookally, called by the English calapever, which is a gigantic mullet often weighing 60 pounds; mullet, cat-fish, sting-rays, and many others. The wide savannas behind the village and the neighbouring forest abound in game; there are also 'turtle banks' 18 miles off the coast, and with all these natural advantages the people are usually well fed.

The village is surrounded with groves of soopa palm, alligator pears, mammee apples, limes, oranges, and cocoanuts. The red clay on which it stands is swept clean and planted with hibiscus, four-o'clocks, marigolds, and other flowers. There are no sand-flies, mosquitoes, nor jiggers, but there are thousands of fleas in the houses, and numerous lean dogs to grow them on. The houses are frames of hardwood, supporting a deep roof of swallow-tail leaves, plaited on poles and tied to the rafters. None of these houses have sides, except that of Sookoo the chief, which is wattled round with laths split from the fan-palm tree.

The village is a pleasant and pretty place at night when the gentle land-wind blows and the stars glitter in the broad lagoon, the quiet surface of which is only disturbed by the leaping of fish or the blowing of passing shoals of porpoises, while the deep roar of the sea fills the night air and relieves the ear from the suspense of silence.

At dawn of day fleets of pitpans are seen crossing the lagoon, each containing a man and woman, some children, and a dog or two; they are going to their plantations on the beach, where the women clear a few weeds with the hoe, and dig enough cassava to last a day or two, while the men walk along through the bush at the edge of the beach to kill the deer and agouti which destroy the plantations, or they fish in the creek with hook or bow and arrow. About 1 p.m. the fleet is seen returning, the men to spend the rest of the day sleeping, smoking, and talking, while the women sit by their fires cooking or spinning cotton. Thus day after day passes in quiet enjoyment, interrupted at last by the hints of the fair sex, when the men are roused to make long hunting expeditions up the rivers or voyages to the turtle-banks, from which they seldom return without a large supply of meat.

All the plantains, bananas, and maize are grown far up the rivers at a distance from the sea and the salt tidal water, which is unfavourable to their growth.

The people of this settlement are good specimens of the pure Mosquito Indian, that daring and enterprising race which was the firm ally of the English and the terror of the Spaniard for 200 years. The men are tall, well made, and strong, with high shoulders and immense development of the chest, features strongly marked, slightly aquiline, with high cheek-bones, prominent chins, and full but not thick lips, countenances intelligent and vivacious, without the stolid look of the river Indians or the harsh features of the half-breed Sambos of the north coast. The village abounds in pretty girls, and one whose portrait was taken by Von Tempsky would be called pretty in any country.

The pure Mosquito Indians are smarter, more intelligent, and more enterprising than any of the numerous tribes which surround them, and it is with some difficulty that they are restrained from domineering over and plundering the more gentle tribes of the interior. They are given to fighting, chiefly with the fist, and deeds of violence and rascality are not uncommon. Nevertheless, it cannot be denied that, although they are subject to very little moral or physical restraint, there is remarkably little crime in the country, probably proportionately less than in civilized countries, and life and property are as safe among these Indians as anywhere else.

In January, at the commencement of the dry season, the Mosquito men of the coast fell and burn off their small plantations, and, leaving the women behind, take their departure for the turtle fishery, or to engage in the mahogany works. By the end of May they begin to languish for their wives and children, and turn their canoes homeward.

The women lead a sort of picnic life while their men are absent. They stray away in parties to visit their neighbours at the mouths of the adjacent rivers, camp out in the bush gathering oil seeds, wander for days among the mangroves catching blue crabs, or go to some distant lagoon to feed on cockles and oysters. Generally they devote a month to camping on the beach, where they keep an immense pot boiling night and day, making salt from sea-water, and they are generally living on the beach when the men are expected to return. Then every sail that appears on the horizon is anxiously watched by troops of little brown children, and women with infants on their backs rush out of the houses whenever there is a cry of a canoe approaching.

At length the expected canoes draw near; the men are blowing conch shells to let the wives know that they are coming. The whole village sallies out, and as each canoe rushes to the beach, borne on the foaming crest of the surf, the women, standing up to their waists in the sea, seize hold of it, the men leap out, and it is hauled high and dry on the land. Then follows the welcome home, which is different from our form of the same greeting. The Indians are not acquainted with the art of kissing, but they sniff or smell the skin of the cheeks, which answers the same purpose. The little child is lifted in the father's arms, and he buries his nose in its stomach. Hand-shaking is as common as with us, but I have noticed that there is always a tinge of melancholy in the character of the Indians, which breaks out where we should expect hilarity. Thus, after a long absence sisters and mothers sit down, and throwing a cloth over their heads, with their hands clasped on the head of the person who has returned, cry over him with their dirge-like song. On the part of the wives, it is supposed to be improper to show any emotion, consequently they take little notice of the husband on his return, but confine their attention to others and to their duties in the meantime.

This apparent indifference to each other is part of the character of the domestic life of these Indians. Husband and wife are not considered to be relations, but the wife is in some respects the servant of the husband, and he is responsible for her proper treatment to her relations, who are frequently very strict in looking after her. She has also

a full appeal to the King through his quartermasters, and in
the few cases where I have seen decisions given on complaints of this nature, the husband has been the sufferer in
having his wife divorced on trivial grounds. She, too, at
once finds another husband, while he, on the contrary, may
have some difficulty in getting another wife, and in any case
loses the money he has paid for her to her relations. If the
wife runs away without good and sufficient cause heard and
determined, the husband may claim the goods he originally
paid for her, as well as an indefinite amount for her maintenance while she lived with him, and if not paid this remains
a debt to be quarrelled and fought over for years. One
method of recovering these debts is common and very peculiar.
The aggrieved creditor, instead of wrangling with his debtor,
simply seizes some property belonging to any other person.
This promptly sets the whole place by the ears, and ends in
popular pressure being brought to bear on the debtor.

If language were an indication of feeling and sentiment,
the relation of husband and wife would seem to be tender,
and even poetical. A young man calls his wife before she
has had a child *keeka*. The woman calls her husband before
that event *mahma*. But the real name for husband or wife
is *maya*.

After a child is born they call each other *loopy ihsa* (my
child's father) or *loopy yaptey* (my child's mother). If the
child die, they call each other *rowka*, which means bereaved.
A man or woman whose wife or husband is dead is called
peearka (widow) ; but the relatives of the deceased call the
survivor by a prefix which signifies ' our widow,' as being
their property, in so far that if the widow is taken to wife by
another man her relatives must be paid for her.

All the Indians have names, but they would rather you did
not use them directly to themselves, while to mention the
name of a dead person is an insult to the near relations, and
is very rude in general conversation unless you add some

expression of regret. They are fond of nicknames, and prefer to make use of them, so that it is often merely by accident that one finds out the real name; in fact, they are so touchy about names that one does not know where to have them on the subject.

When a child is born, the father invites a friend to come and cut the navel-cord; this secures him a faithful friend with whom he can ever after trust his wife with perfect safety, and they are dear to each other as brothers.

The young men and women associate freely together, but if a couple begin to take a liking to each other, it is soon known by their refusing to eat in each other's company, and although they try to conceal the case, it is not long before an *enfant terrible* blurts out:

'I say, mother, so-and-so are not eating together.'

Then it becomes generally talked about; the girl gets still more bashful, and will not on any account look at her lover, but she is always alone in her pitpan, paddling and fishing in the creek, and he is always absent, too. The old women exclaim, 'Just see how these two are going on!' and before long it is known that he has given her father a gun, and her mother such a lot of beads and prints and a lovely Dutch looking-glass! Next you hear that she has moved over with all her clothes to his mother's house, where they will probably live till the first child is born,' and then they will build a house of their own.

The young men and women are continually singing love-songs whenever they feel pensive or melancholy, and it is singular that all their music is melancholy. Cheerful music is quite beyond them. These love-songs are plaintive and sad, always the same time and tune, but the words are extemporized by them with a facility which to us would be almost impossible.

The following is a verse of one which I wrote down on the spot:

(1) ' My girl, some day as you walk with your companions,
  When the mist settles over the river mouth,
And the smell of the pitch-pine woods comes from the land,
  Will you think of me and say :
  " My lad, have you really gone away ?
  Alas ! my lad, have I seen the last of you ?
Shall I really never hear your voice again ?
  Alas ! alas ! alas !"'*

(2) ' My girl, I am very sad for you,
  I remember the smell of your skin.
  I want to lay my head on your lap,
  But here I am lying under a tree.
  In my ear I only hear the noise of the sea.
  The surf is rising in the offing ;
  But I cannot hear your voice.
    Alas ! alas ! alas !'*

The young men are very proud of playing jew's-harps, which they select with an ear to the tone, and tune to their liking by sticking balls of wax on the tongue of the harp. The music they produce from them is so original and different from our music that it is not capable of being described. It has a great charm for them, as well as for Europeans when used to it. Their other music may be called concert music, and is played on large and small reeds as bass and treble ; but this is not practised except on festivals. Their dances are similar to those of all the Indians of the American continent, practised only at festivals, and having rather the nature of ceremonies.

When a Mosquito Indian dies, he is buried in his canoe, which is cut in half so as to form top and bottom of a coffin. A small shed is built over the grave, in which are placed a bottle of water, a calabash, his bows, lances, and harpoons. For some time the grave is kept clean and neat, and the women now and then make offerings to the dead of a bottle of rum, a bunch of plantains, small pieces of new prints, and a few beads. Often in the savannas the graves get burnt by

* See Appendix B.

grass fires, in which case the relatives diligently seek out the originator of the fire, and make him pay the cost of a new hut.

All the mourning is done by the women, who clip their long black hair quite short, under the idea that no one should handle it after the dead person. It is an outrage to a woman to mention the name of her dead husband.

If the death is sudden, or the deceased a person very dear to them, the mothers and sisters make persistent attempts to injure themselves by throwing themselves into the fire, banging themselves against the house-posts, hanging or drowning themselves ; but they are always watched and prevented. Having been frustrated in this heroic sort of mourning, they settle down to the regular form of it for two weeks, and every day from sunset until about seven, and from second cockcrow till daylight in the morning, they seat themselves on the ground, throw a cloth over the head, and, moving the body, begin a sort of crying song or dirge. After this period, mourning is continued for about a year whenever the bereaved woman is sad or is reminded of the dead. In every large village, no sooner has the sun set than one is sure to hear, amid the laughter and play going on, at least one woman take up the wail for the dead. This, however, only saddens a stranger ; no one else takes any notice of it.

The dirge has only one tune and time, but the words are improvised, and practice makes perfect, as one may notice in the young girls, who blunder, halt, and make a mess of it, while others are fluent and tuneful.

The burden of the song recounts the virtues of the deceased, and recalls the happy time they spent together— his skill in hunting, fishing, and making plantations. He is asked what offence his friends have given that he should leave them; the house looks désolate without him in his hammock, his bows and arrows are rotting in the corner, grass overgrows the yard. His friends have forgotten him, but she will never console herself; his children have no meat to eat, and now live, like the game of the bush, on roots and fruit. Naturally, as the woman proceeds to depict her woebegone condition, her feelings are worked up, and her song terminates in sobs and exhaustion, from which she rises to her usual occupations, as cheerful and gay as ever.

Here is a verse of a girl's song for her mother, which I wrote down at the Wawa River:

> 'Alas, mother, poor mother! alas, mother, where have you gone?
> Here are your children crying for you;
> Yesterday we were talking together, but now you are lying there.
> Alas, mother, did you go from among us in anger?
> Did we not love you?
> Your husband sits outside with his head hung down.
> Here the women are sitting with their heads covered,
> All for love of you.
> But you have abandoned us.
> Alas, that I shall never see your face again;
> That I shall never hear your voice again!' *

For some time after the death of a man, and less frequently for that of a woman, once a year the relatives celebrate a festival of the dead called a *seecro*, at which they consume so much of their cassava in making intoxicating drink as to reduce themselves to semi-starvation.

A *seecro* is welcomed by all for the sake of the jollification which accompanies it, and all hands join in digging up the plantations of the bereaved relatives who give the feast, which consists of an intoxicating drink called *mishla*. Great quantities of cassava are boiled and bruised in a wooden mortar, while a small quantity to act as yeast is chewed by the women; both portions are then mixed in immense earthenware pots with a quantity of hot water and some sugar-cane juice. It is left to ferment, and in about twenty-four hours the jars have an immense head of froth and the drink is ready.

Meanwhile two or three men retire into the bush, and

* See Appendix B.

secretly prepare two extraordinary masquerade dresses, having distinctive paintings on the headpieces to denote male or female characters. The dress consists of a head- and a shoulder piece made of white bark, with holes for the eyes, painted with hideous features and fantastic designs. From the base of the shoulder-piece is suspended a skirt of cocoanut leaves, which reaches to the knees of the wearer. To the top of the headpiece is fixed a thin piece of painted wood, 5 feet long and 5 inches wide, with sharp wooden spines fixed along the edge to imitate the bill of the sawfish. While preparing these dresses the men have at hand a calabash containing an infusion of chili pepper and water, and any woman or child who may by accident or design get a sight of the figures is caught and made to drink the burning draught.

When the dresses are finished, two men put themselves inside, and each having placed in his mouth a tube of wax with duckskin stretched across it, they issue from the bush with measured steps. Guns are fired to announce their approach. Presently they appear, and marching towards the house of the late lamented, they bow to it by giving a sweep of the sawfish bill, invoking in a strange voice sundry animals, as 'koontoo yaptey' (mother ground-shark), 'kilkaro yaptey' (mother shovel-nose shark), making at the same time a hideous whistle with the wax tube. The female apparition replies, invoking another beast, such as 'tilba yaptey' (mother tapir), 'kiaki yaptey' (mother agouti), both all the time sweeping with the sawfish bill.

The meaning of this ceremony is to represent the spirit of the dead coming out of the forest to visit his family and friends, and the wailing of the women is to propitiate it.

The figures parade round the house, inside of which the female relatives wail and howl, and the chief mourner (the mother or wife) takes up the usual dirge with the cloth over her head. She asks him with many sobs why he comes to visit them. Has she not kept his grave clean? Does he not see his children playing outside, and his friends laughing and happy? But she is always sad; every night she cries for him. However, a little of this goes a long way, and presently the mourners arise and join the festivities, and may be seen, with eyes red from crying, laughing and joking among the rest.

While the men are parading outside with the figures, a number of others walk round in a circle, with wax tubes in their mouths, singing a strain in what they call 'thick speaking'—that is, nonsense verses, or words with double meaning or unintelligible, at the same time making strange and hideous noises with the wax tubes. This is an important part of the ceremony, and is called *yool inaya* (dog-crying); it is supposed to please the spirits, and induce them to depart without doing any injury to the village. Presently, therefore, the masks depart for the bush.

But now the concert must commence, and will last at intervals until intoxication disables the performers. Two old *sookias*, often ornamented with head-bands of feathers, provide themselves with trombones formed of small bamboos 6 feet long, with curiously formed mouthpieces of wax and duckskin. One end rests on the ground, and through the mouthpiece they blow the most unearthly sounds in measured time, resembling if anything the deep roaring of a bull as he trots along the ground, while with the right hand they scrape time with a stick on notches cut in the side of the bamboo. Inside the houses the men are playing on large clarionets made of reeds 4 feet long and 1½ inches in diameter, accompanied by others on small reeds half an inch in diameter and 18 inches long.

The music produced cannot be described. To a European it would have no meaning until he is accustomed to it and has entered into the spirit of the whole performance, and then it acts on him as it does on the natives, filling them with a thrill of excitement and superstitious awe. There are a variety of plaintive, harmonious notes with a certain fixed time according to the piece. The large flute is bass and the small treble. Most of the pieces are a conventional imitation of the notes of birds, or musical representations of the actions of animals. There is one tune called the Vulture, in which the players hop round with the peculiar gait of the turkey-buzzard. Another is called the Red Monkey, the players imitating the antics of that lively animal, especially its scratching of its back and sides. Another is called the Savanna Quail, and so on.

During all this the young women stand in a half-circle, the left arm over each other's necks, holding small carved gourds filled with seeds in the right hand. They sing a measured strain, keeping time by bending their bodies, uttering exclamations, and rattling the seeds in the gourds.

But this, being dry work, is accompanied by copious libations of the same fermented *mishla*, which resembles butter-milk. I never tasted it, although I have had such pressing invitations that the half-intoxicated girls seized me by the hair, and when I refused to drink have poured calabashfuls of it over my head. Young girls hand round the drink in calabashes, which an old woman fills and skims with her fingers at the great earthen jars. The alcohol in the mixture soon takes effect; weak stomachs get sick, as generally happens to European beach-combers, who are often found living with the Indians and married to Indian women. The stronger get furiously drunk; all grievances are raked up, insults resented, payment of ancient debts demanded, long-forgotten jealousies remembered. The women rush to hide all weapons; fights with the fists are going on all round, women are felled to the ground, men pound and abuse each other, children cry, dogs bark, until, overcome with drink, the whole population collapses and lies drunk on the grass. A dead silence follows the uproar, save where weeping infants crawl over unconscious mothers, vainly trying to wake them, or a fallen combatant groans over his bruises.

Next morning one by one the good folks wake sore and stiff, but good-naturedly laugh over their quarrels, and mutually pay each other for any blood that has been shed.

Very frequently, when a man dies, they cut down his fruit-trees, burn his house and clothes, split up his canoe, and sell his wife ; that is to say, if another man takes her, he must pay the relatives of the late husband for the expense and labour he had devoted to her. Thus, the children inherit nothing but the debts, which are not forgotten to the second or third generation. In addition to this, the bereaved relatives are urged to give feasts of the dead, and an entire plantation of cassava may be consumed in a single night's debauch. Sometimes the intoxicating drink is made of fermented sugar-cane juice, or it may be of pineapples roasted, pounded in a mortar, mixed with hot water, and fermented. These drinks are delicious, and highly intoxicating.

As a result of the wilful ungoverned tempers of such unsophisticated children of the woods, but partly, too, from a mental characteristic of all the American Indians, suicides are very common, especially among the women ; indeed, any pique or annoyance is apt to be followed by a suicide. Among many that I remember, the following are characteristic instances : The King of Mosquito and I were having a Christmas hunt ; that is, just before Christmas we went hunting to provide a feast for that most enjoyable festivity, as was the custom of everyone on the Mosquito Coast. While sitting by my side in the canoe on a blazing hot day, he fell to the bottom with a sunstroke. We hastened home with him—a two days' journey—but he continued for many days unconscious. His mother and eldest sister never left his bedside. One day I asked Dr. J. Green what he thought of the case. He answered: 'The probabilities are he will die.' At the mother's request I translated the answer to her. She jumped up, gave a gasp, and left the room. Half a minute after the sister came in, and said: 'What is the matter with mother?' I told her what I said. She gave a piercing scream, and rushed out in a frantic state, crying: 'Oh, save my mother!' Her two other sisters, her Indian man-servant, and many others, flew in all directions, and after a short while brought in the old Queen, whom they had cut down from the branch of a guava-tree to which they had found her hanging. They brought her to, the King also recovered, and for a long time the old lady had to listen to Parson Pfeiffer on the sin of suicide, and to her daughter's jokes about her unseemly haste.

On another occasion, at the Walpasiksa River, a young man, a great friend of mine, entertained a strong passion for the young wife of a chief. The oldest wife scolded the girl repeatedly, and ended by telling the husband, who gave her a sound beating, and sent to tell the youth that he was prepared to do the same to him when he fell in with him. The girl ran away, the man was missing also, and the pitpans of both were seen drifting on the river. After some days they were found entangled in a snag, bound face to face with his waist-cloth. Of course, there was trouble over this affair, and if I remember rightly the husband had to pay up to the extortionate relatives of both.

The vice of drunkenness is inherent in all Indians, and when they can get intoxicating drink they have neither the power nor the desire to abstain. Fortunately for them, they seldom have the means to buy spirits, and the intoxicating drinks made by themselves consume too much of their provisions to be indulged in frequently. Therefore their drinking bouts are separated by such long intervals of perfect sobriety and temperate living that they suffer little harm from their orgies other than the wounds and bruises they incur. I must say in their defence that, passionately fond of spirits as they are, if they are going hunting, or are engaged in anything requiring nerve and judgment, they refuse to cultivate a Dutch courage, knowing that their skill and faculties would be dulled by drinking. How different from European soldiers and sailors, who break into the spirit-room when the ship is sinking, or plunder the stores of a captured town, and are found drunk at the moment of greatest peril!

The medical faculty is filled by the *sookias*, or medicine-men, whose cures are due to the faith of their patients in the efficiency of their methods, which consist in charms and fumigations to drive out spirits, without regard to the special nature of the ailment. Therefore it may be said that the people have no medical treatment, and that nature alone effects cures.

I have seen a young girl, who was shrieking hysterically in a dreadful manner, carried in a canoe a long distance to consult a celebrated *sookia*. All that the *sookia* did was to erect round her painted sticks with charms tied to them, to blow tobacco-smoke over her while muttering strange words, to make a bubbling with a tobacco-pipe in a calabash of water, which she was then made to drink, and to tie a knotted string round her neck, on every knot of which was a drop of blood from his tongue. For as many days as there were knots she must not eat the meat of certain animals, must suffer no one to pass to windward of her, and must not see a woman with child.

Nature is their doctor, and in a hard but merciful way keeps the race healthy. All weak or sickly persons die, and only the strong live and produce children, the consequence being that they are like the wild animals, of uniform make and appearance. There is little variety of physical or mental development. All are alike of magnificent bodily proportions and perfect constitutions. Abnormal growth, producing

7

a dwarf Tom Thumb or a giant Chang, is never seen, and deformity is as unknown as it is in the wild deer. There are no towering geniuses and no silly fools. A remarkable indication of the mental state is that in savage tribes you may see a harsh or a bad face, but you never see a weak face, such as is so common among civilized people. The price they have to pay for this condition of sound minds in sound bodies is that which all nature pays for the same gifts. Natural selection takes them in hand, and remorselessly weeds out all the unfit, as man himself does in breeding horses or cattle. In civilized communities, on the contrary, natural selection, as far as is possible, is told to stand aside, and let benevolence and humanity work at the problem. There the halt, the maimed, and the blind are carefully nurtured; the weak and the strong, the diseased and the healthy, are amalgamated, with the result that the older the civilization the more weedy the stock becomes, until one sees in the oldest of all civilizations, the Chinese, a people looking like a race in its dotage, in which, as travellers relate, the amount of idiocy, insanity, deformity, and constitutional taint is appalling.

CHAPTER VI.

Voyage up Twaka River—Lower River—Sickness and superstition—
Sailing in a pitpan—Camping in the rain—All night in a canoe in the
rain—Attempted suicide—Voyage continued—Flood in Twaka River
—Camp in flooded bush—Hunting on the way—Cruelties of shooting
monkeys—On the journey again—Flood subsiding—Hunting and
shooting—Boy in a nightmare—Monkeys—Wowlas—Superstitions—
Boat-bill herons—The falls on the Twaka—News on the sandbanks.

HAVING hired four men and a pitpan, we started at 8 a.m.,
and while the men were fresh we went at a brisk pace, the
regular stroke of the paddles causing the light boat to fly
over the water. The sun was very hot in the calm, open
lagoon, but on entering the creek that leads out to the main
river our course was delightfully shady and cool.

This is a winding, shady creek with black water. The
banks are usually overgrown with mangroves; in places
where the banks are higher, dense clumps of papta palm
grow. These have long, crooked, brown stems, which in
the younger trees are comfortably clothed with a soft fibrous
cloth, which is discarded as the tree grows older. Behind
the waterside fringe of mangroves grow many trees peculiar
to the swampy land near the mouths of the rivers, such as
sapodilla, an excessively hard and durable wood bearing
a small and very savoury fruit. This is the original tree
from which the well-known mammee apple has been developed
by long cultivation. The sba-tree bears an oily, bitter nut,
which is the favourite food of peccary, paca, and agouti.
The wood is very like mahogany. The lovely samoo (called

7—2

' somewood ' by the English) grows in great numbers. Its branches droop like those of the weeping ash, and its small dark green leaves contrast beautifully with its large bunches of brilliant crimson flowers.

The kawey and bitter gourd trees growing over the water send large buttresses into the water, forming rooms which are inhabited by pairs of tooba fish, which there watch over their young, and guard the surrounding water from the approach of other fish. Numbers of red-breast and yellow-breast trogons live in these thickets, their favourite perch being over the water in some bushy tree, where, in the heat of the day, they utter their monotonous cry, highly appreciated for its sleep-producing effects. The bootkoo pigeon mourns in every bush, and the singing of the crickets steeps the ear in dreamy sound.

The mud between the mangrove roots swarms with little grey crabs, having one claw nearly as big as their bodies ; this they hold aloft with a threatening attitude, while with their other very small claw they gather food. At low-tide thousands of these crabs come down to low-water mark, eagerly feeding on little water insects and slime left dry. The roots of the mangrove are the resort of troops of little mangrove crabs which feed on the water-grass growing on the roots. These crabs are amusing in their efforts to escape pursuit. They run round and round the root with a smartness that makes it most difficult to catch them, and when hard pressed rush down the root under water, or jump into it and swim ashore. They are much sought after as bait by the Indians. There are also on the wet ground between the mangroves numbers of large slate-blue crabs, the prey of droves of raccoons, which pursue them in and out among the roots, cleverly cutting them off from their holes, and seizing them by the back. White-faced monkeys live in these damp forests by preference, their favourite insect food being found here in great abundance.

Creeks of this character are innumerable on the Mosquito Coast. In this stretch of coast nine principal rivers, descending from the interior, spread out when they approach the level land near the sea, and form deltas enclosing extensive lagoons, often separated from each other by narrow necks of land called ' haulovers,' from the custom of hauling canoes over the land from one creek to another. In rough weather it is possible to travel inland with heavy canoes from one end of the Mosquito Coast to the other through the various creeks and lagoons, and over the narrow necks of land separating them.

About half-way through this creek there is a settlement of six or eight houses, situated on ground elevated above the surrounding lowland. As soon as the people heard us coming they shouted for us to stop, as someone was sick and we must not pass to windward of him. On my telling my men to paddle on, they refused to do so until I assured them I would pay any fine that might be demanded in consequence. So we passed at full speed, receiving a volley of abuse from some old men and women who stood gesticulating and threatening on the banks. In those headstrong days of my youth I did not understand the efficacy of healing by faith, nor reflect that the poor sick Indian might suffer by the violation of the *sookia's* orders that no one should pass to windward until the evil spirit that possessed the sick person was expelled by his spells. I was also possessed by that proselytizing, meddling spirit common to all Europeans, which prompts them to correct and show up what they consider to be the erroneous beliefs of the poor benighted heathen. However, the *sookia* was even with us, for many months afterwards he exacted payment from my men for having weakened his power over the spirits by their action, and I had to refund the amount.

About 2 p.m. it began to look black towards the east. The growls of distant thunder stole upon the ear, and the rising wind made us very thankful that we were not at sea in a small cranky canoe. Taking the warning, we landed and cut a quantity of fan-palm leaves, with which we carefully covered all our things. In another hour we emerged from the narrow sheltered creek upon the wide, open Prinzawala River. We had brought the sail of our sea-canoe, so we proposed to take advantage of the fair wind and sail up the river. This was an innovation, as sails are never used on river canoes or pitpans. Accordingly the men landed and cut two sticks for mast and sprit; we propped the mast in the hole in the flat bow, and two men held on to it to act as shrouds; another held up the lower end of the sprit, the third steered with his paddle. We two whites held on to the sail-sheet, and so we loosed our canvas to the wind, and went flying up-stream. Everyone was delighted at the unexpected sailing qualities of the pitpan. The river was lashed into waves on which the canoe, as it flew over them, dashed its flat bottom with alarming blows. The Indians, relieved from the labours of the paddle, shouted with excitement, cheering every mad plunge of the canoe. We flew round the long reaches, now with the wind close hauled, then dead astern; now on the port tack, then on the starboard, as the river wound along its crooked course. After an hour and a half of this, the wind suddenly freshened, and the canoe sheered wildly over the river, regardless of the utmost exertions of the steerer. As the gusts came roaring through the trees she heeled over, and water poured in over the side. Then we heard, far in the distance, a tremendous roar of wind and rain among the tops of the trees; so we prudently took in our sail and got under the shelter of the banks. Presently the squall came tearing along, announced by the cracking of branches and the thundering fall of trees, while showers of leaves obscured the air. The rain followed in tropical torrents. We had on flannel shirts and straw hats, the Indians thin cotton shirts and no hats; and in half a minute we were as wet as if we had jumped overboard, and all our exuberance and joy were drowned out of us.

We had not eaten since morning, and it was useless waiting till the rain should pass, so we sought an opening in the leafy wall that lined the river, and climbed up the muddy banks into the gloomy, dripping forest. It was with the greatest difficulty that we succeeded in lighting a fire. We had to wander through the dark bush, with mud and water up to our knees, gathering branches, covered with mud and dirt as they were, which we had to carry on our shoulders to the camp. By chipping off the wet outside and cutting fine shavings from the dry wood, we procured the necessary fuel; then with flint and steel the tinder was lighted, and surrounded with a handful of torn-up bark-cloth. After much blowing and coughing the spark was kindled into a blaze, the man who performed the operation being sheltered by swallow-tail palm leaves, which we held over him. As the ground was swimming with water, the fire was raised on the top of a pile of green logs. We then built a shed of leaves about the size of an umbrella over the fire, put the pot on with salt pork and plantains, and seated ourselves in the mud to wait for dinner. An artist could have made a striking picture of us as we sat round our fire, soaked with rain, all with pipes in our mouths, the bowls turned down, the blue smoke curling up among the dark and dripping foliage, the little fire making everything look dreary beyond its cheerful blaze.

After an uncomfortable meal we embarked again. The rain was so heavy that we could not see 60 yards off, and we had to bale constantly to keep the rain-water below the level of our luggage. Soon it became dark, but there was no sleep to be had in such weather, so we paddled on till midnight, when, overcome with cold and weariness, we made the canoe fast to a bamboo which projected over the water, and lay down to rest.

In place of umbrellas, tarpaulins, or waterproof sheets, the Indians use the leaf of a species of musa, which grows in large clumps near the river. Long round leaf-stalks grow out from a root underground ; the leaf is 5 feet long and 3 feet wide, usually without a split in the immense surface, which is tough and pliable, the under surface covered with a white dust. This leaf, called *waha,* grows only above the fine brackish tidal waters, and we were not far enough up the river to find any ; we had therefore nothing to cover ourselves with but the calico sail, which let the rain through freely, although it protected us from the beating of the raindrops. The Indians lay down in their bark blankets, each covering his face with a papta leaf, and so dozed and shivered till morning. We lay for a long time too cold to get up and bale the canoe, until we found ourselves nearly floating. We endured this until the croaking of frogs in the grass at the river-side, and the howling of a monkey, announced the coming of daylight. It came, not in its robes of purple and gold, but struggling in dull gray through the pouring rain, accompanied with gusts of wind which swept up the river, wildly tossing the bamboos and palms. From time to time the watery landscape was suffused with a blue glare, instantly extinguished, and followed by tremendous peals of thunder, which echoed along the reaches of the river, dying away in the distance in a low reverberation, while the continued growling of distant thunder was heard from the east, where all bad weather comes from in these regions. We roused up at last cold and stiff, our skins shrivelled with water, and even the Indians looking as if their ruddy-brown colour would not wash. We rolled off the heavy wet sail, wrung the water out of our hair, let go our fastening, and started on our way.

The exertion of paddling brought back some of our lost heat, and revived our spirits. Of the cold remnants of boiled salt pork and plantains floating in our pot, we made our breakfast, and at 2 p.m. entered the Twaka branch of the river. The main river was clear and blue, but the one we entered began to show signs of a coming flood, and we paddled hard all day to reach some houses before the flood should stop us.

It never ceased raining until we reached the houses at 5 p.m.; then it held up with the calm leaden sky which generally succeeds these rain - storms. We found some families of Mosquito Indians from Walpa Siksa on the coast, who were sojourning here to weed their plantations of plantains and Indian corn. They gave us an unoccupied shed on the opposite side of the river, on the floor of which, a foot deep in mud, we built a stage of logs for our fire. Under the eaves was the usual bundle of poles, which served as a sleeping-place, to which we ascended by a notched log.

While we were cooking, an Indian paddled across to ask us the news, and among other items we told him of the recent death of a young man at the river mouth, not knowing that his sister was in the village at the other side.

Our visitor calmly discussed the news, asked where we were going, and if we had seen any game on our journey, then slowly paddled back to the village. A few minutes after he landed we heard a most alarming scream, and saw a young woman rush down the bank and jump into the river. Several men pursued her and got her out. She broke away from them and threw herself into the fire in one of the huts, but the women rescued her, and watched her until her grief subsided into crying, which lasted the greater part of the night. In fact, she cried herself to sleep, and woke to cry again all the time we remained there. We had to eat our dinner standing up to the knees in mud, and as soon as it was dark we retired to our elevated beds, scraping the mud off our legs with a knife, and washing our feet with a calabash of water handed up to us. However, we slept soundly in spite of the rough poles, which left deep wales along our backs when we rose in the morning.

Having purchased several bunches of plantains and some sugar-cane, we set out at ten in the morning with splendid sunshine and a cloudless sky. The flood was covering the floor of the hut when we left it, but we fondly persuaded ourselves that it would now subside. After paddling three hours against the strong flood, the pungent smell from a drove of warree was wafted out of the forest. We immediately stopped and pushed the canoe to the bank among the submerged bushes. The Indians wiped the rust off the points of their arrows, and I put fresh caps on my gun. We then struggled through the thorny bamboos and tangled vines in water up to the waist, unable to cut our way for fear of alarming the game. We then reached higher land with open bush, and heard the peccary ' singing ' some distance off. All separated in different directions in order to surround the drove. I advanced as quickly as the tangled undergrowth would permit, but fell over a stick and buried the muzzle of my gun in the wet earth. A clashing of teeth and a headlong rush was the result, but fortunately an Indian was crouching in their path, and a pitiful yell announced that he had brought one down. As one was enough for us, we did not pursue the flying drove, but returned to the canoe, and, having carefully washed the mud from our legs, embarked once more on our journey. Thunder was heard, and dark banks of clouds appeared in the east, and soon the rain came down as heavy as ever.

In the evening we landed in the bush to cook, and seeing plenty of swallow-tail palms, I told the Indians to make a house and have a comfortable night's rest, rather than fight the flood, and sleep drenched in the pitpan. They were too cold and hungry to obey, so I set the example by stripping to my trousers and cutting a large bundle of leaves, upon which they set to, and in an hour we had a good shed and a *creecree*, or raised stage of sticks, covered with a thick layer of leaves, to sleep on. On this, after dinner, we reclined,

smoking, talking, and listening to the thunder and rain, and
diverted by the continual glare of the lightning, which turned
the dark bush for an instant into broad daylight every minute
or two. The Indians predicted a big flood, and talked of
the dangers of the river when the flood was on. At last we
fell asleep.

In the morning the floor of our hut was under water, and
our bedplace only an inch or two above it. But the brilliant
sunshine and the cheerful songs of the birds stirred us to
action, and we started on our way, to have a hard day's work
battling against the flood. This was much to the annoyance
of our crew, who could see no reason why we should not stay
and rest until the flood went down.

After mid-day it rained heavily, and the flood covered all
the land near the river. We had to warp the canoe along
by pulling on the branches of the submerged trees, while
taking shelter from the current behind all projecting points.
Frequently we were stopped by rafts of bamboos, grass and
drifting trees. Whenever there was a strip of grassy bank
we poled over it, and then had to pull ourselves along by the
bushes to the next grass patch. In many places we had to
make our way among the branches of the trees, which, growing from the banks and meeting overhead, totally obstruct
the river when the flood is up. Through such obstructions
we had to cut our way with machetes. We saw many snakes
swimming about and resting on branches swaying in the
water.

We noticed a curious effect of the flood, the river over-
flowing its banks and flowing inland in a strong current,
while the course of several of the creeks was reversed, the
river running into them. This phenomenon indicates a
great extent of level land on both sides of the river.

Exhausted with our exertions, sore with blows from the
branches, wet to the skin, and covered with slime and moss
from the trees, we looked in vain for a place to land and

cook. There was no dry land to be found, so we moored our canoe to the trees, and had a meal of barbecued warree meat and raw ripe plantains. When we started again we lost the river several times, and paddled about in the forest trying to find it. As night came on, the rain, thunder, and lightning increased, and we could only make out our course by the brilliant flashes that lighted up the country. The water roared and boiled through and over the trunks and branches, our pitpan frequently becoming jammed, at the imminent risk of upsetting. Our position was getting dangerous, so we cast about for a place to tie our canoe out of the way of drifting logs, and just as we turned a bend we saw by a flash of lightning an expanse of water that looked like a lagoon, into which we paddled, and sticking a pole into the bottom, tied our canoe to it. We then lay down on the bottom of the boat, covering our faces with leaves to keep off the rain; but we were too cold and it rained too heavily for sleep, so we groaned and swore for three hours till the rain cleared off and the stars appeared. We then wrung out our wet clothes and put them on again, produced our blankets quite dry from under their covering of leaves, baled the canoe out, and, laying the benches and paddles on the bottom and ourselves on them, in a few minutes were fast asleep.

About four in the morning I woke, and perceived that we were surrounded with grass. I roused the men, and proposed that we should get back to the river; but we did not know the way. A mist had settled down, and it was so dark we could make nothing out, so we all went to sleep again. In the morning we found ourselves high and dry, and the river a long way off, and it was all we could do to drag the pitpan through the long grass to the water.

The flood having fallen 8 feet, we made tolerable progress. We saw numbers of curassows and quams on the trees, spreading out their wings to dry, and unwilling to fly away;

but we abstained from shooting until a large drove of red monkeys, feeding on the hog-plum trees, excited the Indians beyond all restraint. But as they had no guns, all the shooting had to be done by me. The monkeys made off, but I noted the direction, and darted through the bush until I got ahead of them. When they came up they stopped to look at me, and my first shot brought one down. The next I fired at had its thigh broken and made off, but another shot brought it down. Then I shot an old she-monkey with a young one on her back. One shot went through the mother and one through the young one's leg. She ascended to the top of a high tree, and lay on a branch. Another shot broke the arm of the little one, and the mother moved slowly away. The young one gradually hung its head, then relaxed its hold of the mother's fur and fell to the ground. As we had neither time nor ammunition to spare, we returned to the canoe with the three monkeys, and went on until the men complained of hunger, when we landed under an immense fig-tree that hung over a dark recess in the bank, enclosing it with vines that drooped from the branches into the water—a shady and romantic spot. We soon had two fires going, one to cook our warree and the other to singe and barbecue the monkeys. The process of singeing gives the monkeys a ghastly and horrible appearance; the arms are stretched and the fingers clenched, the lips drawn out into a hideous grin. The Indians, however, cut the heads off, and, having roasted them, gnawed away in the most cannibal fashion, tearing off lips, ears, and scalp in a disgusting manner. Then the hands and feet and tail were cut off, roasted, and eaten as tit-bits to give an appetite for dinner.

The game was then cut open and barbecued to preserve it, as we had no salt. This method of preserving meat, which in the tropics would putrefy in twenty-four hours, is common all over America. A low stage of green sticks is

erected over a great fire, the meat is laid on it, and continually turned until it is thoroughly dried. In this state it
will keep four or five days if the weather is dry; in damp
rainy weather it spoils much sooner.

Having finished our meal, we left this beautiful spot, and
took to our paddles again. That we took to our paddles is
to be understood literally, as we two Europeans did the same
work as our Indian crew day after day, from daylight very
frequently till past midnight. We had a splendid day without a cloud in the sky, now thoroughly cleared by the rain.
The fresh north-east trade was blowing up the river, sighing
among the bamboos, laden with the perfume of the bush
and the flowers, now freshened by the recent rain. The
Indians stripped off their shirts, and, naked but for their
waist-cloths, sat in the broiling sun, with no covering to
their heads but their thick black hair. We were dressed in
blue flannel shirts, duck trousers, and straw hats, and no
more felt the heat than the Indians did. A white man in
this country when properly clad ought never to be distressed
by the heat, even when working in the sun. As soon as the
profuse perspiration bursts out, all feeling of inconvenience
disappears, and my own experience is that I could always
do as long a day's work in the tropics as I could in Scotland.
The conditions are, however, sparing and temperate diet,
and plenty of hard work. I have worked for days in the
sun at a temperature of 84°, and slept for weeks in the open
air, rising in the morning with hair and clothes wet with
dew, and felt all the better for it. The Mosquito Shore is
exceptionally healthy for a tropical country, but I have done
the same in Brazil with equal impunity.

The flood was rapidly subsiding, and all along the river
high up on the branches were immense deposits of drift
rubbish and great logs, perched in positions most dangerous
for people passing underneath. In one place we found a
raft of banana-trees washed out of the earth far up the river,

and collected in an eddy. We ransacked it, and found a great many bunches of ripe bananas. In places immense slices of the bank had been undermined, and had slipped into deep water, with all the trees and bamboos standing erect and shaking violently with the current. We also saw very large silk-cotton and mountain guava trees standing on high banks, with their roots washed bare, ready to fall into the river at the first gust of wind. Places where the land appeared to be as old as the hills were undermined and broken down, exposing beds of leaves and trunks of trees. This shows that the whole country is entirely alluvial, the soil being uniformly of a light red earth without stones, the surface covered with a deep bed of black soil formed from the rotting leaves of ages. The land is covered with heavy timber, the river banks generally with tall cutch grass and flowering bushes, and overgrown with wild sweet potato, a species of convolvulus, and behind that the invariable dense groves of bamboos over 100 feet high, with stems 9 inches in diameter. This gigantic grass, although apparently perennial, is not really so, but obeys the law of growth common to all grasses, completely dying down after seeding. It is said to seed every twenty years, and I have seen all the bamboos for miles shedding ripe seed and all dead; but it is replaced so quickly by the young shoots that this phenomenon is seldom noticed. The seed is $1\frac{1}{2}$ inches long, very like that of rye-grass, and smells atrociously.

As the sun descended behind the trees, it was delightfully shady and cool. After enduring the heat of the day, the evening on these rivers brings an hour or two of pure enjoyment to anyone who can appreciate the deep shade on the calm river, in which the walls of forest are reflected as in a mirror. The sunlight lingers on the tops of the trees, swallows skim the surface of the water, twitting cheerfully, the birds burst into song, and out of the bush the cries of beasts and birds make a deafening noise. The world seems to be alive with excitement and pleasure. There is life in everything; the air, the water, the ground, and the trees swarm with it. The heat and the moisture impregnate the earth, and, like a fruitful mother, she gives birth to living things in myriads.

Paddling has the great advantage over rowing that you sit facing the bow, and you become so accustomed to the regular stroke that you can talk and amuse yourself with as much ease as in walking. The Indians, from their simplicity and excitability, are most amusing companions on a journey, and the time passes much more pleasantly than it would with a crew of our own countrymen. This is the case also with the negroes, who are charming companions when kept in proper control. The reason is that the European is more grave, reflective, and self-contained than these simple, impulsive races, and what gives the charm to their company is the marked mental contrast between them and ourselves. It afforded us endless amusement to hear our crew chatting, chaffing, joking, telling stories, and making the river echo with merry laughter. Every trifle that occurs excites the attention of their keen and observant minds. Loud exclamations and sighs of regret were set up on seeing a great iguana jump from the highest trees and fall into the river, or at a deer feeding on the convolvulus vines, and bounding into the bush just as they had the arrow ready. Occasionally one had a shot with the arrow at a muscovy duck swimming across the river, followed by shouts of laughter and volleys of jokes when he missed it.

'When did your wife last eat fresh meat?' 'Your children must be growing up like squirrels, and living on nuts.' 'Oh, he is quite harmless! If he walked in the bush, the game would sit on his shoulder;' and so on, all received with untiring good-nature.

The keenness of these Indians' senses is marvellous. They were continually pointing to animals or birds, which, though

I have excellent sight, I could not see. Often they detected the smell of animals—even of the curassow, which
no white man could possibly perceive—and amid the thousands of noises they at once perceived the faintest sound
of game.

On passing a very large Indian-fig tree which grew over
the water, the Indians perceived a number of iguanas on the
branches, and as the water was only 3 feet deep below
the tree, there seemed a good chance of catching a number
of them. So the Indians begged me to stop and let them
have some fun. It was useless to represent that we had
plenty of food in the canoe; they had set their hearts on the
iguanas, and it is always good policy to indulge them when
possible; so they all got into the water except ourselves,
who took charge of the canoe. This great lizard has the
habit, whenever there is danger, of jumping into the water,
whatever the height, coming down upon it with violence
sufficient, one would think, to break every bone in the body.
In going up some of the narrow, unfrequented creeks, there
is often quite a shower of falling iguanas, and some danger
of getting one's neck broken.

The men having stationed themselves, one of them
ascended the tree, upon which the iguanas began to jump
into the river, and the men plunged under water in pursuit.
The first half-dozen escaped; then a large one was caught
by the tail, which broke off in the hand, and was flung into
the canoe, where it lashed and jumped about in the most
extraordinary manner. After much exclaiming, blowing, and
laughing, six were caught out of more than thirty which
jumped from the tree. To secure them the men took the
middle toe of each foot, wrung it out of joint, and, pulling
the sinew 2 inches out, tied the forelegs over the back, and
the hind over the tail, by their own sinews; or else they
broke the thighs and armbones, and put the backbone out
of joint, and in that condition flung them into the bottom of

8

the canoe, to keep alive until wanted. We had now a good supply of meat—half a warree, two curassows, two monkeys, and six iguanas, besides a quantity of fish, which the Indians had been killing with arrows since morning.

We paddled until 8 p.m., then landed on a flat ledge of rock, raised 4 feet above the water, and overhung by sung-sung bushes. Above us was a shallow rapid, over which the river rushed with much noise. We groped in the dark for firewood, and, soon having a blazing fire, cooked our supper of warree meat and plantains, washed down by a roasted ripe banana, which we squeezed into a sort of gruel with the hands in a calabash of water. Then we gathered all the spare leaves from our luggage, and spreading them on the rocks with a log for a pillow, lay down to smoke and sleep. The men were asleep in no time, but we two lay awake for a long while, talking of our home.

The moon had set, the stars were shining bright, and the evening star cast a beam of light along the river. On the opposite side the forest was a mass of black shadow reflected on the water under it, but the middle of the river reflected the starlight. On the opposite bank grew an immense cotton-tree with short trunk and wide-spreading branches, in which a wowya, or screech-owl, was hooting to another far off in the bush, and from time to time uttering the most diabolical screams. Lulled by the murmuring of the rapid, I was just falling into a doze, when I was startled by one of the crew, a boy of fifteen, jumping up and crying out: 'Oh, mother! they have gone and left me.' He rushed into the river, struggled across the rapid, flew shouting along the sandy beach, and disappeared round the point. I called to him to stop, but he was gone in a minute. The Indians, hearing me call out, started up and seized their bows; but when they saw the boy in the water they said his demon had seized him. They jumped into the pitpan, and soon brought him back. He was trembling from head to foot, but we gave him a drink of rum, the men joked him, and he soon recovered his spirits.

He told us that he awoke and imagined we had gone and left him. He thought he heard a tiger creeping through the grass, and hoped to catch us by running round the point on the opposite side ; but he only woke in reality when the men seized hold of him. The men said he was subject to being possessed by his demon. A *sookia* had driven it away, and tied a charm round his neck, but he had transgressed some prescription, and the evil spirit had returned.

After this adventure we slept soundly till dawn, when we were awakened by the howling of a monkey and the shrieks of a flock of quams. A thick mist had settled over the river, through which the trees were dimly seen. An immense flock of parrots had taken possession of the cotton-tree from which the wowya had hooted in the night, and they were making a deafening noise, while in the same tree a flock of the beautiful yellow-chin paroquets were uttering their more cheerful cries. Long trains of yellow-tails (*Cacicus Montezumæ*) were seen wending their way through the fog to their favourite feeding-grounds.

We had our usual bathe, shook the dew out of our blankets, stowed the canoe, hauled it over the rapid, and started on our way. The sun began to rise, and shone with a dull glare through the mist ; the land-wind cleared off the mist, and heaped it round us at intervals, giving us glimpses of a deep blue sky that indicated a hot day. Gradually the sun and wind lifted the curtain, and showed the country glowing with sunshine and dew.

After paddling on for a short distance, we saw on a hog-plum tree overhanging the river a large drove of red monkeys taking their morning meal. On seeing us the males set up their loud warning bark, and the boldest congregated on the outer branches, shaking them violently, screaming, and glaring at us with looks of fury. This sort of Dutch courage is usual enough in these monkeys when they are in large droves; they then dare even to threaten the jaguar and puma, their most deadly enemies. But, as a matter of fact, monkeys are courageous animals. I shall relate how, when as a boy I carried my monkey on my shoulder, it would at once spring on anyone who threatened me.

Our Indians begged to be allowed to have a shot at these daring monkeys, but as we had lots of meat in the boat, I refused to let them be disturbed; and while the Indians uttered exclamations of regret and impatience, we stayed to look at the interesting sight of these, the most intelligent, lively, and happy denizens of the forest. We were amused at the angry and indignant gestures with which the young males tried to frighten us, while the mothers with young on their backs took no part in the row, but went on feeding and minding their own business. At times the fighting party would flag in their anger, and set themselves to play. They would hang in the oddest positions, some by the tail and one leg, some by the tail only, others by the two legs, while they played with their tail. Others hung by both arms, and dangled their legs with the tail wrapped round them. Then they would assemble in little groups, and scold and claw at each other, and a strong one would make an angry rush at another, which fled along the branches. Every now and then one would stare at us, and give the usual threatening bark, and all would rush towards us again, shaking the branches and scolding. Finally they tired of the excitement, and resumed their feeding, keeping a sharp eye on us; but meanwhile the mothers of families had come to the conclusion that the locality was not safe, and were streaming away back into the bush, soon to be followed by the fighting party.

We passed on the right hand a small shady creek with precipitous earthy banks and deep black water. This creek

is regarded by the Indians with superstitious dread, for they
assert that an immense wowla (boa constrictor) lives at the
head of it.   In different parts of the country other creeks
are pointed out as tenanted by these dreaded creatures, and
the Indians say that the boa after attaining a certain age
betakes itself to the water, and, living a lonely life in a secluded
creek or swamp, attains a fabulous size.   It is strange that
in Brazil the same idea is entertained by the Indians.

Wise old Indians delight to tell the young ones of the
swarms of game and fish to be found in these creeks, which
no man dare enter.   If a *coopias* (heartless, foolish) person
should do so, loud thunder is heard even in the brightest
sunshine.   Gradually the water of the creek is found to be
flowing towards its source, and before any means for safety
can be taken the current increases to the velocity of a cataract,
and the unhappy trespasser is swept into the jaws of the
wowla.

Concerning superstitions, is it possible for any human
being to look at the plain face of Nature and see things just
as they are and not otherwise?   Certainly no people on
earth have ever yet done so, unless it be the matter-of-fact
philosophers of the German school.   Imagination, and the
vague groundless terrors which it builds up, alter the face of
nature to the credulous races of people, and cause them to
see the light of day as it were 'through an atmosphere of
moonshine.'   Superstition, however, requires its accessories
and stage properties.   It must have dark caverns, gloomy
forests, trackless wilds, foaming cataracts, before which the
play is acted.   An old man sketches the outlines in dreams
or reveries over the lonely camp-fire ; the background is filled
in from surrounding nature.   The tale is disclosed to the
terrified people crouching round the embers on some dreadful
night, when the rain is roaring on the tree-tops, and the
fierce lightning reveals for an instant the wild flood tossing
great trunks in its yellow waves.   Furious squalls yell and

shriek through the forest, their track marked by the thundering fall of great trees; the tiger, terrified and hungry, utters his sullen roar; monkeys scream with alarm, and the great bull-frog sounds his booming note of warning from the depths of the pitch-dark forest. The old man, fearful himself, and playing on the fears of his audience, appeals to Nature in this angry mood; it is enough, they cannot resist the dreadful evidence. Silently in their hearts they beg for protection and comfort. 'Is there no being to love us, to pity us, to shield us from furious and implacable Nature?' The wily old man sees distress and apprehension in their eyes, and he offers what comfort he can. The spirits come to him in dreams to tell him of their intended vengeance. He will intercede; he will put in a word for the people; and so the charms and incantations are invented which shall (for a consideration) soothe their fears.

This digression is not quite foreign to the story of our travels, for it was thus that my sister's husband, Gustav F. von Tempsky, discoursed on the subject of the dreadful creek which the Indians showed us. We did not attempt to intrude our vulgar disbelief on them. This would have been an outrage; it would have been like throwing dirty water over a pretty picture. 'But,' says the matter-of-fact sceptic, 'you should always try to enlighten.' There are no 'buts' about the matter. An Indian is an Indian in his simple faith, and if he dabbles in doubts and reasons without having passed through centuries of investigation and training, he is a fraud. 'But,' persists the proselytizing person, 'you should always try to raise their ideas to a knowledge of revealed truth.' You should no more try to do this to the simple savage than you should try to teach a little child the mysteries of regeneration and predestination. To God a thousand years are as one day, and it is more pleasing to Him to see the simple mind of a savage groping its way to a knowledge of Himself through the first steps of idols and fetishes than mumbling the formula of a highly developed religion which he cannot possibly understand.

In this creek, at its mouth, we found great flocks of the boat-bill heron, which is a ghostlike and uncanny bird. It sits by day hidden among the branches of bushy trees, with its great flat bill laid upon its breast, dozing until night, when it seeks its food along muddy shores, uttering strange cries. On our approach these birds fluttered from tree to tree and set up a hideous clatter, the cry somewhat resembling that of the laughing jackass of Australia, ' ookookok-akakokoko.' The Indians assert that the wowla places them at the creek-mouth to warn off intruders who might be tempted to enter in pursuit of the game which the Great Snake preserves for its own use. Their name for the bird is ookaka.

At 3 p.m. we heard the roar of the falls, called by the Indians Walpatarra (Great Rocks). There is nothing very grand or tremendous in this place, the river being small, and the water not precipitated from any great height; but there is such variety of light and shade and diversity of foliage as to make the scene very impressive. At the foot there are several small islands covered with sung-sung trees, the river boiling round them. Turning a bend, there is seen a reach 300 yards long, down which the river comes roaring at an angle of about 10 degrees, through a multitude of rocks which lash it into white foam from one end to the other. On each side there is a wall of rock about 30 feet high, overhung with dark and strangely gnarled sung-sung trees, which make a complete arcade of foliage, shutting out the sky overhead, but allowing patches of bright sunshine to break through and flicker on the tossing water. The rocks are covered with every variety of fern and moss, and slender palms, great epiphytal plants, wide-leaved musæ, and wild ginger cling to the crevices, presenting all the shades of green from pale pea-green to dark bluish. Numbers of little yellow-back wagtails skipped about the rocks and flitted like yellow butterflies over the raging water. We could hear the cheerful screams of paroquets among the bushes over the falls, and from time to time they swept past in compact flocks, like flashes of green light. This lovely scene would have been peopled by the ancients with nymphs and sirens, but in these days only a few iguanas dozed on the rocks, and the cry of the soaring hawk-eagle (*Spizastus ornatus*) was heard above the roar of the water.

We landed all our things at the foot of the falls, carried them through a narrow path over a hill, and deposited them at a landing-place above the falls. The Indians then gathered a number of strong and very long withes or vines, called congkeewa, which grow hanging down from tall trees; they are white, smooth, round, and have the diameter of an ordinary pencil; each will bear more than the weight of a man. These they fastened to the hole in the bow, and then laboriously tracked and hauled the pitpan through the little channels at the side, incurring numerous falls and bruises, and occasionally running the imminent risk of slipping into deep water and being carried over the fall.

When we embarked again, we found the river still and deep, with occasional rocky banks. After paddling some time, we came to a fine sandbank, on which the Indians desired to land, to adjust their toilet before reaching the Twaka village. While they changed their waist-cloths, put on their shirts, and combed their hair, we strolled along the sand to stretch our cramped legs and read the news—for a sandbank on a lonely river is like a newspaper in a town. On its surface you learn all that has recently been taking place. Here a great trough in the sand shows where an alligator has dragged himself up to bask in the sun. Long winding trails, with little footmarks, indicate the track of the iguana, and you follow it to see whether he has safely reached the bush, or has had to turn and run for the river. Little dog-like tracks are those of the coati or the raccoon;

in this upturned sand he has suspected the presence of eggs, and you see the mark of his nose where he pressed it to the sand to detect the smell of the laying iguana or tortoise. At the edge of the grass you see a large track, the size of a man's hand, where a ' tiger ' has come to the river for a drink. You follow it to the edge of the water, and see that after taking his drink he has walked along the beach and turned again into the bush. Many tracks of bird or beast afford you an opportunity of testing your knowledge of the inhabitants of the forest, and if you are at a loss you call an Indian up, and he interprets for you at once.

CHAPTER VII.

Twaka village—Interview with a cock curassow—News of the day—The
Twakas—Industries and customs—Bathing sports—I go hunting—
The hunting-path—Meet two bush nymphs—Dexterity of Indians in
the bush—A view from a hill—A drove of warree—Gathering the
slain—Hiring men for mahogany works—We prepare our provisions.

WHEN the Indians had finished their toilet with a jaunty
streak or two of red and black paint on their cheeks, we
embarked again, and had not gone far before we perceived
the smell of fire.   Soon after we heard the barking of dogs
and crowing of cocks, and on turning a bend came full in
view of the Twaka settlement of Accawass maya, consisting
of three immensely long houses placed on the top of the
river bank, 90 feet above water.   At the landing-place troops
of women and children were bathing and swimming about.
The women were greatly disturbed and confused, not at
being seen bathing, but at not being in time to run up
and hide away their things, as their sad experience of the
Mosquito Indians of the coast teaches them that such
visitors are accustomed to beg from the Smoo and Twaka
Indians everything they fancy; nor are the domineering
Mosquito men to be put off with one refusal, or two.   While
the women nervously put on their dry wrappers, the naked
children rushed screaming up the bank, dogs sallied out of
the houses and barked violently, and the men were seen
hurriedly secreting their valuables ; but seeing two white
faces, they took courage, and came down to the waterside

TWAKA INDIAN HOUSE AT ACCAWASSMAYA.

to receive us; and while we shook hands all round, the women, with dripping hair, and some with babies in their arms, ran up the bank to the shelter of their homes.

This is a very pretty little village overlooking the river, and surrounded by forest. About fourteen families live in three long houses, which are, as usual, open at the sides, and have stages on posts at the height of the eaves as sleeping-places. Hammocks were slung from the house-posts for the men to sit in, and each of the women had a little wooden stool at her own fireside. Large earthen pots, bamboo-joints filled with water, calabashes, and gourds, littered the earthen floor, and little naked children were creeping about, knocking them down or being knocked down by them, or stumbling over sleeping dogs. Round about the houses the ground was thoroughly weeded, swept clean, and planted with those flowers with which the Indians love to adorn their homes. These are generally African marigolds, purple and white four-o'clocks, the crimson hibiscus, the anatto bush—which bears bunches of flowers a little like the English rose—and the chili-pepper, bearing capsicums of various bright colours. Round about the houses swarms of cocks and hens, muscovy ducks and tame curassows, quams and other birds, wandered about in the most confidential manner, the latter having laid aside their wild habits to enjoy the comfort and security of domestic life. Numerous parrots waddled along the ground, screaming at anyone who passed too close to them; agoutis popped out of dark corners, and sat upright nibbling scraps of food; monkeys chased each other over the house-tops. One might almost think that some form of millennium had come, when the wild animals of the forest were to live at peace with man; but we know that the Indian women and children are fond of taming the wild animals and birds. They are fond, in fact, of all pets, but they have only their dogs and the captured wild animals to lavish their affections on.

Forthwith the noise became almost unbearable, and would
have given a nervous person fits; for these Indians have a
habit of speaking all together at the top of their voices, and
this, with the screaming of tame parrots, cackling of fowls,
barking of dogs, and squalling of babies, made such an
uproar that you could hardly hear yourself speak.

While this noise was going on so that my head was almost
turned with it, I sat down in a hammock, and presently
a beautiful tame curassow walked up to me with perfect confidence, and began to rub its silky black head against my
hand, pecking at my wrist-buttons, hiding its head up my
trouser-leg, pulling at my clothes to attract attention, and
uttering all the while its plaintive, insinuating cry.

After a while our host, the headman of the village, served
us a splendid dinner of boiled warree, fine mealy cassava,
ripe plantains, and plenty of chili-pepper, rubbed up with
salt. The other families in the three houses also sent in
small portions of their dinner wrapped in leaves. Of course,
we could not consume it all, but the four men of our crew
did. Our table was a rough mahogany stool set on the floor
between our hammocks, and little boys with switches
attended to drive away the hungry dogs.

Meanwhile, evening coming on, the absent ones began to
return in their canoes, each received by its own troop of
little children, who rushed shouting down the bank to meet
their fathers and mothers and share the good things they
had brought. The men came up bearing strings of fish and
bundles of game wrapped in leaves; the women toiled up
the bank with great loads of plantains, bananas, maize, and
firewood.

The sun had set, the soft twilight lingered over the river
a short while; then everything was dark, except the gleam
of the river in the frowning gloom of its wall of forest. Our
landlady made up our fire, brought several stools to its side,
and a small billet of fat, resinous pitch-pine.

NEWS OF THE DAY

'What is going to be up?' said Von Tempsky.

'We are going to have a levee to hear the news,' I replied.

Soon all the men of the village assembled, each bringing his little solid mahogany stool, and seating themselves round the fire, they threw pitch-pine into it, which gave a smoky flame sufficient to see each other by. Our crew were the talkers, while we listened. The conversation was animated, but so mixed with metaphor and exaggeration that to an Englishman the information intended to be conveyed would be extremely mixed and doubtful. But the Indians know how to sift the talk, and separate the chaff from the grain. What deductions, for instance, would one of us draw from this style of talk?

Q.—'Is there any game down the river? Is it fat or lean? Is it tame or shy?'

A.—'The game is so plentiful along the river that you cannot land on the banks for the crowds of it. It is so fat that it is impossible to eat it. Curassows and quams are like the fowls in your yard, so tame are they.'

'Yes,' said our old host, 'I just knew that. As I lay in bed the other night I felt a *smaaya* [a twitching of the flesh] under my eye, and my *oolussa* [friendly spirit] always sends me that sign when plenty of game is about; but my *wahmanany* [young men] are very headstrong; they won't listen to their elders nowadays. They say they know better, and they think of nothing but lying all day beside the women, with their arms round their necks. Ah yes! we Twakas are very lazy and *coopias* [thoughtless].'

Q.—'Are there any ships on the coast? Do the white people bring much goods now?'

A.—'This is the year for abundance of turtle, and the white people's ships have come after them in such numbers that they are like butterflies on the sea. All the beach is covered with their goods, and big drunks are going on in all the villages.'

(There were three Jamaica turtle-schooners at anchor on the banks of the King's Keys, and one ship loading mahogany at Wawa River mouth.)

'The King has also gone to the Keys to eat turtle. He has taken his mother and his sisters with him. Everyone knows that this is the year for fat turtle. The grape-trees on the Keys are hung all over with fat, and you can perceive the smell of it a day's journey off. But they say the King is very sorrowful, though his people, with full bellies, laugh around him. He hangs his head, and his hair is turning gray with grief because his children up the rivers [the Smoos, the Toonglas, and the Twakas] do not love him as their fathers loved his father. They forget to bring him presents of canoes, indiarubber, deerskins, and chocolate; and he says when his children from the coast go up the rivers they are half starved, and the girls receive them with frowns, or hide in the bush. Yes, the King's heart is very heavy.'

This was a deceitful piece of special pleading which I promptly contradicted, and our Twaka people said they all loved the King, but they were very poor; large trees, fit for making canoes, were now only to be found in the heart of the bush, where the poor Indians could not drag them out; the indiarubber-trees had all been tapped, and it was difficult to get any now; the peccaries ate up all their maize in the night, and wild parrots at break of day devoured their chocolate, so they had nothing to give the King. Almost all old Indians, especially headmen of the settlements, have the inveterate habit of what they call *smalkaya* (teaching)— that is, lecturing the young people and preaching at them, drawing wise examples and 'modern instances' from the news of the day. This serves the same purpose as our Sunday sermons, and the Indians are by no means free from the tendency to exhort and preach, which is often so offensive among Europeans. On analysing this species of teaching, it is found to be very much the same as that we receive from the pulpit. It is largely made up of exhortations to be honest, to refrain from fighting and violence, not to go after other men's wives, to be kind to wives and children, to be diligent in providing for their families, to respect old people, and obey the King. The examples held up for imitation are usually the hearers' dead ancestors, who are always represented as patterns of virtue and good conduct; and the warnings held over them are the anger of the King and his punishment of evil-doers. Other than this, these people have no restraint on their conduct.

Our host did not fail to improve the occasion after this fashion, but as he lectured his naughty young people in the Mosquito language, it was evident he wished to show us strangers that he was a terror to the scorner.

I received the usual invitation to come and tell stories to the girls and young people, but I was at a disadvantage, as not all, among the women especially, understood the Mosquito language, and there was so much translating and explaining that I became sick of it. At last bedtime arrived; they all scrambled by little ladders to their beds under the eaves, leaving the lower part of the house to the dogs and us.

The Twakas are a small tribe living at the head of the river bearing their name; they are a kind, gentle, hard-working people, and live very happily in this secluded region, surrounded by the boundless forest. They go to the coast about once a year to pay their tribute to the King, and sell canoes, indiarubber, skins, chocolate, maize, etc., for hardware, cloth, beads, salt, etc., which they purchase from the Indians of the coast. They are middle-sized, good-looking, and very fair, some of the women so much so that one can hardly believe they are not descended from white fathers; but it is a beautiful fairness, blended with the natural brown and with the glow of blood, very different from the sickly fairness of the Chinese; the hair and eyes, as usual, are jet black. The hair of the women is remarkably long and abundant, generally reaching below the hips. The men wear their hair down to the shoulders; beards and moustaches they have none. The clothing is the same as with all the Indians of the country: the men wear a waistcloth, the women a wrapper. Little children of both sexes wear a waistcloth, which is substituted as the girls grow up by a wrapper, just as our girls' dresses are made longer when they grow up.

On festive occasions the men are dressed in very gay and pretty waistcloths woven of cotton-yarn in patterns of maroon red, orange yellow, white and black, and thickly fringed with the snowy-white down of the muscovy duck. They also have the leg below the knee, and the wrist, clasped by bracelets of very pretty beadwork, most ingeniously plaited in patterns with red, black, and white beads, strung on strong twisted thread. This, and the painting of their faces in stripes of red and black, is all the finery they indulge in. The bracelet round the leg below the knee is sacred to love, and it is bad manners to allude to a young man's knee-clasp or to question him about it. Yet, when young men meet, those who know of this custom can always see them glance at each other's knees, and often a girl is seen hurriedly to conceal a piece of beadwork she is engaged in plaiting. But most young men have a very small skein or single thread of black cotton-yarn below the knee. This is the sweetest and dearest pledge of a girl's love, and is considered sacred by the man who wears it. It is procured in this way: All women wear, in addition to the wrapper, a hank of black cotton-thread round the waist, by means of which a long strip of the finer kind of indiarubber bark cloth, or English calico, is passed between the legs, the ends passing under the hank of yarn, and hanging down before and behind. This probably is worn for fear the wrapper should by accident be pulled off the body, which, as it is only tucked in at the side, is apt to happen. The modesty of the Indian

woman is passionately sensitive, and I have no doubt she
would commit suicide if she were accidentally exposed naked.
When an Indian girl is secretly in love with a man, the
sweetest pledge of that love is to unloose a few threads from
the skein round her waist and tie them round her lover's
knee ; and I never met an Indian, drunk or sober, who would
betray the giver or scoff at the gift.   Wives are not supposed to perform this love ceremony, so as years accumulate
and love passages become less frequent, the tokens round
the knee bleach white and drop off, and the young fellows
remark, ' So-and-so is getting on in years; his knee-threads
are looking rusty.'

The finery of the women is much quieter than that of the
men, for the simple reason that, as they have to provide it,
they cannot afford to dress themselves and the men too.   On
festive occasions the women smear their whole body with
oil, coloured a light red with anatto and scented with pantipee
gum or the root of the aromatic rush.   They may or may
not wear some feathers in their hair, but they always carry
round their necks heavy masses of red, black, and white
beads, and necklaces of the teeth of tigers, raccoons, and
monkeys, and sometimes of small sea-shells like cowries.   If
their husbands are poor or lazy, they must be content with
wrappers of *toonoo*, otherwise it may be of blue twill or
Manchester print.   Their long thick black hair is oiled, and
hangs loose down their backs, affording a most convenient
handle for their husbands when drunk to haul and pull them
about by.   It is only fair to say of the Smoos and Twakas
that their drunken bouts are much rarer than among the
coast tribes, and when they are drunk quarrelling does not
often take the form of fights, but, strange to say, oftener
results in trials of endurance.   In such contests one man
bends his back and clasps a post with his hands, while his
enemy digs violently into his back with his elbow.   When
he can stand no more he cries off, and his enemy takes

his place and allows his back to be similarly maltreated. All over America the Red Indian displays a singular propensity for stolidly enduring pain. What excellent raw material they would furnish for martyrs! I have seen little Indian boys lighting the ends of twigs in the fire, and seeing which could best stand holding the burning stick against the calf of the leg.

The Twakas raise quantities of plantains, bananas, cassava, maize, and sugar-cane. The bush and the streams furnish them with abundance of animal food. Indeed, food is never scarce with them, and the coast Indians, knowing their abundance, are always glad of an excuse to go up to the Twaka settlements, as they are sure of a good blow-out. The Twakas grow quantities of chocolate, alligator pears, mammee apples, papaws, and soopa palm. This last bears bunches of orange-coloured nuts, the size of a small orange, which, when boiled with meat, have a peculiar and delicious flavour. Humboldt, in his 'Views of Nature,' mentions this palm as growing in the Orinoco region, but he gives its height as 70 feet, whereas in Central America it grows only about 20 feet high.

The Twakas speak a dialect of the Smoo or Woolwa language, but most of the men can speak Mosquito. They are much more industrious than the coast people. The men are always out hunting or fishing, or else cutting canoes, splitting mahogany slabs, or making paddles, bows and arrows; while the women are as constantly occupied weaving cotton cloth, spinning yarn, or beating out cloth from the inner bark of the *Siphonia elastica*. Their villages often sound as if machinery was at work, from the continued hammering of the women.

The next day I sent two boys in a pitpan to the villages higher up the river, to call the men to come and talk business, and then, the day being very hot, five or six young men accompanied me to have a bathe. We went up the river to a small rapid, landed upon a beautiful pebbly bank shaded by sung-sung trees, and indulged in our bath for about three hours. The Indians amused themselves by swimming across the rapids, throwing white stones into the deep parts, and diving to find them, chasing each other under water, coming up like porpoises for breath, and diving again ; but the favourite amusement was to walk to the head of the rapid and swim down it at a speed of 12 or 15 miles an hour. This is their favourite form of the tobogganing practised by the Canadians on snow-slides. In the evening I amused myself with the young men shooting and throwing spears at marks, while Von Tempsky took portraits of the girls, which greatly surprised and interested them, so that they sat like statues for their likeness.

As I lay in my hammock in the evening, one of my men said to me :

' Do you know what these Twaka women are saying ?'

I said : ' What is it ?'

' They say that they have heard that wherever you go no " meat hunger " is felt, and that they are hungry for meat.'

So I said that if they would send some young men with me to the hunting-path I would give them a feed of *rakboos weena*, *i.e.*, gun meat, and at the same time they were to show me a grove of mahogany-trees which were reported to be worth cutting.

And here let me digress on the derivation of certain Mosquito names, which are used by all the tribes. The Mosquito name for a gun is *rakboos*, and one might be puzzled to discover the origin of it; but the Smoos and Twakas call a gun *arakboos*, which is no other than the old name of 'arquebus,' which they must have heard the weapon called by the buccaneers 200 years ago. A bullet or shot they call *rakboos mahbra*, gun egg, which is an odd idea. A machete is called *issparra*, which is the Spanish *espada*, a sword. A spoon is called *koostarra*, which is the Spanish *cuchara*. A pig is called *queerko*, the Spanish *puerco*.

A fowl is *caleena*, the Spanish *galina*. Their connection with the English is shown in their word for cattle, which is *beep*. A ship they call *slowp*, our 'sloop.'

At dawn next morning one of the wives of our host blew up her fire, and prepared for me a calabash of chocolate and a roasted ripe plantain. Having partaken of this simple breakfast, I embarked in a pitpan with six strong young Twakas. We poled for an hour and a half up the river, and landed at the foot of a precipitous bank. On scrambling to the top, the Indians laid down their arrows, sat on the ground, and commenced to scrape the rust off the iron tips; then tightened their bow-strings, hitched up their waist-cloths, and one, taking a machete, led the way, while we followed in a line. To one not practised in bush travelling there was not the slightest indication of a path. Every here and there a twig had been cut or bent down, but the cuts were old and overgrown and difficult to detect. Nothing, however, escapes the eye of an Indian; he follows these obscure marks as easily as he would a beaten track, and so pursues his way swiftly and silently through the trackless forest. There is no more fit and proper sight than to see a man exercising those faculties which he has trained to perfection, and an Indian in the bush is such a sight. Our men, though young, were masters of their art, and were at home in the forest. Every sense was on the alert. Though strong and active, they husbanded their strength for the proper occasion, and showed neither precipitation nor hurry. Every sound was noticed and understood; every scratch among the dead leaves was examined, and at times they stood still to listen. An agouti sitting on its haunches had an arrow through its back before it could make up its mind which way to turn; it was then wrapped in swallow-tail palm-leaves, and hung to a branch against our return.

The path led through a fine specimen of tropical forest; the ground was rolling, with some pretty high hills with dark and deep ravines between them. The undergrowth was not very thick, but the land was covered with large trees of great height, thickly interspersed with the beautiful mountain cabbage-palm, called by the Indians sileena, with patches, too, of the short little swallow-tail palms and groves of tall palms with horrid prickly fronds, which the Indians carefully avoided for fear of their feet. Here and there a tremendous silk-cotton or copal tree stood like a tower out of the ground, with great withes. wrapped round it and hanging from its branches, which were clothed in a perfect forest of parasitical plants, among which, no doubt, many raccoons, quashes, and arari, or bush dogs, peeped down at us in passing.

We walked till about noon without seeing anything, and then descended the sloping ground to the banks of a clear stream, the opposite gently sloping bank of which was covered by a beautiful plant with purple hairy leaves and bright blue berries, which looked like a bed of velvet. We did not sit there, for fear of snakes, but rested on the sandy beach close to the water. Having nothing to eat, we took out our pipes, and had a smoke and a drink of the clear water. While lying on the sand and talking, one of the boys suddenly stood up, and, motioning for silence, gazed through the bush down the creek. Soon the others heard something, and stood up. Of course, I could hear nothing. They gave me a quick glance to be prepared, and silently stood ready with their arrows. Presently, sure enough, I heard the crunching of gravel under feet, then I heard talking, and the men whispered, ' Women are coming,' and kept still. Then I saw two young women walking up the creek. The foremost caught sight of the men, and both flew up the bank and hid behind a tree. Our men laughed, upon which the girls came towards us with perfect composure. These girls were sisters, and were the handsomest Twaka Indians I had ever seen. They had nothing on but a *toonoo* wrapper, which clothed them from above the hips to the middle of the calf of the leg, and each carried a machete. Their long black hair was tied up in a bundle at the back of their heads. They were tall, slim, and beautifully proportioned, with shoulders, neck, and bust like the Greek statues. Their colour was so fair that I was astonished, thinking they must be half-breeds, and, like all Indians, they had feet and hands elegantly small. They were the wives of the headman of the next Twaka village up the main stream. They said they were gathering keeso nuts to make oil, and that their husband and some others were camped at the mouth of this creek preparing a cedar canoe to be hauled out of the bush. We had nothing to offer the girls but a smoke of our pipes, which they enjoyed. They were very demure and inclined to be silent; but our men knew them, and had a long talk. But as the girls seemed a little uneasy, I told our men to come on. I gave them some tobacco and made them a present of my pipe, and we went on our way.

We walked up this creek a long way, and inspected a patch of mahogany-trees. These were small and much scattered, so I decided they were not worth cutting. While resting here it struck me that I had not the most remote idea of the direction in which our canoes lay, and I asked the Indians if they could tell. They looked up through the trees at the sun, and at once pointed out the direction. This singular faculty of the Indians, by which they know, as it were instinctively, their way through the boundless forest, has often puzzled white people. I believe it may be accounted for in this way: In travelling through the bush the Indians are always glancing up at the sun, or observing which way the clouds are drifting, which in this country is always from north-east to south-west. I believe they intuitively keep in their minds a chart of the route they have travelled, and so have a mental picture of the direction they came from, besides which they know more or less intimately the physical geography of the whole country in their district. They know where every creek enters the main river, and they have a fair knowledge of the course and direction of the creeks, the character of the country, and the variety of the vegetation on the banks.

We now left the creek, and travelled towards the northeast over some hilly country, ascending a high hill, which near the top was very rocky and overgrown with rushes and cane brakes, and so thinly covered with trees that when we climbed a high rock we had a glorious view of the surrounding country. Towards the east and south as far as the horizon was an extensive plain, dotted here and there by small hills. To the north, at ten miles' distance, was a low line of hills, which, rising towards the west, formed a hilly country, but the hills were not very high. The whole was an unbroken forest of sombre green in the distance, but in the foreground showed an endless variety in the tints and in the shapes and masses of the foliage. The broad shadows of drifting clouds followed each other swiftly over the vast landscape, throwing into relief inequalities of the ground, which are hardly distinguishable in the glare of the sunlight. My fancy brooded over this most unusual view, for the Mosquito Coast is so flat and so densely wooded that one seldom sees an expanse of country spread out below one's eyes. Could I only see through these impenetrable woods, what herds of game might be disclosed, with tigers prowling about or reposing in the thickets! Perhaps even the camps of wild Indians might be there concealed, for no civilized foot had ever trod this luxuriant wilderness to lay bare its mysteries, and everywhere there are traditions of wild tribes living in the depths of the forest.

I stood dreaming like this till an excitement among the Indians drew my attention. Their ears had caught the sound of a faint and distant cry—one of those loud yells which the peccary occasionally utter, probably when fighting among themselves. They stood attentively listening for some time, until they detected another cry, which, however, I could not hear. Then, eagerly uttering the impatient sipping noise with their lips which is equivalent to the yelping of the hounds when they have scented the fox, they started off down the hill at a trot, going through the bush like cats, bounding over branches, bending under others almost to the ground, winding in and out through tangled thickets, so as hardly to touch a leaf. Having got to the bottom of the hill, they halted to listen, and at once detected the ' singing ' of the warree. This threw them into a sort of fever of excitement, each sipping with his lips, and eagerly pointing to the direction in which he heard the noise. They arranged their arrows and drew their waist-cloths tight, while I put fresh caps on my gun ; then we all separated and advanced cautiously.

I had not crept far through the bush when I heard the snapping of teeth and the barking snorts which the warree make when alarmed. Immediately afterwards a piercing scream, a great rushing noise, and presently the whole drove burst out upon me. I was hiding behind a clump of swallow-tail palms, and stood up immediately, upon which the drove stopped, snorting and raising their bristles. I fired both barrels at the two best-looking beasts, and stood still to see the drove fly past. Just then one of the Indians came running up with bow in one hand and arrows in the other, and seeing a warree darting through the bush, he squatted flat on his heels, in an instant fixed his arrow, and pierced the animal through the belly. It made off, however, at full speed, and he came up to see what I had got. He then whistled in their peculiar way to his companions, and on their answering we went up to them.

We found he had killed his animal, but the others had made off with the arrows in them. We therefore laid the three dead ones together, and started to track the wounded.

There was only a small drop of blood to be seen sprinkled on the dead leaves at intervals of 6 or 8 feet. These indications the Indians followed at a quick pace, first finding one drop, then another, until, after going about half a mile, we saw the wounded animal lying down and panting. It jumped up, but an arrow pierced its vitals, and it lay down again for the last time. The men pulled down a lot of withes, with which they tied each fore and hind foot together, and the owner, putting his arms through the loops thus formed, with the beast's head downwards, as if shouldering a knapsack, walked off with his prey. We waited a long time for the other three men who were tracking the rest of the wounded, but they returned with nothing. One of the boys, however, had fallen down in a patch of skunk cabbage, the acrid juice of which had got over his face and neck and into one eye, causing him to suffer much agony. They took him to a little rill of water, washed the parts poisoned by the juice, and cutting open one of the warree, took some of the fat, with which they rubbed them. This gave him relief, though his eye was bad for some days after.

We were now many miles from our canoe. We had travelled over hills and through swamps, scrambling up and down steep ravines, and now the task before us was no light one—to carry out four warree, each weighing from 50 to 90 pounds. The young fellows seemed confident of their strength, for they did not disembowel the game, but tying the animals in the peculiar manner above mentioned, and supporting each by a spare waist-cloth tied round its body and crossed over the forehead, four of them shouldered their loads, and, leaving the boy with the sore eye and myself to 'spell' the others, set off on the long tramp. They made a strange picture, trudging laboriously through the dark forest, each with a dead grizzly animal on his back, and all covered with perspiration, blood, and dirt.

After many rests and much smoking of pipes, and some

amount of help from us two spare boys, we reached our pitpan, with grunts of relief, at about half-past five. We were very tired and ravenously hungry, for although we had discussed the advisability of roasting and eating our agouti, which we picked up as we passed, we agreed that we had better push on, and not get benighted in the bush. So we plunged into the water to make ourselves decent-looking, and, embarking in our pitpan, made off down the main river.

Arrived at the landing, it was already dark, but the women had heard the sound of our paddles, and were waiting for us at the waterside. To them we delivered our game, and after a dinner of roast fish and plantains, and a calabash of chocolate with chili-pepper in it, we composed ourselves to rest in our hammocks, listening to endless stories of hunting adventures, the prospects of game on the path, and the comparative merits of different creeks in that respect, related partly in the Mosquito language to my men from the coast, and partly in Twaka language among the Indians themselves.

The next day a number of canoes came from the villages up-river, and we had a long talk about hiring men for the mahogany works on the Toongla River. They all seemed backward in agreeing to come, but after they had retired to cook some food, the headman of our village, accompanied by two others from up-river, came in, and, having seated himself near me, began a long story of his young men's desire to accompany me to the mahogany works, saying they had a great regard for me, and considered me as one of themselves; I had only to call them, and they would follow me like dogs, for their hearts were strong when I was with them. They were poor Indians, and were cheated and abused when they went among the proud Mosquito men; but when they had me with them they could hold up their heads like King's soldiers. Yes, the young men were impatient to go. They were ashamed to hear their women asking for beads to put round their necks, and English cloth to wear round their loins, when they had none to give them. ' When we old men were young, we used to lead the young men to the river and to the sea to take care of them, and bring them back safely to their mothers and their wives; but we are too old now; we must sit by the fire like the women, and the young men now grow up headstrong and foolish, and won't listen to us old men. They laugh at us and tell us to shut our mouths, for our day is done. But now our English boy has come to take care of the people. All the rivers know the English boy, that he is young like our own youths, but his heart is wiser than the hearts of our oldest men. His heart is full of books, and he knows all things.'

He then said that the old men were quite willing to let the young men go with me, but there was a great *sookia* (medicine man) at the Wanx River, who had sent round to tell the people that there would shortly be a *teemia tarra* (great night, probably meaning an eclipse of the sun), and he warned all people against being away from home at that time, as it might last a long while, and they would not be able to find food in the darkness. ' Now,' said he, ' you English know all things from your books; tell us, then, if this is true.'

Accordingly I looked into my book for some time, and then said: ' The sun himself only knows this thing, but he will tell it to the book.' So I laid the open book on a slab in the sun, and poured a little gunpowder beside it. ' Now,' I said, ' if the sun sets the powder on fire, there will be no great night; but if the sun cannot burn the powder there will.'

I waited until the rumour of this magic had drawn the whole village round me. Then I gazed at the sun, and said in English: ' Oh, sun, answer these people '; then, on holding my sun-glass to focus over the powder, it exploded. The women and children yelled with surprise; the men looked at

each other and grunted their astonishment.   This experiment
decided the question ; the old men said it was a false *sookia*
who had tried to deceive them, and the young men might go
with me.   To confirm in their minds the idea of my powers
over the supernatural, I showed them my pocket-compass,
and told them it was my ' road-spirit,' and would guide me
in the bush or on the sea, and would lead me to my country
wherever I might be.   I said it would follow me like a dog,
to prove which I made it whirl round when I passed my
knife over it.   Nothing more was needed to establish my
reputation among them.   When doing these miracles I had
asked my brother-in-law to go away with the Mosquito men
who had come with me, as the coast Indians are much more
sceptical of pretensions founded on such evidence.

We were delayed some days to allow the men to take
leave of their wives and children, some going hunting for
meat to leave with the women, and some bringing in a great
store of barbecued fish with the same object.   Having
engaged twelve men, the women on their part loaded them
with parting gifts.   Our canoes were stuffed with great *oosnoos*
(baskets woven from warree withes) of *bishbaya*, which is
maize steeped in lye of wood ashes to remove the outside
skin from the grain, then soaked in running water till it
partially ferments, and finally dried in the sun ; with cakes of
chocolate wrapped in waha leaves, bunches of soopa palm
nuts, of plantains and bananas, and with loads of sugar-cane.

CHAPTER VIII.

Birds of the morning—Shooting the rapids—Tapir yarns—Poultry of the
spirits—Clamorous land-rails—Night on the river—Night talk—
Overcome with sleep—Attacked by wasps—Fight with mosquitoes
—Insect pests—Goods arrive—Toongla River—Alligator yarns

AT eight in the morning we started down the river in four
pitpans. As usual in these rivers, the morning mists hung
over everything, so that the walls of forest on each side
looked like shadows, glowing with the sunlight which
struggled through. The air was alive with the songs and
cries of birds and beasts, among which the song of the banana
bird was distinguished by the variety of its sweet notes,
sweeter and more varied than that of the nightingale or any
European bird. The banana bird should be called the bird
of the morning, which it loves more than any bird. It thinks
the morning was made for it alone. From earliest dawn all
along the riverside you see its yellow plumage flashing in
the sunlight as it flies from bush to bush, or perches on the
drooping bamboos, pouring out its soul in a song which
almost drowns the hundred voices of the other birds. As
the sun rises it ceases to sing, and retires to feed silently or
to rest in the thickets. It loves the beauties of the interior,
refusing to live near the lowlands of the rivers, and it is said
of it that it will not stay where the tide makes the river
brackish.

Although we were wrapped in white mist, the tops of the

high trees were bathed in sunshine, and here many birds had perched to enjoy the sun, and make themselves heard far and near in answering each other's calls.   There are many birds in this country which call and answer each other with rhythmical regularity for half an hour at a time ; and on this occasion one delightful bird called out in a high musical note, heard half a mile off, ' What am I to do ?' while it was answered from some distant tree in clear, ringing notes, ' Poor man, Jacko.' This rendering of a bird's song may seem foolish and overfanciful, but that it has a foundation in fact is shown by the Creoles of Blewfields, who always notice the loud musical notes of this bird the first thing in the morning.   They also render its song in words as above.

We could hear droves of white-faced monkeys quarrelling among the bamboos, and the small querulous barking of the male squirrels.   Macaws flew past overhead with deafening screams, and, together with flocks of parrots and paroquets, made such a noise as one hears in the crowded streets of London.   Amid this deafening but cheerful uproar from thousands of living creatures, man is silent.   He is not heard in this concert of joy.   The birds look down and see him silently passing in his canoe, or elsewhere creeping like a thief through the bush.   We go to London, and what a reversal of the picture !   A plague of men crawling and swarming below like our ' marching army' ants when they are out for the rains.   The hideous uproar has no notes of joy and exhilaration ; it is stunning if not brutal, and Nature retires ashamed at the sight.

At noon we arrived at the falls, and Von Tempsky and I walked through the bush while the men went down the rapid in the pitpans.   As we trudged along, we could hear their shouts as they swept past us down to the bottom.   We embarked and drifted down the river, the lazy Indians doing the smallest possible amount of paddle work.   They passed the time drinking copious draughts of bruised corn and water, and chewing sugar-cane, with which the boats were half filled. They also plied the rod and the arrow, and secured a great quantity of fine fish.

As night was falling we passed the scene of an adventure I had with a tapir the previous year, and after recognising the scene, our conversation turned on this subject, the Indians having lots of tapir yarns to tell. One told how, while he was quietly fishing and his wife steering, he saw a tapir rush out of a clump of bamboos and bound over a steep bank into the river, with a puma hanging on its neck. The tapir made for the shore, and they rolled over and over and struggled terribly for a long time ; but at last the tapir was killed, and the puma walked round it panting for breath. The Indian then moved up in his canoe, the tiger retired, and he loaded his canoe with the tapir and went home.

A few years ago two Indians, friends of mine, were paddling up the Prinzapalka River, when they heard the noise of a tapir browsing on the bank above them. One of them landed with bow and arrow ; the other, armed with a lance, landed a little farther down. The tapir, hearing the first man coming, fled in the direction of the second man, followed by its calf. This man was imitating the cry of the calf to attract the mother, and seeing her coming full at him, he let fly his lance and missed her. She knocked him down with a blow from her nose, and tried to trample on him, which would have finished him. He got up, however, but was again knocked down by her nose, and she again tried to stamp him under foot, when the other man came up and put an arrow through her.

One bright moonlight night ten or twelve of my men had to camp on a sandbank in a small creek overhung by trees. About midnight one of the men happened to wake, when he was alarmed at seeing a big black object standing right in the middle of the sleepers. He seized a lance and buried it in the tapir's side. It fell on its knees, knocking one man down and trampling on his thigh; then rose and rushed over the beds of the others. In the morning it was found dead close by.

The tapir does not seem afraid of fire. Several times when I have been camped on the banks of a narrow creek, a tapir has come in the night to the other side, stamping, snorting, and gazing with wonder at the fire, until a firebrand thrown at it has driven it away. Often it is heard in the night in the bush on the banks, uttering its shrill whistle, and crashing through the long cutch grass on its way to the river, where it swims about in the moonlight, enjoying the water. When alarmed, it snorts like a horse. It is a timid and awkward beast, which makes a great noise in travelling through the bush, and so betrays its presence to its habitual enemies—man, the jaguar, and the puma. It makes great havoc among the maize, cassava, and sugar-cane of the Indians, for which depredations it pays a heavy price, being often tracked for many miles and killed with arrows. It weighs about 600 pounds; the flesh is dark and coarse, but is very good eating.

As it was falling dark, we saw a flock of very singular birds on a high dead tree, where they were giving out the most unearthly screams in false cracked tones, as if they were all husky from bad colds. Perhaps it is from these dismal, uncanny cries that the Indians call the birds pnamaka yoola, which means the poultry of the spirits, and refrain from killing them, believing that they have a keeper invisible to man, who would bring trouble on any person molesting his poultry. The Indians say it feeds only on wasps. This bird so much resembles a young cock curassow that on first shooting one I was surprised. They go in flocks of from ten to thirty, and are found only in the interior. In April they make their nests in hollow trees. It is 20 inches long; the upper part is of a deep black, the belly and under tail-coverts pure white, the bills and legs horn colour.

As night closes in there are many birds which by their cry display regret for the parting day. Chief of these is the bird called by the Creoles topknot chick and by the Indians watabree. Before concealing themselves for the night, they take the precaution to ascertain where other birds of their kind are hiding, and that done, they wish each other a clamorous good-night. First a covey of birds in some dark thicket, having selected comfortable branches, sheltered by dense foliage from rain or the attacks of owls or 'possums, set up a peculiar cackling, which is answered by coveys from the other side of the river, and telegraphed, as it were, to the most distant parts of the bush; then suddenly they burst out with the evening salutation, 'coong, coong, bucket, bucket, bucket,' each bird trying to make himself heard above the others. After awhile they quiet down, except that every now and then some excitable young cock bursts out again; but the old birds, getting sleepy, we may suppose say, 'Shut up there,' and all is quiet. The watabree is a land-rail, and is the most beautiful of its species. It seldom flies, but runs swiftly, with its head low and hind-parts raised.

Night had now set in. We had had a good rest and a sumptuous repast, so we washed up our pots and calabashes, replaced them in the canoes, lighted our pipes, and shoved off, drifting down the river. Soon the moon rose in splendour, first lighting up the tops of the trees, then illuminating the river, while the banks remained in deep shade. Lots of bats flitted over the water with shrill cries. Some very large ones occasionally flew past, leaving a disagreeable smell in the air. The night herons startled us with their loud groans, the wowya owls made the night resound with their loud 'coo, coo, wow,' and we heard several tapirs browsing and whistling in the cutch grass.

The lovely moon beguiled the birds from their sleep; we heard the snake-hawk calling 'wahkah, wahkah' from the distant forest, and parrots every now and then set up screams from the trees they were roosting in. Frogs croaked and bleated from the grass by the waterside, and the ringing sound of millions of insects filled the air. Once we ceased our chattering to listen with awe to the hoarse half-purr, half-roar of the jaguar calling to its female, as our tom-cats do in the back-yards of towns. The land-wind was gently blowing, wafting the smell of the bush, laden at once with miasma and the odour of flowers, and rustling among the drooping bamboos which lined the river banks. Not a cloud was in the sky, and the stars glittered feebly as they swept past the lofty forest trees, which stood like a dark wall behind the feathery bamboos.

The Indians now made up their minds for a night of enjoyment. They stripped off their shirts and paddled slowly along, telling stories, and making the woods resound with merry laughter. The pitpans kept together so that all might join in the talk, which was in the Mosquito language, so that all might understand. The conversation was infinitely varied, highly animated and vivacious; there were no bores and no drivellers. The subjects were social, business, and political.

Social subjects comprised discussion of the girls who were growing up, and the question who was likely to get them to wife; the qualities and character of the different women known to the speakers; the village gossip and intrigues of the young of both sexes; the peculiarities of the different families, their odd ways and tempers; the skill or want of skill of the men in hunting and fishing.

Business subjects related to the respective values of different kinds of bows and arrows, and the comparative merits of firearms beyond arrows and lances; the value of iron tips to arrows as compared with mere hardwood points; the value and durability of bows of the soopa palm as compared with those made of lignum vitæ; the dangers of hunting, and the known accidents arising in that line of business; the small profits made by selling rough canoes, which involve heavy labour, as compared with the great value they acquire after they have been trimmed by the coast Indians; the exorbitant extortions of the middlemen who bring English goods to the interior.

Political subjects included the conduct and exactions of the headmen of the villages; the tribute of canoes and skins paid annually to the King; discussion as to whether the King really gets the said tribute, or whether the Mosquito quartermasters keep it themselves.

In their simple fashion they have a great range and variety of talk, and after listening to the conversation of the European working classes, I am at a loss to know where any difference comes in.

After the moon began to pass the meridian, conversation began to flag, and some abandoned it altogether. At length, finding it impossible to resist sleep, half of the crew lay down, and the rest paddled, relieving each other after a short sleep. We had brought a large piece of bark with which to secure the waha leaves that covered our luggage from being blown away by the wind. This was laid on cross-sticks on the bottom of the canoe, and on the bark we two whites slept soundly, scarcely disturbed by the tight fit of the narrow canoe, nor did we wake till dawn aroused us, bathed in dew and thoroughly refreshed.

The morning mist hung over the river, and the moon delayed in the west to see the sun rise, when we landed on a large sandbank to stretch our legs and have a run. We two boiled some coffee, and the Indians roasted each a ripe plantain, which, having squeezed and mixed in a calabash of water, they drank, and on this frugal breakfast we started again. About mid-day the Indians perceived the smell of warree, and all landed while we stayed in the pitpans. After being away a long time, they returned with three fine warree, and we paddled away in great spirits for Sowpee Falls, which, when we had passed up the river, were smoothly covered by the flood, but were now a roaring fall 6 feet high. The fall is made by a bar of white limestone, from which it gets the Indian name of *sowpee*, meaning white earth. We hauled the canoes over the rocks to the calm water below, and cooked our dinner on the rocks. We had reached the low lands, where bamboos and thickets take the place of the lofty forest, so we hurried the Indians on, passing over reach after reach of the winding river, with its monotonous sameness of banks and vegetation. The men were disgusted when several indications of the presence of warree and three or four droves of fat red monkeys were passed without stopping; but towards evening a large flock of curassows coming to roost on the bamboos, I landed and killed seven, while an Indian who had a gun killed two more, and this restored us to good humour.

The river being now wide and clear of rocks, we kept no watch when night came on, but all slept and allowed the pitpans to drift. When day broke we were all separated and out of sight of each other; but being close to the rendezvous, we paddled on, and got there by nine in the morning. Soon afterwards the rest joined us, all having passed a quiet night, except one canoe, which, while the men slept, had drifted broadside on into a bush in which was a large wasps' nest. When they woke up the wasps attacked them in the clear moonlight, and everyone had to jump overboard and swim about until the canoe had drifted clear of the wasps, when they got in again, and took such rest as their stings would allow of.

Our rendezvous was a high bank at the junction of the Twaka and Toongla Rivers, and here we had to wait for some men coming from the coast at the mouth of the main river, which is called the Prinzapalka. Here we landed, and the Indians cleared a space to erect a hut of palm leaves. As I was looking on, one who was working close to me roared out, ' Snake !' and sprang back. I sprang, too, and, looking back, saw just where I had been standing a tomagoff 6 feet long, neatly coiled on a large head of rushes, the root of which the Indian had cut, tumbling it down, and with it the snake, which showed no sign of anger, merely turning its head from side to side to look at us with its cold stony gaze.

Having put up a lean-to shed, and dined off boiled curassow, with curassow soup to finish with, some of the men went fishing, and the others rested on beds of swallow-tail leaves spread on the ground. The day passed, the fishers returned with plenty, but there were no signs of those we were waiting for. We resolved to sleep here, so after chatting till dark, we spread our respective bundles of leaves on the ground, with blocks of firewood for pillows, and thought of passing a pleasant night. But after dark the mosquitoes swarmed out of the bush and banished sleep. Each person made a fire by his side, piled leaves on it, and surrounded himself with smoke ; but it was no use. Some defended themselves with leafy twigs, others tried to rest with their heads covered up in their bark blankets; but after an exhausting fight we beat a retreat to the canoes. We paddled up the river as noiselessly as possible, and quietly made our canoe fast to the branch of a snag in the middle of the river. The Indians particularly warned us not to make a noise, as that would at once bring the mosquitoes.

Although this is the Mosquito Coast, I can say, after long experience in nearly every part of the world, that this country has fewer mosquitoes than most tropical countries. The lower parts of the rivers, where the land is often swampy, and where the water is brackish from the tide of the sea, are infested with mosquitoes ; yet the Indian villages on the coast, and on the banks of the lagoons adjoining the coast, have none ; nor are there any in the interior above the influence of the tides. Stinging flies are, however, more common, and are most tormenting on the coast. These are of many kinds, from great yellow horse-flies an inch long, to the innumerable 'short jackets,' which are black flies with short gauzy wings. Flesh flies and blue-bottle flies swarm in the bush. They are a terrible source of agony and death to wounded animals. We used to have the greatest difficulty in Blewfields to keep our goats, pigs, and dogs free from maggots, which swarmed in the most trifling wounds ; and a wild animal receiving a wound must certainly die in lingering torture. And then it is so disgusting to return to camp and find one's flannel shirts and blankets fly-blown, and all white with eggs glued fast to every hair. There are plenty of insect pests in this country ; yet we are thankful for some blessings. We have no leeches, that terrible annoyance in the Eastern tropics ; we have no gadflies, that deposit a horrid hairy worm in one's shoulders or neck, as has often happened to me in Brazil ; we have no tape or Guinea worms. Ticks are not common, as in Jamaica or Brazil, where they make life almost unbearable to man, beast, and even fowl.

We slept soundly in our canoes, undisturbed by anything except the want of room, and at daylight heard far off the faint sound of a conch shell. We were soon joined by two large pitpans, with eight men and three women, and loaded with my goods, consisting of blue *dungaree*, unbleached calico, white cotton drill, cotton long-cloth, prints of various patterns, handkerchiefs of various colours, boxes of machetes and axes, powder and shot, flints and percussion caps, red, white, and black beads, Dutch looking-glasses, fish-hooks, bundles of hoop-iron to make arrow-tips, files, straw hats, ribbons, jew's-harps, and knives. This was the wealth for which all these men were undergoing the risks and hardships of the mahogany-cutting.

After a rest we all started on our voyage up the Toongla River. This was a change for the better. Instead of a narrow, rapid stream, we had now a fine open sunny river with endless reaches of bright-green grassy banks, with the usual fringe of bamboos, and the lofty forest, with every variety of foliage and shade of green, towering over all. This stately and magnificent forest the Indians call the real forest, to distinguish it from the dense jungle of the lower parts of the rivers.

We passed numerous large sand and gravel banks, on which many alligators were basking in the sun with their mouths wide open. They were always reluctant to move on being disturbed, and, dragging themselves slowly down, plunged into the water, there to float watchfully with the eyes and back-crest out of the water. Sometimes we stole quietly upon them, but they were wary, and always wakened in time to avoid a shot. One, however, we found so fast asleep that we paddled up to just far enough from him to avoid his capsizing us, and I fired at his eyes with B.B. shot, without any result but wounding one eye. He gave his tail a fearful sweep and dashed into the river, nearly swamping us.

When I was a little boy, and almost lived in the water, we had regular set games there with troops of red-skinned Indian children. One game is called *oolee poolaya* (playing turtle). One boy is chosen as the turtle, and swims away to a fixed distance from the rest ; then, at a signal, he dives, and the other boys try to catch him. As the water of our lagoon was usually a little muddy from the dashing of the small waves on the half-mud, half-sand of the beaches, it was not easy to see the diving boy in, say, 5 feet of water ; besides which, we were very skilful divers, and could keep long under water. The boy dives to the bottom, and keeps to it. Drawing up his right leg, he buries his toe in the sand, and kicks out violently, sending his body flying along

the bottom, to rise finally to the surface in some most unexpected position. On seeing his black head above the water,
the *quatmuss* of the boys (a corruption of the English word
'quartermaster') speculates as to the probable direction the
turtle will next take, and orders his boys to cut him off,
surround him, or pursue him, as the case may require. The
turtle waits to rest till his pursuers are too near, then dives
again, and possibly shoots between them, rising to blow far
behind them. Shrill yells and laughter and the shouts of
the quartermaster again recall the boys, and pursuit is
resumed in another direction, till, utterly exhausted, the
turtle is at last caught and brought to the quartermaster,
who is supposed to kill it by slapping with the palm on the
top of the head.

Another game is called playing at shark. In this the
diving boy, representing that fearful fish, stealthily dives
among the others, and pinches or bites them under water.
This is a favourite game, which fun and fear combine to
make very exciting.

One day, when forty or fifty children were bathing, a large
alligator, which had crept among them unperceived, seized a
boy by the hips and for a moment held him above water,
shrieking in its jaws. The children rushed screaming to the
shore ; the noise brought several men quickly to the spot,
who shoved off in a canoe with a fish harpoon, and pursued
the alligator, which was swimming swiftly away on the surface
of the water. Getting within reach, the bowman threw the
harpoon and speared the alligator, which dropped the boy
and made off. A pole was shoved into the mud where this
happened, and pursuit of the alligator resumed, but the line
broke and it got away. Returning to where the pole was
stuck in the mud, the men dived in about 12 feet of water
and found the body of the boy, drowned, but very slightly
wounded.

I was not bathing that day, but ran down to the landing

on hearing the fearful screaming of the women. The poor
mother had got her dead boy, and, shrieking in the most
awful manner, rushed into her house to injure herself, as is
customary with Indian women. Everyone knew what she
would do, so the men and women pursued her and saved her
from throwing herself into the fire. They also prevented
her from dashing her head against the house-posts, although
she did succeed in hurting her face. Several women and
two or three men sat by her all that day and part of the
night ; they did not tie her, but kept watch to prevent her from
escaping to hurt herself. She had remarkably long hair, but
next day her head was cropped like a boy's, and she looked
very queer.

Next day the same or another large alligator was seen
swimming round our bathing-place, but it was too shy to be
harpooned. However, a negro who lived in the village made
a toggle, or spindle of hard wood sharp-pointed at both ends,
about 10 inches long. This was fastened in the middle by a
dozen strands of fishing-cord, and then attached to a harpoon
line of strong silk grass about 10 fathoms long. The toggle
was tied up with thread lengthways of the strands of string,
and the whole was covered with a great piece of turtle meat
and entrails, leaving the sharp point of the upper end of the
toggle sticking out. Next an empty canoe was provided ; the
bait was suspended at the surface of the water from the end
of a pole, the end of the line made fast to the bow-thwart.
In the evening this canoe was sent adrift near the cruising
ground of the alligators, and all the village assembled to see
the result.

For a long time nothing happened, but at last the canoe
was seen to move. It was pulled forward, and then turned
round, and at last it made off at a considerable speed. This
success was hailed with shouts of delight from men, women
and children, and several canoes were manned and shoved
off in pursuit. The drifting canoe was soon caught, the

alligator was pulled in, and half a dozen fish harpoons were stuck into his back. With the toggle in his throat and the harpoons in his back, he was dragged to the landing-place. The men jumped ashore with the lines, and the canoes were removed for safety. As soon as the alligator touched ground the battle commenced. On land an alligator's most dangerous weapon is his tail, and with it this one lashed out furiously, doing, however, no harm to anyone. He made desperate efforts to turn towards the water, but the men held him steadily. Then he tried charging his opponents, but, as they retreated, this manœuvre only brought him farther ashore. The captors called on the women to come and beat him, bidding some men, who were going to help, leave off and let the women do it. These set to with ungoverned fury, and, armed with sprits and boat-poles and blocks of firewood, they gave the creature a bad quarter of an hour, not, however, without considerable risk to some of them, who were pushed over by the crowd or fell near the beast by their own awkwardness. For although it was harpooned in the head, neck and shoulders, and held tight by the lines, it was not possible to prevent it from making furious lunges from side to side, and snapping at the people with its immense mouth. At last the men lost their temper, not at the slow death of the alligator, but because the women had broken many of the valuable hardwood poles, which are much prized. Several men then came among the women and forced them back, taking the poles from them. A strong man hit the beast a crushing blow on the head with a heavy billet used for skidding canoes, and this put an end to all conscious struggles, though it still continued to lash its tail and open its jaws. Its head was then cut off with an axe to save the teeth, and the body was pushed into the water, towed about a mile away, and left there. This was a very large alligator. I do not remember the length, but it was probably 18 feet.

Once, when staying at Quamwatla Lagoon, I had to take a canoeload of goods up the Toongla River to the mahogany works there. We left the village in the afternoon. There were three Indians and myself in the pitpan, which was loaded with provisions and goods, protected from the weather by a thatching of waha leaves, laced down with cords to the skids on which the goods rested.

We paddled along gaily while it was daylight, and soon entered a narrow deep creek, by which the Prinzawala River communicates with the lagoon. The creek was walled in and overshadowed by lofty forest, which, as the night came on, made it very dark. We paddled wearily along this intricate creek till near midnight, when we suddenly emerged on the broad main river, when, being very tired and sleepy, we tied the pitpan to a snag and disposed ourselves to sleep. The men took the thwarts and their paddles, laid them on the bottom of the canoe, and covering themselves with their bark blankets, called *toonoos*, were soon fast asleep. I endeavoured to find a place in a similar position, but the bottom being dirty and wet, I lay down on my back on the top of the pile of luggage and goods, and, covering myself with my blue woollen blanket, was soon asleep also. After sleeping some time, I was awakened by feeling a shower of water over my face, and heard a plunge in the river. I sat up suddenly, and thought one of the men had fallen overboard, when the man in the stern, who was sitting up, said to me very calmly, ' If I had not waked in time, you would have been killed by an alligator.' All were now awake, and sat up to listen to what had occurred.

The man in the stern then said that he had wakened and raised himself to see if dawn was coming. All was dark and still, but he noticed what he took to be a drift log in the river, and while he gazed dreamily at it, he saw that it was approaching the canoe, and presently came close to it. He then noticed that I was sleeping on my back, and that my left foot was hanging over the side close to the water. The alligator came up to within a foot of it, when the man suddenly recognised the danger I was in, and gave the side of the canoe a bang with his hand. Hearing this, the alligator lashed his tail, sent the water all over us, and disappeared. Thus, by the most providential accident, I was saved from a horrible death.

CHAPTER IX.

Charming the wind—Smoo Indians—'Thunder's mooring-post'—Piakos-Maya—Story-telling—Night scene—Sucked by bats—Jaguar adventure.

WE paddled on till midnight, and then slept on a pebbly island, where nothing disturbed us; but towards morning it rained heavily. The Indians, hearing the rain coming by the noise in the distant bush, vainly tried to keep it off by blowing with their mouths and driving the breath away on either side of their faces. They also spoke to the rain, telling it of the uselessness of its coming to wet them, thus: 'Pass on—pass on; we are all wet already. You need not come here; pass on to the head of the river. There is gunpowder and tinder lying uncovered on the rocks. A man is burning a plantation there; pass on quickly, lest another shower wet it before you.' They believe these incantations send away the rain. Often when they hear a shower coming they push their canoe quietly under a thick bush to hide till the rain passes, and are much annoyed if you talk or make a noise.

This may seem very silly, but it is no more so than whistling for the wind and invoking 'Sant Antonio,' as Catholic sailors do. However, their invocations were useless, and we were drenched as we lay. Daylight brought the sun, which soon dried our clothes, and we went on our way. We passed numerous plantations of plantains and Indian corn (maize) belonging to the coast Indians, and noticed that the peccaries and tapirs had done much damage to the crops. Coming upon a large drove of monkeys, we killed five, and landed at a large plantation to cook them.

While seated on the ground with our waha leaves in front of us, we heard the noise of paddles coming down the river, and hailed the strangers, who pulled up beside our canoes. They were twenty men of the Smoo tribe, who were taking two rough canoes to the King as tribute. One of these was a splendid boat, 36 feet long and 7 feet beam, without a crack in it, and most of the sapwood cut away; it must have been a grand cedar-tree.

The quiet, docile manners of these Indians were a striking contrast to those of the Mosquito men I had with me, who were boisterous, alert, and self-assertive. These Smoos had their faces painted black and red in stripes and diamonds, and wore only waist-cloths. They were rather short and thick-set, with the usual extraordinarily high chests of Indians. Their limbs were muscular and beautifully modelled. They had the stolid wooden look so characteristic of the river Indians, yet their eyes gleamed from their half-closed lids like beads of jet. They had hair reaching to the shoulders and tied in a queue. Their headman was a quiet old fellow of few words, who sat in the middle of his pitpan, dressed in a long shirt of thick cotton cloth of their own weaving, without sleeves, and striped with red, orange, black, and white stripes. This was evidently a reception dress, and he must have prided himself upon it when he saw the old faded calico shirts of such of our men as had shirts on.

Their pitpans were loaded with plantains, bananas, sugar-cane, cassava, and pineapples, with many *oosnoos* (withe baskets) of soopa palm fruit. They had also quantities of deer and tiger skins, and great cakes of indiarubber. Each man had beside him a large roll of waha leaves to lie on, and for shelter from the rain. Each was armed with a powerful bow of either soopa palm wood or lignum vitæ, and bundles of arrows neatly tied together. They had just killed several fat warree, of which the old man presented me with a side, while I gave him some tobacco.

We paddled on till near midnight, when we tied to a stump in the middle of the river, and slept comfortably till waked at dawn by the howling of a monkey, which preceded a heavy shower of rain. We loosed our canoes, and proceeded on our voyage. This day the scenery of the river was very beautiful. There were many rapids, and occasionally low cliffs of rock, or red and white clay, while everywhere the grassy banks were crowned by the beautiful mountain guava, with its silvery bark and dark-green leaves. Every here and there enormous silk-cotton trees grew on the banks, bearing an immense spread of huge gnarled limbs covered with innumerable parasitical plants. In places a great Indian fig-tree bends over the river, sending hundreds of roots down to the water, which afford luxuriant shady retreats from the mid-day sun, while if the tree is in fruit abundance of fine fish are to be caught under such trees by baiting the hook with figs.

One place we particularly admired. The Indians call it Alwaney-ta-Wilkan, meaning Thunder's Mooring-place. Out of the water stands a rock with a top like the head of a nine-pin, to which the *sookias* (medicine-men) say that Thunder (or the Almighty God) tied his stone canoe when he lived on this world. There is a wall of rock extending along the left bank of the river, which is rent at intervals by deep clefts, out of which creeks flow to the river. The whole is beautifully overhung by bamboos and sung-sung trees. The other side of the river is a sloping grassy bank, illuminated by the sun, making a beautiful contrast with the deep shade under the rocks.

Beyond this the river becomes filled with gravel-banks

and grassy woodland islands; the banks are very high and covered with cutch grass, among which are many clumps of wild bananas. Here we noticed great signs of recent floods; enormous pieces of the bank had in places slipped down into the river, carrying trees and bamboos, which waved about in the water. Vast piles of driftwood were stranded on the islands, and we saw great logs lodged among the branches of the trees.

In the evening we arrived at the Toongla village of Piakos-Maya, but the village was empty. We were much disappointed at this, as the next village is a day's journey up the river; but as all the cocks and hens were about, we concluded the people could not be far off, so we paddled on, and found them three miles farther up on a large gravel island, inhabiting a number of small sheds thatched with swallow-tail-palm leaves. The old people were sitting outside the huts chatting, the young men were throwing spears at marks for amusement, the girls were reclining on the ground watching the play, and troops of children were playing about the island. The setting sun threw a yellow light over the water, the forest, and the brown skins of the people, and we remarked what a pretty picture of sylvan life this was—a scene of innocent peaceful life without wants or cares of any kind.

Here the Toonglas had just killed two deer, some meat of which they covered with quantities of delicious white cassava and soopa nuts, and set before us in large mahogany troughs of rectangular shape. Beside each person was a calabash of *peelala*, or meat soup thickened with maize, and a waha leaf containing salt ground up with chili-pepper. After dinner we had a bathe in the river, and talked news till late at night; then we slept on strips of bark in the open air, as the little sheds had no room for strangers.

Next day we and the whole Toongla village went down to the settlement we had passed. The name of Piakos-Maya means 'the mouth of the Piakos,' and is derived from

TOONGLA RIVER FROM PIACOS MAYA.

a large creek flowing into the river just below, the name of which is Piakos Tingney, or the Creek of Toucans. The village is situated on the top of a very high bank, so placed as to be out of the reach of the floods, and consists of four-teen well-built houses, open at the sides as usual, and surrounded by a very large clearing planted with sugar-cane and plantains. Round about the houses were little gardens of the gaudy flowers the Indian women love to grow. The ground round the houses was swept clean, but inside them the floors were littered and untidy. From the high bank there was a view of a long straight reach of the river, with the usual brilliant green cutch grass, groves of elegant bam-boos, and the wall of forest behind them. It was a beautiful scene which we never tired of looking at.

This village was the nearest on the main river to our mahogany works on the Wakna Creek, about 12 miles off; so it was our headquarters and sanatorium for about two years. Here we sent our fever patients from the forest, to inhale the fresh trade wind on the open river, and when we were sick of the gloom of the bush we would make holiday trips to Piakos-Maya, to enjoy the sunlight and the wind. The people were hospitable, friendly and kind, and when I was at death's door with fever they treated me as a mother treats her infant.

We stayed some time at the village of Piakos-Maya awaiting the return of a canoe which I had sent to the coast for some barrels of pork and flour, and some of our goods which we had left behind.

The Toongla Indians speak the Mosquito language, which I spoke quite as fluently as themselves, and most of the men had known me from my childhood. So I was quite familiarly received, without any of that reserve which Indians always show to strangers. One of the sheds of which the little village consisted was inhabited only at one end, by an old man and his wife, and the girls and young men were in the habit of congregating at the other end of it in the evening after dark to joke, laugh, and tell stories, as is their custom, reclining, some on the ground on strips of bark, and some in string hammocks. Shortly after my arrival, my brother-in-law and I were reclining in our hammocks about eight o'clock in the evening, when a little boy touched me, saying, ' Oopley Saaley, Mire-nanny beela man eyeney bal wow cumtaia storea eyesahya' (Friend Charley, the women say you must come quickly and tell book stories). So, not to be ill-natured, I had to attend as ordered, and found over twenty young men and girls and women sitting round a large fire in the above-mentioned house. I sat down among them and told stories, to the intense interest of them all, especially the women.

From my experience in many parts of the world, I have come to the conclusion that the negro is the only race that can tell stories effectively, and as they ought to be told, but I may add that the Indians of the Mosquito Coast are the best listeners in the world. During the telling of a story to them their interest is intense, and the feelings even of the most reserved are of necessity betrayed by the eager sympathy and excitement of the women, who act almost as if the occurrences were real, and taking place before their eyes. There are no doubts, no balancing of probabilities ; they are credulous, sympathetic, and unreserved as a little child, but with the strong feelings of grown people. The men are much more reserved than the women, but I noticed that however sorrowful a tale might be, even the latter never cry or sob, although sympathy and distress are evident in their eyes ; the fact being that crying with Indian women is a set affair, and always accompanied by a song or dirge. They may yell or scream in the first moments of great sorrow, but the crying is only done when sitting on the ground with a cloth over the head, and is accompanied by a song with words composed on the occasion.

The Indians can relate an occurrence in the most animated manner, and with the additional effect of the most telling gesticulation, but they are deficient in the ability to invent tales or stories, and in this art the negroes have no equals. The most effective stories I used to tell my Indian friends were animal stories told by the negroes. These generally relate to the forest and to personified beasts. With the negro there is generally a thread of example running through the stories ; that is to say, the passions or loves of men are set forth by the actions of animals. The Indians fail to perceive this intended drift of the tales ; they take everything just as told, and I never knew even thoughtful old men to utter the wise saws and modern instances which the negro story-teller delights in deducing from his ' *hanancy* stories.'

The bow of human feeling cannot be long kept bent, so after the intense excitement of one or two stories my friends suddenly wearied of the amusement, but many nights I had to return to tell more stories, and I learned to make my stock of them go a long way.

Before retiring to my hammock I stood on the high bank in the moonlight. Before me was a straight reach of the river, calm and peaceful in the soft light ; the moon illuminated the feathery plumes of the wall of bamboos that lined both banks, until they looked as if frosted with silver ; while the forest behind the bamboos looked mysterious and dark, and out of it came those wild, weird, and often unknown sounds which never fail to inspire one with a thrill of dread. Horrid great bats flitted about, emitting a vile smell as they passed, and every now and then the unearthly yell of the screech-owl was heard in the depths of the bush.

After finishing my pipe, I turned into my *creecree*, or bed of bark laid over a stage of sticks, and drew my blanket over me. There was a faint glow from the dying embers of the fire, and by it I noticed many small bats flying about under the roof of the house. Just as I was falling asleep I felt a

11—2

cool wind on my toe, and a soft pressure as if something had alighted on it. I knew what it was, and gave a violent kick, and then covered myself all up, notwithstanding the heat. I woke in the night, and all was dark and still; I felt my cheek wet, and feeling with my hand I thought it was oil. I smelt at it, but it had no smell; my neck and forehead were wet, and I felt uncomfortable, but could not think what it might be. It was certainly not water, because it was so soft. I came to the conclusion that a gourd of oil must be hanging to the rafters and leaking over my head, and so fell asleep. In the morning I woke and went to sit on a stool by the fire, where a woman was blowing it up and several children were crowded round to warm themselves. The woman started with fright, and the children exclaimed, ' Oh, look at the blood !'

I said to the woman, ' What are you looking at ?'

She said, ' Your head is covered with blood. Were you fighting last night ?'

My brother-in-law woke at the same instant, and said, ' Charley, what the d——l is the matter with your head ?'

I had not the least idea, but got a little looking-glass out of my box and beheld a ghastly sight. My head and face were covered with blood, and my hair also was matted thickly together with clotted blood, dried to a sort of glue. I then examined my pillow, and found it all smeared, and on it a place where there appeared to have been a pool of blood. I felt my head with some alarm, but everything was sound and in good order, so I went down to the bank and had a good bathe in the river, and washed all the blood out of my hair. On returning to the house I noticed that the lobe of my right ear was a little sore, so I asked the woman of the house to look at it.

She said, ' Why, it is a bat that has sucked your ear.'

The bat had indeed sucked my ear and gone away, leaving it to bleed on to the pillow, and when a puddle of blood had accumulated, I had evidently rolled my head about in it. I felt no harm from the loss of blood, but on subsequent nights I was sucked several times on the toes, and began to imagine I was getting weak. The people of the settlement were seldom sucked, and did not seem to mind the bats. After I left, the children found the hole in a tree where these bats lived, and they were burnt up.

Some time afterwards there was much rain with thunder and lightning, and one night as I sat talking with the Indians they suddenly said, 'Listen, there is a leemey [jaguar] roaring.' It sounded a long way off, and I took no notice, but finished my talk and went to bed. In the midst of a sound sleep I was wakened by the woman pulling at my arm, and saying in a frightened tone, ' Get up quick, and protect your friend's wife ; you will never look him in the face if the girl is carried off by a jaguar.'

I jumped up and got down my double-barrelled gun and loaded it with buckshot. The people were all awake now, and kept calling on me to be quick, for at intervals of a quarter of an hour or so the sullen grunting roar of the beast was heard in different parts of the pitch-dark bush. Then the girl called from her shed in the bush, ' Oh ! is no one coming ? I will be eaten up !' I seized two great waha leaves to shelter me and the gun from the rain, and in a great state of trepidation I groped my way through the dark to the shed just within the bush, where the girl, as the Bible says, ' according to the custom of women,' was temporarily secluded. Usually another girl had come and slept beside her for company, but this night she had been left all alone. From my own experience, I can say that it requires some amount of courage to sleep alone in the bush in Central America, even with a fire and dogs about you ; but this young woman had not asked for protection until this alarming occurrence. She was about sixteen years old, and was the wife of a young Indian who was a great friend of mine because we had travelled and worked together. Both were from the village of Quamwatla, on the coast, and I had sent the husband back to the coast for goods.

When I dodged under the eaves and got inside the low shed, I found the girl had made all the fire she could, and was exceedingly nervous and frightened, saying, ' Oh, Saaley, why did you not come sooner ? I am very frightened.' The actual words, which I give to invite the criticism of those who know the language, were, ' Alai, Saaley ! deea can man ihney balruss, young sowra seebrin I dowkey sa.'

Just then the ' tiger,' not far off, gave a long series of his dreadful grunting roars. The girl jumped up and seized me round the waist, trembling, and I confess that I was as frightened as she was. Forgetting the conventionalities in my fright, I said to her, ' Come away out to the houses ; I'll carry your things.'

She answered : ' No, no, I could not do that ; I will let the tiger eat me first.'

To make the situation worse for us two cowards, there was no more wood, and soon the fire went quite out and it was pitch dark ; also the encouraging bark of the dogs was not heard, for they would not bark at their most dreaded enemy, but only hid behind things and growled. Again the jaguar roared ; this time he was very near. We certainly passed a *mauvais quart d'heure.*

But things are sure to mend when they are at the worst, and by this time the men in the settlement had all roused out of their respective beds, or had torn themselves away from the arms of their terrified wives. They began to shout and yell, and throw firesticks into the bush. Some were whistling and setting on the dogs, which, plucking up courage, began now to bark, taking care, however, to keep inside the houses. Presently I heard the stentorian voice of Von Tempsky, my brother-in-law, ' Why don't you fire off your gun, you d——d fool ?'

I yelled back: 'I can't load again; I have not got my shot-bag, and the fire is out.'

Then I saw the waving of firebrands, and he with some Indians brought more firewood and my shot-bag. They made up a fine fire, and my brother-in-law went back to his bed, saying: ' Now blaze away till morning.'

I fired off both barrels, and then a few more shots. The girl and I lay down back to back, I with my gun in my arms, and soon talked ourselves to sleep.

Next day we went into the bush and saw the large tracks of the jaguar in the soft ground, and found that it had come within forty or fifty yards of the bush hut, but had there turned and gone off. The following night I prepared to camp out again with the girl, but I found two girls with her who told me to go away, as they were all coming out, which I was very glad to hear.

CHAPTER X.

Proceed up the river—Lazy voyage—Small village—Hospitality—Hunting
warree—Carrying the game out—Feasting and stories of the hunt—
Sentimental reveries—A fishing journey.

ONE day two Indians in a small canoe came down from the
next settlement, about a day's journey up the river, with a
message from the headman, saying, 'Would I come up and
"talk law "?' which meant, to discuss affairs generally, and
adding that there was plenty of game in the Wakna track,
and the women were 'dying to taste my hand.' This doubtful compliment really meant that I should undertake the risk
and labour of a day's hunting that they might guzzle; but,
reflecting that it would be necessary to get the headman's
consent before I could engage and take any men from his
village for the mahogany works, I consented to go with the
messengers sent for me. Early in the morning I started off
with the two Indians. The white fogs were just lifting off
the river, and the sun broke them up into patches, which
the wind rolled over the tops of the trees. All nature was
joyous and happy; the lovely song of the banana bird was
heard among the cutch grass on the banks.

I was much interested and amused to see small parties of
the white-faced monkey eagerly seeking for spiders or other
insects on the lofty bamboos which lined both sides of the
river. Occasionally they thrust their arm up to the armpit
into holes in the joints, to feel round inside for their prey,

pulling out handfuls of spiders, beetles, or grubs. Sometimes two would fall out, and utter loud screams, when immediately the rest would rush up to share the fight.

They always kept a sharp look-out on the canoe passing by, and now and then one would give the warning cry of danger, when all would fly together and gaze all round to see what was to be feared. Soon they got tired of searching the bamboos, and moved off into the forest which always grows behind the avenues of bamboos.

The breeze was very light, and the sun on the river was roasting hot. We kept as close to the banks as we could, to avoid the current and get some shade if possible. All is hushed in the middle of the day; the birds are asleep, or drowsily preening their feathers in the thickets; the noisy monkeys are now stretched idly on the branches, each cleaning the other's fur with nimble fingers and teeth. Only the lizard tribe and the river tortoises enjoy the noonday sun. Every now and then we see an alligator lazily crawling off the sandbanks at the sound of our poles. Hiccatees, or river turtle, lift their heads as we approach, then suddenly tumble off their snags into the water. A drowsy heat and brilliant sunshine seem to hold the forest in a lethargic embrace. The long reaches of the river glisten with an intolerable glare, which not even the brilliant green of the cutch grass and bamboos, nor the sombre green and deep shadows of the lofty forest-wall, can alleviate. Nature seems to protest against the unseemly activity of man, who alone breaks the rule of universal repose at mid-day. The ringing sound of innumerable crickets, or the drowsy, monotonous call of the trogons in some bushy tree, soothe the senses and gently urge repose. With a waha leaf in my hat, and my head wet and dripping with river water, I was just falling asleep, and so were the men, when one whispered to the other, ' Be quiet ! I smell fire !'

From long experience in past days of rough usage and

plundering at the hands of the coast or Mosquito Indians, the river Indians have got into the habit of making cautious investigation before approaching another party. So we poled noiselessly along, till, peeping round a bushy fig-tree, we saw a man, his wife, and three children asleep on the sand under the shade of a sung-sung tree, and their pitpan made fast to its branches. We roused them with a shout, and, having joined them, made an exchange of provisions, receiving some fish and steeped maize in return for two fat monkeys.

With the declining sun we continued our journey. After a while we found the river banks getting higher, and occasionally composed of low rocky cliffs, overhung by the forest, and clothed with ferns and creepers. At last we came to a rapid, which it took all the strength and skill of the Indians to get through with their poles. Arrived, breathless, in smooth water at the top of the rapid, we heard the barking of dogs and crowing of cocks, and as we rounded a point saw a village of five or six very long houses on a high bank 60 feet above the water, and on the crest of the bank all the people assembled to greet our arrival. The houses were, as usual, open at the sides, and string hammocks were suspended to the posts, while the sleeping apartments were stages of sticks covered with a sheet of thick bark, and erected at the height of the eaves, or, say, 7 feet above the floor, so that the only way of getting into bed was by climbing up a notched pole. The floor of the houses is only clay, beaten smooth ; the furniture consists of hammocks, low stools of different sizes cut out of solid mahogany, three-legged iron pots, many calabashes, clay pots of their own make, and joints of bamboo to hold water.

The village is in a small clearing in the forest, but it is surrounded with alligator-pear, mammee-apple, and other fruit trees, and clusters of the prickly soopa palm, which yields bunches of a very nourishing fruit. Round the houses

were the usual flowers, with fruit of every hue, and many
bushes of anatto, from which they make red paint.

I was soon installed at the end of one of the long houses,
where the headman's two wives sat beside their respective
fires, and as I reclined in my hammock I related a pre-
liminary portion of the news to the men and boys. Soon a
lot of little children came, each bringing a small complimentary portion of food from the fireside of their mothers.
One sent a ripe plantain squeezed up in a calabash with
water, another a small roasted catfish and boiled plantain
wrapped in a green leaf. Others brought a morsel of deer
meat or a piece of iguana, and so on. Of course it is
expected that they shall also have a taste of my provisions,
and when the two women had cooked our monkeys and
iguana, they sent round portions to all the firesides of the
village.

In the evening all the village assembled round a blazing fire
to hear the news, and I had enough to do to satisfy their
inquisitiveness. At last all retired; the headman's wives
climbed to their elevated beds, and the man passed the
babies up, except such as were old enough to sleep in
hammocks below. Presently I heard two women singing
their dirge. The elder sang well, and composed good words,
but the younger, poor girl! was new to the business of grief.
Her song was jerky and hesitating, and the words were
nowhere. This was over the death of a man who died a few
months before this time.

At dawn I was wakened by the dirge of the same two
women, but they went to sleep again, and so did I; for I
woke the second time to find the sun was up, and five or six
men impatiently waiting to accompany me to the hunting-
ground. They were armed with arrows only, and each
carried a machete stuck in the waist-cloth, which was his
only clothing, for they were without shoes, hats, or anything
to protect their naked skins from thorns or stakes.

As we poled the pitpan to the hunting track, which is nearly four miles higher up the river, the Indians explained to me that the kawey-trees which abound there were now ripening their seeds, and that great numbers of warree were in the track.

We came to the landing and tied our boat up, then climbed up the bank through the long cutch grass, and soon found ourselves in the forest, where we halted to put everything to rights. Arrow-tips were scraped, bow-strings examined, waist-cloths tightened, and pipes lighted, for we were not on any account to smoke when we got farther into the bush. After walking about a mile over dry ground, densely overgrown with very tall reeds resembling small bamboos, with trees growing only here and there, we descended into lower ground more or less swampy, with a heavy growth of trees, among which were innumerable clumps of swallow-tail palm. We now walked in Indian file, as usual, silent and watchful, the Indians observing everything and hearing every sound. As we travelled we met abundance of smaller game—monkeys, curassows, and deer—but the Indians would not have me fire at any of them. At last we saw tracks of warree in great numbers, and soon the Indians stopped suddenly, and began to get excited, pointing eagerly in various directions. They heard what is called the ' singing of the warree '—that is, the low buzzing sound of innumerable beasts grunting together. I listened hard, but could hear nothing. After agreeing among themselves, the Indians started off into the bush in various directions, and I followed an old man who seemed the least excited. We advanced at a half-run in a stooping position, so as to get through the bush with the least obstruction. We had not gone far before the presence of the animals in a large drove was evident enough ; the united grunting made a sort of low roaring which seemed to fill the woods, and in all directions we heard the cries of such as were fighting with each other.

My man told me not to fire until the Indians had a chance with their arrows, as he feared the drove would make off at the sound of the gun.

Suddenly I heard the distant snapping, or rather clashing, of teeth, which is the signal of alarm, and all the other sounds ceased ; presently came a loud yell as of a dying pig, and then the angry singing and clashing of teeth seemed to fill the bush. My man darted forward to have a shot, and I heard several yells announcing that the Indians were among the drove with their arrows. I was advancing quickly to get a shot, when my man came running towards me, crying, ' Look out! the drove is going to charge.'

We retreated at once, seeking a tree to climb, and most fortunately came upon an old fallen tree, into which we mounted, and got among the dry branches. The Indian with me, after seeing me safe, got down and again advanced, and in half a minute I heard the twang of his bow followed by a dying yell, and the next instant he rushed out and sprang into our tree. A portion of the drove charged after him and surrounded us. I fired both barrels, and killed with both. The report caused the beasts to disappear, each one hiding behind a thicket and watching ; but presently, being reinforced apparently, they charged us again with loud barking. I had two more good shots, and my Indian brought down one with his arrow. All this time the loud clashing of teeth and angry grunting and barking were heard over acres of bush, and over all the shouts of the men from different parts announced to each other that they were still alive. The warree charged repeatedly to the bottom of our tree, sometimes in twos or trees, sometimes twenty at a time. I fired many shots, but did not kill all I fired at, and my old man killed two or three and wounded others. At last we agreed that we had better not disturb them any more, and presently they retired. When all was still we shouted to the other men, and soon we were all together

and unhurt, except one man who had failed to get up into a
tree, and he had received several cuts from the tusks of the
peccaries on his arms and legs. Not being able to get up
a tree, he had taken refuge between the large spurs of one,
and there defended himself with his machete. He said he
thought his last hour was come, as they repeatedly charged
him in great numbers ; but he cut and stabbed at them
desperately, and wounded great numbers, but killed none.
He took us to see his fortress, and there was evidence
enough of a great struggle, the ground being torn up and
spotted with blood. We now collected the slain in a heap.
I had killed about eight, and the Indians as many more.
While we were tying up the dead, the Indians heard the
coughing of two, which they traced to where they were lying
wounded by arrows, and these they killed and brought to
the heap. One or two of the young fellows wished to start
off and track those warree which had gone off badly wounded,
but we agreed that we had enough. One of the dead warree
was a sow with a number of young pigs, which were hiding
in the bushes close to where their mother was lying. They
kept quite still, watching us with their fierce little eyes.
The young fellows rushed at them, and after a good deal of
running and many falls caught three, which they secured
with withes, intending to take them home.

It was now getting towards evening, and we were very
hungry, so we lighted a fire, singed and cut up one of the
smallest of the game, and made a meal off the choicest
bits, roasting the flesh skewered on green sticks. We had
nothing to eat with the meat, not even salt, but the Indians
at least did not mind that. We finished with a soothing
pipe, and then the men proceeded to tie up the warree for
convenience of carrying. Before leaving we tied all that we
could not carry ourselves up to branches, out of reach of
prowling animals. I insisted on carrying my share of the
load, so they lifted on to my back a small warree of about

50 pounds weight (the largest might weigh 80 pounds). It was quite enough to carry through a bush track, where one has to climb over or crawl under fallen trees, wade deep creeks, and climb up the steep banks, and sustain innumerable stumbles and falls, and all under a temperature of 82°. I stumbled along, streaming with perspiration, and getting rapidly exhausted, until we were startled by the sharp metallic ' pink, pink ' of a flock of curassows, and immediately they flew one by one into the trees with sounding wings. The Indians stopped and looked at me, and I, glad to get a rest, threw down my load and crept into the bush to get near the birds. I shot two, and the rest of the flock flew into another tree, to which I followed them and shot two more, nor did the birds disperse until I had shot about ten of the flock, which was the largest I had ever seen.

It was near sunset when we reached the pitpan, into which we cast our loads, and then had a refreshing bathe in the river and started homewards with great zest and rejoicing. All was dark, but for the bright stars and the shiny surface of the river, when we reached the landing-place below the river, and here we found a number of women and children waiting to see the result of the great hunt. These carried the warree up, and very soon they were being singed and scraped over a fierce fire on the cleared ground in front of the houses.

The night was devoted by the Indians to feasting, and all the culinary art that they possess was put in practice to prolong the joy that food affords. Many went to sleep to wake and eat again, and by morning there was nothing left. Being a fine night, the whole village sat round the fire in the open air, and the hunters related the events of the day in the most exaggerated and animated manner. The pigs that the men had caught they had abandoned in the path, and the young women now bewailed the loss of them, as they are very fond of making pets of animals. I had given them my young monkeys, but the infants could not be induced to adopt a human foster-mother; they had died for want of milk. I was sick of hearing the tiresome details of hunting adventures, so I strolled with my pipe down to the landing-place and sat in an empty canoe to meditate.

Here I was alone in the grand temple of Nature, so soothing and yet so awe-inspiring after the mean frivolities of jabbering men and women. One would think it impossible to be silly and thoughtless in presence of the imposing forest, the silent river, and the glittering eternal stars. Everything here is solemn, or even melancholy. The lofty plumes of the bamboos, and the outlines of the forest shaded in the blackness of night, tell of loneliness or death. The strange sounds of the woods have no touch of joy in them, but only of wailing, threatening or distress. There is no merriment here now, no joyous songs, no cheerful chirping, no cries of exhilaration and pleasure; but in place of these there is the sad wail of the far-distant wood-partridge, the hideous rolling hoot of the wowya owl, the demoniacal yell of the screech-owl, the melancholy and monotonous cry of the goat-sucker, and the occasional screams and howls which are heard out of the dark depths of the forest.

Next morning at daylight a number of women in two pit-pans, with two of the hunters of yesterday as protectors and guides, went up to the path to bring the remainder of the game left by us hanging to the trees. They returned about mid-day, and great joy reigned in the village. The headman told me he was going up the river to fish and cut some bunches of wild bananas. I said I would go with him to pass away the time; so he, his two wives—one with a very young baby—and myself got into a pitpan, and he poled away up the river while I steered and the women sat and talked. Arrived at a place where the current was not too strong, he laid down his pole and I and one of the women paddled, while the man sat on the flat bow of the pitpan, bow and arrow in hand. When he saw a likely place, such as where large snags were grounded in the water and shaded by overhanging trees, we stopped and guided the boat according to the signals he gave with his hand. The man kept up a continual low plaintive whistle to call the fish, and every now and then transfixed one with his arrow. This required considerable skill, as I had found by experience, for by reason of the refraction of the light through the water the position in which the fish appears to sight is not the true position, and the correction, which is only properly estimated after long practice, varies with the distance of the fish, as also with its depth under water. This phenomenon in optics the Indian learns how to deal with when he is a boy. We, on the contrary, learn it, if we ever do, from philosophical treatises. Our man proved very skilful, and shot quite a number of fine fish, greatly to the satisfaction of his wives, as the Indian women estimate a man principally by his skill in hunting and fishing, while the agricultural department more properly pertains to the care of the women. It is a great reproach to a man if it is said of him that his wife suffers ' meat hunger ' (opanwowaya), an expression to indicate the craving which comes over one when long confined to vegetable diet.

Paddling lazily along by the grassy banks overhung with the feathery bamboo, at last we came to an Indian-fig tree. This tree usually grows overhanging the water, and this was the month when the figs ripen and drop in great numbers on to the banks, or into the water, where they are forthwith eaten by the fish. So one of the women landed and gathered a calabashful of windfalls, which the man used as bait. His style of fishing may appear most eccentric, but it is precisely adapted to the requirements in this case. Taking an unripe fig, he fixes it firmly on his hook, and with it flogs the water slowly, like a coachman touching up his horses. The fish, accustomed to hear the sound of the figs falling from a height, and also to scramble for the prize, dart forward and

12

swallow the bait with the least possible delay. This style has also the advantage of not requiring the tiresome and lugubrious whistling which is indispensable in fishing for tooba with bow and arrow.

When we had exhausted the resources of this fig-tree, we paddled slowly along, stopping at every eddy and dark shady corner, while the tempting fruit was popped by the rod into every likely spot with good results. At other places the patient Indian laid down the rod and resumed the bow and arrow, and, to crown all, he finally jumped overboard and caught in his arms a large kooswa, or river turtle, that was browsing among the water weeds. We then landed on a sandbank, and lighted a fire under the shade of sung-sung trees, and while the man and one wife went away to look for wild bananas, I stayed with the other and the baby to help at the cooking. Having no pot, she cooked the fish in a most excellent manner. They were wrapped in waha leaves and buried in hot ashes. By this means all the fat and juices are preserved and concentrated in the flesh. I assisted to erect a stage of green sticks over the fire, and on this the woman barbecued the remainder of the fish.

In about an hour the man and woman returned laden with bunches of wild bananas, found growing among the cutch grass, where they are drifted by the floods from plantations of the Indians further up. I was much amused to see the mother feed her baby, which she did just like a pigeon. She chewed up the banana and fish, and, putting the infant's lips to her own, made the necessary transfer of material. I concluded that there are important advantages in this mode of feeding an infant, as the baby gets all the benefit of the saliva of the mother, greatly assisting digestion, which is always delicate in a young baby.

Towards evening we paddled and drifted down the river homewards. When we landed, I got out of the canoe first and walked up the steep path, which is bordered by high coarse grass. A tame cat was lying in the sun in the middle of the road, which on seeing me leaped into the grass, and I heard it give a slight scream. I thought nothing of it and passed on, but not long afterwards it was found lying dead on the path, and on searching about a very large poisonous snake, called a tomagoff, was discovered and killed. I cut off the head of this snake and took out its poisonous fangs, which I kept in a phial with pieces of soft root on the points. These teeth were about an inch and a half long, beautifully curved, and pierced with a fine hole down the centre to the point. The poison gland, which is a sac about the size of a pea, I left attached to the base of the teeth. Years afterwards I showed the phial with the fangs to some people in a drawing-room in London. I left the room for a minute to get some other curiosity, and on returning found that a young lady had taken the teeth out, removed the corks, and was trying the sharpness of the point against her finger. It was a pretty picture to see blooming young life playing with grim death, but nevertheless I roared at her in a rude and startling manner.

CHAPTER XI.

Cupid—Drift down the river—Howling monkey killed—Yowya Creek:
beauties of the forest — Sleep on a tomagoff — Wakna Creek:
camping—A tapir—Morning start—A jaguar—A pretty waterfall—
Our head camp.

HAVING engaged some young men to go to the mahogany
works, and told them to go by way of the hunting-path
already mentioned, I returned to the lower village, where I
assembled all the men engaged to work for the season.
There were some from this village of Piakos-Maya, some
Twakas from the Twaka River, and some Mosquito Indians
from Quamwatla, on the coast. Several men took their
wives with them, and the headman came also with three
wives, two being middle-aged women, and one a very young
girl—too young, in fact, to be a wife at all. I had also a
small, dwarfish, but strong, active young negro, named
Cupid, with a very pretty, young, pure Indian wife. Cupid
had been with my father and myself for years, and was useful
on account of his versatile talents, especially in cooking, and
his irrepressible activity and cheerfulness. His spirits seemed
never to flag, his stories and yarns were inexhaustible, and
no canary-bird in its cage sang half so cheerfully. I could
tell stories to the Indians, but when Cupid was about I was
nowhere in that department. He spoke English and the
Mosquito language with equal fluency, and often in my
loneliness among the Indians my soul has yearned towards
Cupid because I could speak my own tongue to him, not-

withstanding that his English was that grotesque form of it used by the negroes of the West Indies.

In telling stories to my men, the lies and exaggerations he wove into them were shocking ; and once when I said, 'Oh, Cupid, how can you tell the people such lies ?' he replied, ' Maas Charley, dem Ingin too jam fool; dem lub lie better dan victual.'

One day in camp at the works I came upon him surrounded by an admiring audience of women and young men, to whom he was explaining the science of hydraulics in this wise : 'Water always falls down; of course it does. Did any of you ever see water run up the river ? Does not rain fall down ? If not, why do you put a waha leaf over your head, or get under a tree ? Look here ! You people know no more than the game in the bush about these things. In my country' (he came from Belize, in British Honduras) ' we make machines to send rain up into the sky, and when the birds come at the sound of the water to wet their feathers, they drop down dead with fright to see the rain falling towards the tops of the trees. But that is nothing; I myself can make water climb upward. Some of you just hold a calabash of water to my mouth.' Thereupon he stood on his head, supported by his hands, with his legs straight in the air ; then, asking for the water, he drank some, having called on the people to notice it going up his throat. This feat was received with roars of laughter, and seriously discredited his rain story.

Cupid's wife had some difficulty in reconciling herself to her position, and the girls used to jeer at her on account of her jet-black husband, but her answer was always quite satisfactory, namely, that he gave her plenty of meat to eat and lots of cloth and beads.

We left the settlement late in the evening, and drifted down the river, at first laughing, talking, and singing, making the solemn woods echo the merry sounds from side to side of the river, and frightening the night herons and boat-bills from their usual quiet haunts. Towards morning all had collapsed into sleep, until even the man steering at the stern failed to keep the pitpan from running under bushes and bumping against snags. A white cold mist settled down on the river, and one after another, scattered far apart, the canoes were tied up to branches overhanging the water. I was wakened at daylight by the howling of the howling monkeys, called coongcoong by the Indians; but although the birds were piping up, and the quams flying down from their roosts to the ground with loud shrieks, the mist was over everything, and my blankets were soaked with dew. So I pulled them over my head and fell asleep again. When I again woke, the sun was up and the fog lifting, so we untied the pitpan and went on down the river. We were alone; the others had gone long ago.

As we paddled along, we saw on the left bank a howling monkey, sitting warming itself in the rising sun on the branch of a very high trumpet-tree, which grew on the edge of a vertical bank of earth 30 feet high, so that the monkey was about 100 feet above the river. I said to one of the Indians: 'Lend me your bow and arrow, till I have a shot at the coongcoong.' They all remonstrated that to kill that kind of monkey is sure to bring rain; but an old man said, 'Let the white boy have a shot; he can't hit it,' and himself offered me his bow. When the pitpan was directly below, they stopped. I took good aim, and, drawing the bow to my cheek, let fly the arrow. It entered the monkey's body just over the hip-bone, and the point came out under the armpit. The monkey gave a loud scream, broke the arrow in two, and pulled out the piece that was in its body; then crawled slowly along the branch towards the trunk of the tree, bleeding profusely. Then it stopped and lay down on the branch, and after a little rolled off and hung by its tail. We waited some time to see it fall; then, as it did not, we went on, but had hardly gone 100 yards when it fell into the river with a loud splash, and we left it to the alligators.

They all grumbled at my killing the monkey, although they passed flattering remarks about my skill with their weapon. The old man gave me a lecture, saying: 'Friend Saaley, when you come among us you must not be so heartless and deaf. Now your poor soldiers' backs will be wet with much rain. You may know all about books, but you do not know the bad spirits that live in the bush. That monkey belongs to the Water Spirit, and it will be very angry at us for what you have done.' It did not rain more than usual for a long time, but whenever it did I was sure to be reminded of the death of the howling monkey.

We soon came to a large tributary of the main river, or creek, as by the English all over Central America such tributaries are called. This one, named Yowya Creek, offers the most beautiful sylvan scenery imaginable. It is about 40 yards wide, and arched over by trees, mostly of the kind called sung-sung, the most beautiful of all riverside trees, which never grows anywhere except on the banks of rivers, and prefers narrow creeks, which it can cover up from the glare of the sun, and protect from rough winds, so as to make a sacred leafy aisle for its beloved water to flow through.

We assembled, and had our breakfast on a gravelly beach, and then proceeded, poling the pitpans up the stream. I myself and my brother-in-law, with four men, went about an hour's start of the others to cut away fallen logs and clear the creek for the more heavily-laden canoes. The Indians pointed out to me the camp where, the year before, I had had a perilous adventure.

In the month of June we were going up this creek, and pushing on to get up before a flood should come on. At about eight at night we put ashore at this place, and by the light of pitch-pine torches the Indians cut bundles of swallow-tail leaves to sleep on. We lay down, each on his own bundle of leaves. There was much distant lightning and thunder, and, wondering whether or not the flood would come down, I fell asleep. I was wakened at break of day by feeling water running into my ear, and, putting out my hand, found I was surrounded by water. The Indians were just getting up on making the same discovery. We looked for the pitpan, which had been tied up against the bank, but it was now 20 yards out in the stream. So one of the men jumped into the water, untied it, and brought it close in. They then put all our things into it, and finally took the leaves they had slept on to cover the luggage. When one of the men lifted the bundle of leaves on which I had slept, a poisonous snake, called a tomagoff, 6 feet long, uncoiled itself and made for the water. As it was swimming out into the flood, one of the men pierced it with an arrow, and immediately it knotted itself up in such a manner as to break the arrow in pieces, in which condition it drifted down the flooded creek. On examining the place where I had slept, I found it had coiled itself in the loop of a large root, which had kept me from pressing on it, and, feeling warm and comfortable, it had remained quiet under me all night.

We had a hard day's work chopping branches and logs that obstructed the creek. We entered the Wakna Creek, a tributary of the Yowya, and were poling up a rapid, when a very large iguana, frightened at the boat, let itself go from the highest branches of an Indian fig, intending, as is their habit, to drop into the water and swim away. By an extraordinary chance it fell head foremost into our pitpan, and smashed its head on the bottom of the boat. This was a male 6 feet long, and must have weighed over 30 pounds. If it had struck any one of us, it is probable his neck would have been broken.

As the rest of our people did not turn up, we made up our minds to encamp on a most suitable clean flat rock, nearly surrounded by the creek.

After dinner we cut bundles of leaves, and made up our bed on the rock, but as the stars were shining brightly we did not concern ourselves to thatch a hut. We sat round the fire till we were sleepy, and then retired, each to his bed of swallow-tail leaves. I lay on my back gazing at the stars through an opening in the trees, and listening to the strange noises of the forest. I was just falling off to sleep, when one of the men laid his hand on me and said, ' Tilba owla ; walse' (A tapir is coming; listen). I heard the breaking of sticks and the shrill plaintive whistle, and, getting my gun out, prepared for its coming. It came with much heavy tramping and brushing of leaves and breaking of sticks, and seemed to be quite regardless of secrecy, although it must know that it is always in danger from its numerous enemies. It came to the edge of the creek close to us, and every one of us kept quite still, but do what I could I failed to see it in the dark. It evidently saw us, however, for after three or four minutes' delay it uttered its shrill whistle and plunged into the creek, and mounting the opposite bank went off with great clatter.

At daybreak we resumed our tiring cramped seat, the Indians taking to their poles and propelling us up the creek. We were seated in contemplation of the scenery, and the man in the bow was poling the pitpan past a cliff of earth about 12 feet high, when he suddenly planted his pole ahead so as to stop the boat, and, pointing with his finger, crouched down in the boat. Looking to the top of the cliff, we saw a jaguar standing half hidden among the leaves, but gazing at us with its large, fierce, and threatening eyes. I got my gun out from under the luggage, and just as it turned to go away I fired at its shoulder. In an instant it jumped down into the creek with a splash and disappeared under water, but immediately it rose to the surface, and, strange to say, instead of attacking the boat, seized hold of, and partly climbed up, a very thick vine which hung from the trees into the water, and terminated in a great tuft of roots. The jaguar was biting the vine and growling as if it had its enemy in its jaws. Then commenced a ludicrous struggle, over which we laughed many times afterwards. My brother-in-law, with a cutlass in his teeth, seized a paddle and made frantic efforts to pull the pitpan close to the beast. The Indians, on the contrary, made equally vigorous efforts with their paddles to keep the beast at a safe distance. Von Tempsky roared at them to let him get near; they yelled out, 'No, no; it will kill us!' Meanwhile, I was fumbling in my agitation to put a load of buckshot into the gun, when suddenly the jaguar let go its hold and disappeared under water. Next instant it emerged on the opposite side, sprang up the bank on three legs, and disappeared. I loaded both barrels heavily, and went after it with an Indian. We found the trail of blood, and followed it into a dense thicket of bamboos, the thorny roots of which greatly obstructed our advance. After tracking the blood for some distance the courage of the Indian gave way, and he refused to go on, saying that if it attacked us, stuck up as we were among the thorny roots, it would kill us. So, as I was not game to track it alone, we returned crestfallen to the riverside.

We soon came to a beautiful waterfall 6 or 8 feet high, where the stream has cut a gap through the beds of sandstone which obstruct it, the water tumbling over boulders and large fragments of the rock. The banks of the stream have here a growth of tall elegant reeds, resembling small bamboos; their edges and the waterfall itself are shaded by sung-sung trees. Here we had to unload and haul the boat over the rocks, and having cooked something to eat, we embarked on the stream above, which for a long way is wide and deep. Von Tempsky made a sketch of this fall, and has placed the jaguar on a tree above it as a reminder of the incident related above.

In the evening we arrived at the mahogany camp which we had come to occupy for the season. The camp consisted

WAHKNA CREEK.

of a large house 35 feet long by 20 feet wide, built of stout
posts, rafters, and ridge-pole, open all round, and neatly
thatched with swallow-tail palm-leaves.   There was also a
similarly-built but smaller house for myself, and a thatched
lean-to shed to cook under.   The forest all round the camp
had been felled to the extent of one-third of an acre.   The
branches and logs were chopped up and burnt, but the
stumps of the largest trees still stood all over the ground.

At the foot of the sloping bank flows the Wakna Creek,
about 20 yards wide and a few feet deep.   The opposite bank
slopes gently upwards from the waterside, thickly covered
with forest trees and carpeted with slender ferns.   Immediately above the camp the creek forked, but the branches
joined again a mile further up, enclosing an island between
them.   The branch farthest off descended through a series
of rapids, under the dense shadow of enormous trees, whose
roots obstructed the current and twined among the rocks
and boulders.   The branch nearest the camp occupied a still
and placid channel, winding through banks covered with tall
reeds, swallow-tail palms, and heavy trees scattered here and
there ; but at its mouth, close to the camp, it tumbled through
some great brown moss-covered rocks, among the clefts of
which it roared unseen, and against which in time of flood it
had piled great trunks of dead trees and a vast accumulation
of brushwood.

Here was to be our home for a long time, and it was not
cheering to see the deserted place overgrown with weeds,
and strewed with rotten timber and the decayed fragments
of former occupation.   However, it was of no use feeling
lugubrious, so we strewed the floor with dry leaves, to which
we set fire in order to burn out scorpions, centipedes, and
ants, and set to to erect new stages and to cover them with
sheets of bark for our beds.

The rest of our party arrived next day, and after they had
built huts for the married men, and put the place in order,
we settled down to the routine of our work.

CHAPTER XII.

Our work—Mahogany-cutting—Pleasures of evening at camp—Mahogany
—Truck-passes—Log-driving.

MY own occupation may appear light and attractive, and so
it was, and so it might have continued to be but for the
weary sameness of every day, and the longing which often
possessed me for a change, and to see and hear about the
outside world.   Day after day I had to wake at daylight, and
rouse the sleeping Indians by blowing a shell, or going round
and scolding them for sleeping so long.   Day after day I had
to walk with my whole working gang in Indian file to the
upper end of the island, and there embark in a pitpan and
pole up to the different parts of the forest, where the mahogany-
trees were being felled, cut into lengths, and the logs rolled
to the creek and tumbled into it.   My business during the
day was to walk from one party to another, or jump into a
little canoe and pole up to the other gangs and look after
them.   This was sufficiently unpleasant to spoil the temper
and ruffle the serenity of any man.   The Indians would
skulk, go to sleep, or hide in the shade, and it was with difficulty that they could be kept steadily at their work.

Only such mahogany-trees were cut as grew at a reason-
able distance from the creek, and our work was thus extended
sometimes to many miles from the camp.   Where the stream
was too rocky to be navigable, we had to walk long distances
to and from the work ; but where the stream was passable

we all enjoyed the long distance, for in the morning we were poled up by six or eight men, and in the evening we leisurely drifted down with the current, shooting any game that appeared along the banks.

On arriving at the part of the forest where the works were, the men were dispersed to the various occupations assigned them, and forthwith the woods resounded in all directions with the blows of the axe and the monotonous hiss of the cross-cut saw, interrupted from time to time by the thundering crash of a fallen tree, an event always hailed by those within hearing with cheers and shouts.

The Indians are not powerful nor enduring workmen, yet they ply the axe with great skill. But when they come to the heavy task of rolling the great logs with hand-spikes along the truck - pass to the creek, their strength and endurance are taxed to the utmost, and they cheer their toil with diabolical shouts and yells. In the dreamy stillness of noon, when all nature reposes from the overpowering heat, anyone wandering in the silent woods who came within hearing of these busy sounds would be struck with wonder at the restless activity of white men, whose requirements reach even to this lonely wilderness.

The scene of operation presents a most picturesque bit of landscape. The long vista of the truck-pass admits a blaze of sunlight into the dark forest, and at the end of it is a small cleared space, surrounded by foliage, in the midst of which stand the great black trunks of one or two mahogany-trees, their tops waving in the cool trade wind, while the air below quivers in a sultry calm. Round the huge spurs of the trees is reared a slender stage of poles, and mounted on this, often 20 feet from the ground, two brown figures, naked to the cloth round their waist, ply with measured stroke the glistering axe, from which chips fly in all directions. Through the long hours the blows fall on the tree; already a huge gap is opened in the red wood; now and then a

faint sound is wafted from the distant part of the forest
where another party is similarly occupied, and is immediately
answered by all within hearing ; then the men ply their
strokes with renewed vigour. On one side, where a great
trunk has already measured its length on the ground, and
lies prostrate amid a ruin of torn branches, a party of six
men, three on each side, draw the long saw backwards and
forwards with a measured pull. Their brown backs, covered
with sweat, glisten in the sun ; beside them is a little fire
of mahogany chips, and the pipe and the joke are passed
merrily round. Presently a loud crack is heard, and the
axemen are seen hastily scrambling down from their stage.
The fellows seated so comfortably at their saw have already
fled ; a volley of cracks succeeds ; the lofty top of the tree
slowly inclines over, and the monarch of the forest yields to
its fate with a roar of broken branches and a thump that
shakes the earth for half a mile round about.

So the hours pass until the cool shades of evening lengthen
along the path ; the men begin to slacken their efforts,
anxiously waiting for the signal to cease work. At length
the conch shell resounds through the forest, and immediately
all busy sounds cease, while the cheerful notes of the birds
and the shrill ringing of the crickets again fill the ear. The
men tie their shirts round their necks by the sleeves, shoulder
their axes, trudge down the truck-pass to their canoe, and
paddle merrily home to the camp.

Arrived at camp, they all go down to the creek, and,
plunging in, swim about to wash off the dust and cool their
heated blood. Soon half a dozen fires are blazing under as
many pots round the huts, and the men wait patiently till
the welcome meal is spread on broad green leaves, when,
seated in a circle on the ground, they fall to with appetites
sharpened by toil. As darkness comes on, the men seek
their beds, not yet to sleep, but to smoke and tell stories.
The old men tell wonderful tales, heard from their fathers,

of bloody wars that used to be waged between the tribes; of raids to some distant river to capture slaves, and the fearful scenes of bloodshed that ensued; or they tell of adventures with all sorts of animals, some real, some imaginary. The younger men chat about love adventures or hunting episodes, or of strange sights they have seen in their travels to Belize or to the Spanish countries in the interior. Their stories are long-winded, but told with such spirit and expression of voice and gesture that they seldom fail to interest one.

The mahogany is a very fine tree, growing frequently to 27 feet in circumference, the trunk being without branches for 80 feet. It has a thick black bark with deep longitudinal ridges. The inside bark is stringy, soft, and pink, excescessively bitter and astringent, and is often used to tan leather. The leaf is 3 to 4 inches long, oval, glossy, dark green, the web on one side of the midrib much wider than on the other. It bears brown winged seeds, very much like those of the sycamore-tree of Europe, which lie on the ground and sprout, surrounding the parent tree with thousands of young plants, which, however, seldom grow up. The largest and soundest trees grow on low, often swampy ground, but the hardest wood with the finest grain only on dry or hilly land. The mahogany never grows without spurs or buttresses, which are sometimes of great size, joining the trunk at 20 feet above ground; and contiguous spurs form recesses capable at times of sheltering twenty men. Its range of growth on the mainland extends from Yucatan to Blewfields River, south of which it is not found; and I believe it is confined to the watershed facing the Caribbean Sea. There are many trees of extremely limited range of growth in this country, and for no obvious cause.

The mahogany-cutters waste a vast quantity of the best wood, utilizing only the part of the tree above the spurs and below the branches, and rejecting the closest-grained and most ornamental wood. Logs with a bad split or a rot hole are abandoned. If a tree, on being cut into, shows a rotten heart, it is usually set fire to in the expectation that it will only burn as far as the rot extends; but if the tree is old and seasoned, the fire will extend through the sound wood to the branches.

In large well-regulated mahogany works, where negroes or Caribs are employed instead of Indians, the work is carried on with method and regularity, and though laborious is by no means excessive. All operations, except 'driving' in the creeks and rafting the logs, are done by taskwork, which good men soon perform, and so have the rest of the day to themselves.

They then take their guns and stroll away into the bush 'to look fo' piece o' fresh meat.' They generally resort to the old truck-passes, which, the mahogany having been taken out, are abandoned to silence. These are the most delightful hunting-places imaginable. They are grand avenues 30 feet wide, which extend for miles through the forest, having all the creeks and ravines bridged with rough logs, overlaid with fascines and covered with earth. The celebrated Avenue of Palms in Rio Janeiro cannot compare in beauty with these truck-passes, in which you enjoy the ever-pleasing contrast of dense shade in the bush with the most brilliant sunshine in the pass, and a foliage combining massive grandeur with the greatest loveliness of detail. Here are enormous standing trees covered with innumerable parasites, roped about with cable-like vines and tangled hanks of withes; slender graceful palms 100 feet high; vast massive palms, with leaves 30 feet long springing from a thick stumpy stem; palms 40 feet high supported on numerous roots like stilts, in the centre of which one can stand like a gorilla in a cage; delicate feathery palms with stems 1½ inches in diameter; parasitical palms growing only on the trees; climbing palms with hooks in the fronds; while tree-ferns and ordinary ferns in endless variety,

bamboos and bamboo reeds, lend additional grace to the
more massive foliage; and leaves of every variety of size
and colour decorate the ground below the trees.

In these abandoned truck-passes, if anywhere, game is
likely to be found. All the stumps and roots are springing
up with fresh young shoots, and game of all sorts comes to
browse or enjoy the sunshine. I have often seated myself
on a log in the shade, and observed the game come out of
the bush and stroll about the path. Deer emerge cautiously,
gazing up and down, then quietly feed on the young shoots,
lifting their heads continually to see if all is safe. Curassows
and quams saunter out of the bush and lie down in the sunshine, stretching out their legs and covering them with an
outstretched wing. I have seen small droves of peccary
come boldly out, and forthwith begin to frisk and play in
the sun, grunting and barking as they assailed each other in
fun. Lizards of the most beautiful colours creep about on
the ground, searching industriously for beetles and grubs,
disappearing under the dry leaves, and popping out again to
have a look all round. Once I saw a lovely pea-green whip-
snake 8 feet long, which was sliding over the leaves and
fallen branches, when a large blue butterfly passed it. At
once the snake gave chase, gliding swiftly down the pass
close behind the butterfly until both were out of sight. On
another occasion I saw a beautiful tiger-cat crossing the
pass with two kittens. I started up and pursued it, thinking
to catch a kitten, but they were gone in an instant. I have
also seen the beautiful bush dog, called arari, trot out
into the pass, gaze all round with his nose in the air, surprised at the unaccustomed sight of an opening in the bush,
then disappear. This beautiful animal is not often seen.
It belongs to the fox family, and is the size of a fox, black
with a long sweeping tail. It frequents the sandbanks of
the rivers at night, and with unerring instinct digs up the
nests of the alligators, turtles, and iguanas. It is also de-

structive to cultivated fruits. Occasionally it hunts in small packs, and pursues the smaller animals. I have heard of it attacking people, probably when it had its young under its care.

When the trees have been felled and cut into logs, and the passes cleared and bridged, the trucks are brought into requisition. These are immensely strong, framed of timber, with broad, solid wooden wheels. From twelve to thirty bullocks are yoked to each, according to the size of the log, and there are generally six or eight trucks employed on a camp. They all start from the camp at two in the morning, making a most picturesque party, torches blazing, men shouting and swearing, cattle lowing and wheels creaking, while the forest is illuminated by the red glare of the pitch-pine torches. On arriving at the logs, a gang of men lay strong beams from the ground to the edge of the trucks, and roll the logs up them on to the trucks. All the logs are first trucked out of the branch passes to their junction with the main pass, and then drawn down to, and thrown into, the creeks or rivers. In soft ground a sledge called a slide is employed instead of a truck, to convey the logs. The trucking is done in the dry season, and by the time it is completed the rainy season has commenced. When a freshet comes on, whether it be night or day, the men at once commence 'driving' the logs. Each man takes charge of two or three, and seated on one he guides them with a long pole past the rocks and shallows as he drifts down the creek. He is wet during the day with the cold creek water, and at night sleeps in a damp bed, for it is impossible to keep dry in the open thatched huts which are hastily built as night comes on. The log on which the man rides is continually rolling over and throwing him into the water, and after a long day's wetting it is ludicrous to see the grim faces of the men every time they tumble into the water. Finally they become so chilled that they are shivering and almost powerless, and nothing will induce them to jump into the water to release a log that has grounded.

The logs often get jammed between rocks, or, if the flood is high, among the branches and trunks of the trees. Often it is impossible to distinguish the creek from the flooded forest, and the freshet, subsiding, leaves the logs stranded in the bush, from which they have to be again rolled into the creek. Generally several freshets are necessary before all the logs are driven to the main river, where in a secure eddy they are stopped by a boom made of logs, chained together and fastened to trees.

The logs are made up into rafts and floated to the mouth of the river, where they are rolled on shore and squared with the broad axe. Then they are tumbled again into the river, made up into small rafts, and drifted with the ebb tide out to the ship, which is riding at her anchors off the mouth of the river.

CHAPTER XIII.

Dry weather—Our women—Our hunters—The puma—Monkeys—Eagles
—Hawks—Owls—Goatsuckers—Pickwa.

A LONG period of dry weather came on ; even the dark damp
bush got dry, and many fires spread in the woods.

On one occasion the bush all round our camp was on fire,
and we spent an anxious night for fear of being burnt out.
The creek became very small, and the usual roar of our
waterfall near the camp subsided to a gentle murmur ; our
creek became filthy from the refuse thrown into it, which
lodged against fallen bamboos ar.d refused to drift away.

I was so weary of the shade and gloom of the forest that I
used to gaze up at the blue sky through the trees, envying
even the light clouds, driven by the brisk trade wind, their
freedom. I longed to have wings to fly out of this shady
pit, to see the wide world, the busy haunts of men, to cross
the beautiful ocean and get among my own people in distant
Scotland, to take my place in the race of life instead of
dreaming and fretting among these wild men of the woods.
After many years I did get out into the busy haunts of men ;
I ran my race, and when I was wearied I wished I were
back in the beautiful forests of Central America, to dream
and rest and fret no longer !

I do not know what we should have done without Cupid.
His songs, his loud whistling, his jokes and laughter, poured
oil, I believe, on many a ruffled temper. The Indians seldom

use drums, but no negro can get on without one. So Cupid stretched a deerskin over a pork barrel, and found no end of pleasure in loudly whistling jigs, fandangoes, and carabinis, while beating the drum with the tips of his fingers. Often, carried away by his feelings, he dropped his drum and pranced round the shed in the elegant steps of the waltz or the Spanish punta, till, breathless with the exertion and whistling, he lay on the floor, and commenced to taunt the astonished Indians with their boorish ignorance of the elegant amusements of civilization.

Our womenfolk caused us some little trouble. They stayed in camp, and we found that men often complained of being ill, and returned to the camp during working hours, really to amuse themselves with the women. This the husbands found fault with, and some of the men took their wives with them to their work, where they were again found to be great disturbers of business. One day one of them got bitten on the instep by a snake, and as we had none of their *sookias*, or medicine-men, in camp, they wanted to take her out of the creek to the main river settlement. I took a great responsibility on myself in preventing their doing so, by telling her husband that she would probably die on the journey, and offered myself to do what I could. So I tied a cord round her leg, cut a gash in her foot over the two punctures made by the teeth, and sucked the wound till my cheeks refused to act from exhaustion. Then I applied a rag soaked in hartshorn to the wound, and gave her some to drink. Her leg swelled very much, and gave her a great deal of pain, but after getting very low she gradually recovered.

One day three young men had been sent hunting, and on returning in their pitpan they suddenly came on several of our women bathing in the creek; news of this soon leaked out, and the husbands made a great row, and insisted on being paid by the young men for seeing their wives naked. I took the part of the young men, explaining that it was an accident, and therefore the men were not at fault; but the husbands insisted on payment, and all I could do was to mitigate the amount of the fine. However, so many quarrels cropped up on account of our women that we had to get rid of them, and they were packed off to the main river. This step did not entirely alleviate the trouble, for now the husbands kept coming for leave to go to the village on the main river, and then delayed returning under the excuse that they had to devote a day or two to hunting in order to provide some meat for the women, who, as they described it, were 'dying of meat hunger,' having only plantain and maize to eat, with what few fish the feeble skill of woman sufficed to provide.

We had one or more men who were selected to do our hunting, and provide fresh meat for the gang. They were away in the forest from morning till night, but seldom brought much game; frequently I accompanied them, and with my double-barrelled gun I generally killed twice as much as our hunters could, although they were also armed with guns.

One day, when our hunter and I were on the hunting-path, we sat down on a log to rest, and he told me to stay where I was until he went down to the creek to see if there were any tracks in the sand. I leant my gun against the log and sat looking on the ground. Presently I felt as if someone was looking at me, and, raising my head, saw a large puma standing ten yards off, gazing at me with that fearless, penetrating look which is characteristic of the felines. I seized my gun and stood up, but it never moved, except by giving its tail a sweep. I was spellbound and did not know what to do, though I had the sense not to fire at it, as my gun was only loaded with shot. I turned my head for an instant to see if my man was coming, and when I looked again the puma was gone, vanished like a ghost, without a sound. When I told the man of it, he approved of my discretion in not firing at it, as he said it would have killed me if wounded.

The puma is certainly the most beautiful of all the cat tribe; it has long, elegant legs, a rather slender body, a long neck, and a beautiful head, which it carries proudly raised. In Central America the colour of the puma is a reddish-brown, like the colour of the African lion. In South America the same animal is mouse colour.

The puma presents a great contrast to the jaguar, which has short, very thick legs, and a stout muscular body, thick neck, large heavy head, while its attitude is crouching and treacherous. The puma is very active, and most destructive to cattle, pigs, dogs, and even to fowls. It occasionally attacks man, but only when he is alone.

When the Indian joined me, we sat on the log to rest and smoke a pipe. He told me that he was hunting one day, when he heard the clashing of teeth and barking of a drove of warree; he crept cautiously up till he saw a deep ravine spanned by a fallen tree, on which was a large puma with a young warree in its teeth, and on each bank of the ravine a drove of peccary were rushing about in great fury; occasion-ally some of them charged the puma on the tree, but always slipped off and fell into the ravine. At last the puma dropped its prey, and, creeping towards the butt of the tree, bounded over the heads of the peccary and disappeared, followed by the drove at full speed. Knowing the dangerous state of excitement they were in, the Indian did not follow them up. A month afterwards he and several others hunting in the same place followed up the direction the chase had taken, and found the skeleton of the puma surrounded by three or four warree.

One day, when our men returned from their work, one of them related that he was alone, felling a large tree, when he saw a drove of white-faced monkeys approaching along the bamboos between him and the edge of the creek. He laid down his axe, and sat down to look at them. They were feeding on the seeds of the bamboos, and presently he saw a puma creep out of a patch of swallow-tail palms, and crouch down below the monkeys, with its head on the ground. The monkeys, alarmed at first, took courage on seeing the beast lie so still, and came nearer and nearer, chattering and shaking the branches as if to frighten it. At last one came pretty low down, scolding and barking; the puma sprang at it, seized it in its paws, gave it a crunch with its teeth, and bounded into the bush to eat it at its leisure.

While the men were at their work felling trees, cutting passes, or rolling the logs to the creek, I often wandered about the bush to observe the beasts or birds, without any weapon to defend myself. I often crept through the thickets and hid myself under a tree to observe a drove of red monkeys resting during the heat of the day.

Such an active creature as a monkey takes little rest even in its leisure moments. They are the most sociable of animals. Sometimes they lie sprawling on their backs on a branch, with the arms and legs relaxed, but always holding on by the tail. More frequently one lies on its face, while another parts its hair with a quick nervous action, catching and eating its parasitical insects. Then a number of them hang by the tail and fondle and kiss, making a crooning, affectionate noise. Every now and then one makes a loud, shrill, crowing noise, something like the so-called crowing of the human infant. This is a note of joy or exhilaration, and corresponds to our laugh. Every now and then the younger ones pursue each other over the branches; then return and sit down beside the rest, dozing for a while with their heads bent down between their knees. But one can perceive that they are watchfully on the alert. Now and then one gives a loud roaring sort of bark, a note of warning, and the whole drove is on the watch for enemies; but presently it relapses again into play and amusement. Let a shout be uttered, and they are instantly in motion, streaming off towards the ends of the longest branches, and thence throwing themselves on to the branches of other trees. If pursued, they take the most astonishing leaps from tree to tree. When travelling leisurely, they seek the end of a long branch, set it swinging, and when it has reached its highest momentum, they let go and plunge into the branches of the next tree. Occasionally one misses its hold and falls to the ground. The Indians say that one thus disgraced is not allowed to rejoin its troop, and, in fact, occasionally solitary monkeys are seen in the bush, which the Indians say are such as unfortunately have had a fall. The young ones cling to the hair of the mother's back, and she takes the baby's head under her arm when giving it suck. When at rest, the young one lies in its mother's lap to be cleaned and attended to, but it gets on to her back the instant there is an alarm given.

Monkeys are very numerous in the forest of the Mosquito Coast, and form one of the principal articles of food alike of Indians, negroes, and white people. The red monkey is the species preferred. The white-faced monkey is seldom eaten, the howling monkey never.

The howling monkey stands about 3 feet high; the lower part of the body is black, the shoulders, neck, arms, breast, and belly are dark brown. It has short, fleshy arms, and its legs have calves to them, a most unusual thing in the monkey tribe. It is also distinguished by having a thumb, whereas the red and white-faced monkeys have only four fingers, with a rudimentary thumb under the skin. The male of the howling monkey has a thick and bushy black beard and whiskers, black fiery eyes set deep in bony sockets, and except for its compressed lips it looks like a bearded negro. The most remarkable peculiarity about this monkey is its astonishing voice. It has a tube of bone in its throat, with two projections pointing upwards, which gives to its throat the appearance of a hen's egg sticking in it. This monkey is slow and deliberate in its motions, and shows little fear of man. It goes sometimes in parties of six or eight, more frequently in couples, male and female.

Its roar or howl is a most alarming sound, and can be heard two miles off. It delights to howl at break of day; but in the rainy season, after a day of thunder and lightning, and torrents of rain with frequent tearing squalls, towards evening the rain ceases and Nature seems at rest; the sky settles into leaden streaky clouds, and the sun casts a feeble ray before setting. Then the thundering roar of the howling monkeys is heard far and near over the forest. The sound resembles these syllables sounded in a deep, sonorous bass: ' Googn, googn, googn, googn—goong, goong, goong.' The first four sounds are a sort of roaring shout, the last three are in a higher key, like strokes on a gigantic drum. When several are together, confabulating, as it were, the males sit facing each other, roaring in a low muffled tone, the noise being like a sonorous, rolling growl or croak; the females do not roar at all.

So fearless are these monkeys that they used to come to our camp, and, sitting on a high branch, gaze at the people for a long time without moving. It has a habit of in-variably roaring when it hears the distant noise of approach-ing rain, and travelling at night one is often given timely warning to get under shelter by the far-distant roaring of this monkey.*

The red monkey (*Cebus patuellas*) is about 2½ feet high when standing upright. Among different droves its colour varies from very dark brown to a light dun colour. The face, palms of the hands and feet, and bare prehensile part of the tail, are covered with black and wrinkled skin. Its eyes are hazel brown, and its appearance when pleased is intelligent and friendly; but it is easily enraged, and then

---

* The above description of the roar of the howling monkey does not necessarily apply to other parts of tropical America. In Brazil I found it s o different that I scarcely recognised it.

its eye is threatening and fierce. It goes in troops of from 20 up to 200. It is extensively hunted for food, and its meat, which is red with saffron-coloured fat, is delicious. In fact, I know of no such tasty meat as a fat she-monkey.

When tamed it is sociable, cheerful, and most affectionate to its master. When I was a boy I was seldom without a pet red monkey, and no dog could be so attached, so playful, and so prompt to defend me. I used to lie on the grass and play with it. It would jump all over me, pretending to be in a great passion, and biting in play. Its favourite trick was to jump suddenly on my head, bury its fingers in my long hair, and pretend to worry me. It was only with great trouble that I could get it to let go my hair, and when I at last got it off I would throw it on its back in my lap and tickle its ribs, at which it went into a sort of hysterical laughter. When tired of playing, it would sit upon the ground, and make the shrill crowing noise mentioned already as being like the crowing of a human infant. It often went about with me, sitting on my shoulder with its tail round my neck. If anyone touched me it would glare fiercely and roar at him, and if in fun I were roughly handled, the monkey would scream out, jump on the aggressor, and bite him savagely. It was exceedingly fond of company of any kind, and would sit for hours on a pig's back, searching in the bristles for insects, and enjoying the ride on the pig wherever it went. It was very fond of getting hold of a kitten, which it generally detained by holding it round the neck with its tail. It seemed puzzled when the kitten pricked it with its claws. On the first occasion it gave a bark and jumped aside in great alarm, but immediately captured the kitten again and examined its paws intently. After that it seemed content to suffer an occasional scratch so long as it had the kitten to hug; but we had to take it away, as it kept it so tightly in its arms that it would soon have killed it. On several occasions it captured fowls in the most wily fashion. They used to come and eat the fragments of food which it dropped. The monkey lay on its side with its head on its arm as if asleep, its tail extended over the crumbs, and it caught the hen by the leg with its tail. It then pulled the hen in, held down its wings, put its tail round the hen's neck, and sat on its back. On one occasion we found the hen dead, and 'De Zaacamo' got a good beating. He was exceedingly fond of having his fur parted and searched for insects, although he had not one to bless himself with, for we kept him very clean. He was ready at any time to do the same for any-one, and would part the hair and search most diligently, making a sipping noise with his lips while so employed.

The only other species found in this country is the white-faced monkey. It is much smaller than the red. It is black, with white face and breast. Its expression is gentle and innocent, and it is very timid when tamed. This monkey feeds extensively on spiders, grubs, insects of all descriptions, and even wasps. One of my Indians told me that he was watching a drove of white-faced monkeys feed-ing in a tree, when he saw one of them quietly place itself at the opening of a large paper-wasps' nest attached to a branch. The monkey picked up and devoured the wasps as fast as they appeared at the hole. At last it was satisfied, but on leaving it clawed an immense hole in the nest, and ran for its life. The wasps in clouds assailed the drove of monkeys quietly feeding in the tree, and they made a hasty and precipitate retreat.

One Sunday a young fellow borrowed my gun to go hunting. He had not been gone long, when he returned with a yacal, or harpy eagle, which he had shot, as well as a sloth which it was eating. This magnificent bird lives only in the densest forest, where it kills deer, peccary, quams, curassows, etc. It is a dreaded enemy of the monkey tribe. It never leaves the forest, but sits in the trees watching for its prey, or takes stealthy flight from place to place. This one measured 3 feet 9 inches from the beak to the end of the tail, and 7 feet 4 inches across the wings. On the crest are several long curved feathers, which are raised when the bird is excited. One of the men in camp told me that he and a party were hunting, when they heard at a distance a great disturbance among a drove of red monkeys. As these monkeys frequently make a row on seeing a drove of warree, following them, barking and shaking the branches, the Indians made haste to get near the spot. On getting below the monkeys the noise was deafening, and looking up into a large bushy tree, they saw the whole drove of monkeys plucking an eagle, tearing the feathers out with their teeth and hands, and holding it fast by the head, feet, and wings. On seeing the men the monkeys made off, and the eagle fell to the ground and hobbled away. Several days after, some other men passing the same place saw the poor bird still wandering about, and nearly dead with hunger.

In our town of Blewfields, many years ago, a lot of Creole women were washing clothes at Gunboat Creek, a beautiful stream in the forest near the town. One of them had her baby lying asleep on the bank, when they suddenly heard a rush of wings, a loud scream, and an eagle was seen flying through the trees with the baby in its claws.

The yacal sirpey, or little eagle, known as the white snake-hawk, is very similarly coloured to the harpy eagle, but is much smaller. It is frequently seen flying through the forest, or perched on trees overlooking the river, on the watch for iguanas, snakes, lizards, and small animals. At our mahogany works, on a branch of the Wawa River, an Indian pointed out to me a very high tree, with a nest of these birds in a fork of it. I had the tree felled, and found that the nest, which was a platform of sticks covered with a bed of leaves 2 inches thick, contained a young bird, which, though not fledged, was about the size of a duck. Beside it was the skeleton of an uncommonly large bull-frog and other bones. I took the young bird to the camp and tied it by the leg to a post.   It was ungovernably fierce, striking with its claws at anyone who came too near, and when more closely pressed throwing itself on its back with its talons in the air.   Whenever it saw food, it set up a shrill plaintive whistle, and if a bird or piece of flesh were thrown to it, glared fiercely, and, approaching to within 2 or 3 feet, sprang on it and buried its claws to the roots.   If a person gave it food with the hand, it looked suspiciously into his face, and suddenly struck the food out of his hand.   Once in doing so it tore a boy's hand severely, and he immediately cast a noose round it, and hung it up by the neck, but I discovered it in time to save its life. I let it loose now and then, when it repaired in the heat of the day to a distance of 20 yards from the hut to clean its feathers, and in the evening to the branches of a fallen tree to sleep.   Every evening when I returned from the works I brought it a pigeon or other small bird, and at more than 20 yards it would see at once if I had a bird in my hand, and would set up a shrill whistle and run towards me.   If it had left any of its supper, it returned at break of day to the same spot to look for it.   It was nearly able to fly when we left that camp, and it was left there to look out for itself.

The istapla, or large fowl-hawk, is a fierce and powerful bird, and I have often known it to fly off with a full-grown hen from the fowl-yard.   I have observed that the poultry know the character of the different species of hawk.   Thus, if the great wispilpil, or crab-hawk, or the white-headed fish-hawk fly past, they stand and look at it, uttering a precautionary cry, but if a fowl-hawk sail over the yard, the poultry fly shrieking and cackling to the nearest shelter.   Even the stately gravity of the old cock breaks down, and he partakes in the indecorous flight.

The great forest owl, called by the Indians wowya, often visited our camp by night.   They seemed to come along in pairs, and their ghastly hooting used to give me a cold shiver of undefined dread. Sometimes I had a touch of ague and lay awake at night with a bad headache, and at such times the owl was my pet aversion. I could stand its hooting, but I was always nervously anticipating the horrid shriek. One would begin with a hollow sepulchral ' wow,' and the other would answer, ' koo-koo-koo-wow,' and so on for a long time. Then one would fly over the camp with an awful yell like a man receiving his death-wound. Then it would perch on another tree and resume its hooting.

In paddling along the rivers on a still night, one passes numbers of them, each hid in a dark bushy tree and hooting to another on the opposite side. Every now and then one flies across with its terrible shriek, which makes the blood run cold down your back. It is only by a rare chance that it is ever seen, but one day an Indian and I were poling our pitpan up the creek, guiding it among the mahogany logs that had been rolled into the water, when, on approaching a bushy tree, the man stopped the canoe, and said, in a joking way, ' There are two spirits [*oolussa*] in that tree.' I looked up and saw two wowyas sitting on a branch, half blinded by the light, nodding and staring as if much amazed. I shot one, and the man cut the claws off it to be hung round his child's neck as a charm. This bird is 20 inches long, and 48 inches across the wings.

Another visitor we had which disturbed the superstitious Indians very much. This was a large goatsucker, which for many mornings just at daybreak came and perched on the stump of a tree close to the hut. The Indians did not like it at all, saying it was an *oolussa yoola*, or spirits' tame pet. *Yoola* means any animal kept as a companion or pet. They persistently flung stones and sticks at it, but with its soft, noiseless flight it evaded them easily, and always returned to the same perch. When day brightened it flew away, but in the dusk of the evening it was back again to its stump. Both negroes and Indians fear this bird. Indeed, its actions are rather ghostlike. It sees badly by day, and relying for protection on the marvellous likeness of its plumage to the dead leaves, it lies flat on the ground until nearly trodden upon, when it flits away without any noise and squats again, so that it is impossible to see it.

On one occasion I started the mother from beside a young one, and found near the latter a mouse nearly dead, yet having no wound. I was at a loss to think how the mother could have caught it, or how the young one was to eat it, unless by swallowing it whole, for the beak and claws are small and feeble.

One day at Blewfields I was out shooting with a negro boy, when I shot a who-you, or goatsucker, and, picking it up, placed it in the crutch of a tree. On returning that way next day, the bird flew lamely away from near the same place. The boy on seeing it began to cry, declaring that one of us would be sure to die soon. It makes its nest on the ground, merely scratching the earth a little, and lays two white eggs. If the nest is disturbed, it carries off the eggs in its mouth.

The call of this goatsucker on a still moonlight night is pleasing and soothing. It helps to relieve the gloomy silence, or contrasts pleasantly with the disagreeable or strange sounds and cries which reach the ear out of the forest depths. A pair generally cry together, answering each other with great regularity for hours at a time. One cries in a shrill voice, 'koo-wee-yoo,' and presently the other answers from a distance in exactly the same note. From this note the bird is called 'koo-yoo' by the Indians, and 'who-you' by the Creoles. In different parts of America the note of this bird varies greatly. In Brazil its cry is hoarse and hollow, and resembles the word 'bakoorāo, bakoorāo'; consequently that is the name it is there known by. I have never heard any variation of its cry which could be called musical; nevertheless, the Yankees find it to be so, and have made a pretty song to the ladies out of it called the 'Whip-poor-Will Song.'

There is another bird about which my Indians are sometimes very much exercised in their minds. This is called the pickwa. Its length is 18 inches, of which the tail alone is 10 inches, and the expanse of the wings is 12 inches. The upper parts are of a beautiful chocolate brown, the under parts slate colour, delicately shaded off with brown ; the tail feathers are shaded off into deep black, but terminating in white, the bill and feet bluish, the iris madeira colour. It is light and graceful, and leaps from branch to branch more like a squirrel than a bird. It searches all through the tree for its insect food, with an intentness and set purpose quite different from the thoughtless frivolity of the other birds ; then sails away on its short, soft wings to another tree, and occasionally in a quite unexpected manner utters its loud triumphant cry of ' peekwaa.' It delights in the noonday glare, and bounds and leaps about regardless of the overpowering heat ; but on a cold dewy morning, when all the other birds are about, and filling the air with glad music, it may be seen huddled up in its soft downy plumage. It does not love the shady forest, but seeks the grassy banks of rivers and the open glades, where dense patches of reeds take the place of high trees.

The Indians are very superstitious about this bird, and are often much concerned about the interpretation to be put upon its loud crow ; but they generally conclude that the bird gives a flat denial to any assertion made at the instant of its crowing. For instance, if an Indian should chance to say or think, ' I wonder if my mother is well,' and just then the bird calls ' pickwa,' he gets alarmed and despondent. If they are discussing a hunting journey, the cry of the bird will cause them to put it off. They have only one remedy, which is considered at best of doubtful efficacy—that is, at once to call the bird a foul name, or jeer at it by imitating

14

it in a peculiar kind of whistle. The pickwa sometimes utters its cry at night, and this is a very ominous sign, foreboding death or some serious misfortune, especially if the cry follows discussion of some person or subject.

One beautiful moonlight night our gang of Smoo, Toongla, and Twaka Indians were amusing themselves after the hard day's work of rolling mahogany logs, some listening to the adventures of one of them who had made a voyage in a ship, and who was telling the river Indians how the ship sailed night and day, and was never hauled up on the beach at night ; how they never used paddles or poles, but the wind carried them wherever they wanted ; how the white man prayed to the sun every day to show them where the country was they wanted to go to. Suddenly a loud ' peekwaa ' was heard from a tree on the other side of the creek ; all were silent for a moment ; the young men giggled as if the traveller was telling lies ; but all concluded that there was something of more serious import in it, and an old man came to me and asked me to consult my books to know if anyone was to die. I replied that, according to what I inferred from the books, no one in camp was likely to die, but I could not tell what might take place far from here on the main river. This reassured them, and if I had not undertaken to interpret the bird in this way, I believe they would have left the camp. I have tried to make the Indians disbelieve in this bird by reminding them how often its warnings have been false, but their reply always was that some birds cry according to their nature, but that others are inspired by spirits.

CHAPTER XIV.

King vulture—Curassow—Quam—' Sun-down' partridge—Quail—Twee
—Woodpeckers—Red-rump blackbirds—Peetooyoola—Formicivora
—Wagtails—Warree-yoola legend—Alwaney, the thunder-god—
Pursued by a snake—A snake in the canoe—Boas—Quash.

ONE morning we were early at work. The sky, seen through
the trees, was beautifully blue; light wisps of clouds floated
at a great height, and a fresh land-wind was blowing, making
the morning cold and raw. I was with the men who were
cross-cutting a large log, $5\frac{1}{2}$ feet in diameter. They had
made a stage to raise themselves high enough to handle the
saw. Feeling cold, I joined in the work, and was dragging
the saw backwards and forwards, when suddenly I heard a
roar in the air like the passing gust of a hurricane. I gave
an inquiring look at the men, who said that an opum, king
vulture, had come down from the sky, and looking up they
said, 'Here comes another.' I saw a small object at an
immense height growing rapidly larger, and presently again
heard the roar of its wings through the air. The bird had
its head straight down; its wings were rigid, and it fell like
a thunderbolt until a short distance above the trees, when it
glanced away horizontally, and, giving several sweeps, alighted
in the bush. We all left the work and went in the direction
the vulture had taken, and presently heard the flapping of
wings. Getting close up, we saw several black Johnny crows
in the trees, and the two kings tearing at something on the

14—2

ground. We drove them off, and found the body of a fine deer which had just been killed by a jaguar. It was partly eaten, and much torn by the vultures, but the Indians carried off the remains joyfully.

The king vulture is a magnificent bird, about the size of a large turkey-cock. It measures between 8 and 9 feet across the wings, and next to the condor is the largest of the vultures. It is usually considered to be a distinct species, but I believe it to be the same bird as the common turkey buzzard, and that one out of several eggs laid by the black vulture turns out a king. The young kings are black, and exactly like the common bird.

Our hunters were in the bush every day, but the game became very scarce in our neighbourhood, and usually they got nothing but fish and birds. One day they brought in several curassows, and among them a lovely queen curassow.

It appears that one egg in every eight or ten of the ordinary curassow turns out 'a queen,' as it is called, which is always a female. Curassows go in flocks of six or eight or in pairs, and a queen is often seen among them. The curassow is fully as large as a turkey, but with a shorter and thicker figure. The chickens of both sexes resemble the hen bird, but the cocks assume their distinctive plumage as they grow older.

These birds are very plentiful all over the country, but keep to the forest. In the morning and evening they take to the ground in search of food. If surprised, they run very swiftly, and only fly up in the trees if hard pressed. They are therefore easily hunted with dogs. During the heat of the day they resort to the shadiest trees to repose. In the months of March and April the cock sounds his love-note, which, scarcely audible at first, rises to a low, tremulous moan, like the gentle lowing of a cow; but although the note can be heard a long way off, it takes a practised ear to distinguish it at all.

It is a curious fact that during the months from November to February the bones of the curassow are very poisonous to dogs. Five or six hours after the dog has eaten them it becomes melancholy and moping, howls and rolls on the ground, then rushes about in a delirious state exactly as if in hydrophobia, and finally falls down exhausted, and dies in about eighteen hours after eating the bones. I have seen all the dogs of a village poisoned at once by eating the bones. The Indians believe that the spirits of the birds enter into the dog and possess it. The Mosquito Indians call the bird coosoo, which, I believe, is a corruption of our word 'curassow,' as there are many English words in use by them.

Our hunters frequently brought in a bird called quam by the English, quamoo by the Mosquito Indians, and jacu by the Brazilians. This is one of the most graceful of the gallinaceous tribe. The body is considerably larger than a common fowl. Its colours are not brilliant, but rich of their kind, and harmonize with the delicate figure and elegant gait of the bird. The upper parts are a rich chocolate brown, shaded into very dark brown at the shoulders. Its step is graceful and elastic; it carries its beautiful neck and shapely head proudly raised, and picks its food with dainty elegance. This bird frequents the trees more than the ground, and loves the interior, where the forests are more open. They go in flocks of six to eight, or in pairs. It is more shy and more alert than the curassow. On being pursued it flies into the highest trees, and there remains beyond the reach of shot. They are very sympathetic and affectionate, and the Indians with diabolical treachery imitate the cry of the wounded quam, which attracts the whole flock, when they are picked off by the silent arrow.

At break of day the first sounds which are heard far over the forest, to waken the birds and beasts in the gloomy shades below, are the howling of the monkeys and the loud cry of the quam. He is no sluggard to court sleep. As soon as he inhales the life-giving air of morning, there is no more folding of wings to sleep, no more hiding his head under his soft armpit. He is wide awake at once; he sees the faint straw-coloured streak in the east; he flaps his wings with a loud noise, and flies with piercing shriek into the highest tree, there to bathe in the cool and scented land-wind. Sleep has renewed his life; he feels pleasure in every nerve; the vast forest at his feet is his to enjoy. Eager to taste the new day, he flies from branch to branch loudly calling his own name, 'quam, quam, quam,' interrupted by a low inquiring cry of 'quamoo, quamoo.' As the sun rises he settles down to business and is silent. In the heat of the day the quams sit close in a shady tree, lulling each other with soft endearing notes, resembling the sound 'wheeyou, wheeyou,' repeated till they fall asleep, and resumed from time to time as they wake.

The quam is frequently tamed by the Indian women, and becomes much more attached and more domesticated than ordinary poultry. I remember noticing the actions of a tame quam in a village at the Wawa River. It delighted to nestle close to anybody it knew, to hide its head in the folds of his clothes, or tug at buttons to attract attention, uttering continually a plaintive insinuating cry; but if any stranger approached, it raised its crest and shook its head from side to side with an odd jerk, as if preparing to fight. With the poultry it was good-natured and passive, allowing the pullets to chase and bully it; but if a strange fowl came near, the quam would chase and peck it, making a hideous noise, not unlike the braying of a donkey. So persistent was its attack that, if not rescued, the strange fowl would soon be killed. Even hens that had been absent for a while sitting were attacked, and had to be protected at once.

Seeing how easily domesticated are the curassow and the quam, it is a pity that the people who have the means and the time do not turn their attention to this subject, as these birds would be a most useful addition to the poultry-yard. I believe the curassow was not uncommon in the farm-yards of Holland previous to the irruption of the predatory legions of the French Republic.

Our vesper bell in these wilds was the singular cry of the bush partridge (tinamu). As soon as the sun had set and the shades of night were darkening the bush, all round and from great distances was heard the melancholy wail, resembling the words ' sun-down, sun-down, sun-down.' Every now and then all through the night this cry is heard, and no sound is heard in the bush, so sad, so forlorn, unless it be the cry of the smaller species of partridge. This bird is about the size of a common hen, but plumper in shape. It lives on the ground, and when surprised rises with a loud, whistling noise, and alights after a short flight. It lays on the ground, generally concealed behind the spur of a tree, from ten to eighteen sky-blue eggs. When wounded the meek, gentle submission of this bird would touch the heart of anyone not a sportsman. Without a cry or a struggle it patiently awaits the termination of its sufferings, and when its head falls on the hand in death it seems to have died with forgiveness in its heart.

This partridge is called sooar by the Indians. There is a smaller species very like it, but very rare, called oonkoore. This bird has a most distracting, sad, and melancholy cry, enough to make one commit suicide if in a despondent mood. The Indians imitate it in a peculiar whistle, as a signal to each other in the forest. They refuse to eat the bird or its eggs, believing that he who does will go wailing and lost in the bush, like the desolate and lonely bird.

We have plenty of quails in the bush. One species called cookrung goes in flocks of eight to twenty, and is very common in the bush. In the evening they roost in low trees, and the cocks of all the flocks set up a loud, extraordinary sort of gabble, resembling the words 'cook rung' rapidly repeated. When the Indians fall in with a flock, one of them whistles in a peculiar manner through a little cylinder of bone which they carry about, and with which they can imitate various animals and birds. This whistle greatly distresses the quails, so that they rush among the men with raised feathers and drooping wings, uttering cries like that of a turkey-hen when frightened. While one man whistles to keep up the distress of the birds, the others stand round and shoot them with their arrows. Usually, however, when the quails are disturbed the flock instantly disperses, and while some escape by running, others hide behind bushes and roots.

Another species is called waang. It is only 4 inches long, and 7 inches across the wings. The habits of this bird are very similar to those of the larger species. In the evening, just at sunset, they seek the low trees to roost, and give out a mournful and pleasing cry, which is also heard through the night. The Indians are proud of telling of the good old days when there used to be deadly wars among the tribes ; how, when their forefathers used to conceal themselves round the villages of the enemy for a surprise, the password or signal by which they used to ascertain if their party were ready and in their places was the weird night-cry of this bird.

'Whene'er I take my walks abroad' in the bush to look at such beasts and birds as will trust me with their presence, I generally have a quiet interview with a dear little bird called by the Indians twee. I summon him by whistling his cry; he seldom fails to attend, and we mutually inspect each other. It comes singly or in pairs, and must be fond of company, as it comes quite up to my feet, looking around for the one it supposes to be replying to its call. It is a consequential little bird, and evidently studies deportment in all its actions. In walking it raises its foot quite up to its body with its toes shut up, then makes a long stride, reminding one of little boys playing at marching. It is heard a long way off replying to my call, and presently appears striding along in its methodical way, now and then making a little hop, and stopping occasionally to stand upright, cry and listen. If I am dressed in white or make a movement it keeps at a safe distance, parading round and looking up in an inquiring manner ; but if I close the interview by rushing forward, it flies off with a ' cleek, cleek, cleek,' and no whistling will bring it back.

The drudge and servant of all work in the bush is the woodpecker. His lot seems a hard one, but his conduct is most exemplary. Whenever seen he is busy, plodding and earnest, and he seems to waste no time in singing or amusement. The great redhead woodpecker is the king of this tribe. It is 14 inches long, and 20 inches across the wings. The bill is 2 inches long, wedge-shaped, very hard, and ivory-coloured. The feathers of the head form a peaked crest of a deep crimson.

When the tops of the highest trees are tinged with the golden light of morning, while in the forest below all is still dark, this spirited bird spends a few of his precious moments in letting the forest know that he is about to commence his labours. He selects a high dead tree, and, clinging to the trunk, gives out his loud, cheerful, trumpet-like cry, alternating with a long rolling r-r-r-rap, which can be heard a great distance, and is answered by all the others within hearing, who then fly to meet each other. This signal rap is quite different from the tapping for food, and is a means of communication, like the beating of a drum to a soldier. When the bird is thus rapping, his head strikes so fast as to be invisible. On skinning the head of this bird, there is seen on each jaw a large white gland, which supplies to the tongue the glutinous saliva by which it secures its prey. Two remarkably strong sinews pass from the upper jaw over the head, and end in a large muscle at the nape of the neck.

The brain is enclosed in a very tough membrane, sufficient to prevent the bird suffering from concussion of the brain while striking with its bill.

The woodpecker only remits his labours when the powerful noonday heat demands from all animals a short period of rest; but scarcely has the sun declined to the west than our busy bird must be at his labours again, nor does he cease until dark compels him to take his needful rest.

The Indian when hunting delights to hear the woodpecker tapping ahead of him. The bird is letting him know that he will have to cut firewood to cook his game; but if it purposely deceive him, a hawk will tear its head off before evening. If the tapping is heard behind, he is discouraged, and it is doubtful whether game will be killed.

At pairing time, in the month of March, the woodpeckers excavate a deep hole in a soft dead tree. The hole is chiselled and smoothed off with great skill, and lined with feathers and fibres.

The brown woodpecker, sometimes called the mangrove woodpecker, from its frequenting the swampy land at the mouths of rivers, is occasionally seen in the forests of the interior. This is the same bird which in South America frequents the ground, to the astonishment of Darwin; but in this country the abundance of trees gives no occasion for it to practise the unnatural habit of living on the ground.

Most of our small birds object to the gloom of the forest, and prefer the sunny river banks or the open savannas. Those which abide in the forest are seldom vociferous or noisy. They take their pleasures sedately, as more suitable to the solemnity of their abode. There are some, however, which have lovely notes, clear, resonant, and musical. Thus, in strolling through the bush one is often attracted from a distance by a number of clear tinkling cries, interrupted now and then by a very extraordinary yet pleasant rolling whistle, like a person running quickly over from the lower to the higher notes on some shrill tinkling instrument. On approaching, he finds these to be the notes of a flock of ten or twelve red-rump blackbirds, busily feeding on berries or insects. They disperse, but are soon heard in another direction, giving out their sweet shrill notes. They are exceedingly elegant and active, darting from tree to tree, pursuing each other through the branches, or descending on the wing in beautiful spiral curves after some falling insect. In the heat of the day they desist from feeding, but amuse themselves and keep awake by unremitting chirping and whistling.

In the height of the dry season the sociable little flocks separate in pairs, each seeking some dark and lonely part of the forest, where they take great pains in selecting a suitable place to build their nests, often up an obscure and shady brook, sometimes over the main river or a mahogany truck-pass. They choose the end of the hanging leaf of a slender palm, the end of a withe dangling from the gnarled branches of a silk-cotton-tree, or the drooping tip of the graceful bamboo. They take particular care that no branch is near, nor any access to the nest available to mischievous monkeys, gliding snakes, or the stealthy night-prowling opossum. With untiring activity they scour the bush for suitable building material, and weave out of thin roots and fibre a bulbous pouch-shaped nest 18 inches long and 6 inches in diameter at the bottom, decreasing upwards till it terminates in the fibres by which it is suspended. It is closely and strongly woven, and the entrance hole is halfway up the side, but after all the labour of making it the birds never use it a second time, and it swings in the wind till it rots. The Indian young men often warned me not to molest the nests, as whoever does so will never be fancied by any girl. The whole plumage is jet black, with yellowish-white bill, but the cocks have a patch of glossy orange-red on the lower part of the back.

The peetooyoola (pineapple bird) is shy and seldom seen,

but during the rainy season of June and July, and occasionally at other times in the still evening, after a day of tropical rain, one may hear, apparently at a great distance, a chime of sweet silver bells, just as if Bow Bells of London were softened by a few miles, so that all the loudness and deep tones were taken away, and the same note reached the ear in a sweet silvery key. The notes begin low, rise and fall again just like the church bells, and perfectly correct to the musical note. So sweet and solemn is the little chime in the quiet bush, still softly dripping as if the evening were weeping now after the stormy passion of the boisterous day, and calling on the little bird to sing a sweet Angelus to the setting sun. The Indian name of peetooyoola may be extended to give an idea of the note, thus—pee-too-kee-yoo-la.

Like several species of small forest birds scientifically classed as Formicivora, this bird follows up the armies of foraging ants which invade the forests just before heavy rain and devour every living thing they can secure. But I am convinced that the birds do not eat the ants, but rather, like camp-followers, share the plunder and pick up the unfortunate insects that are flying for their lives. In fact, I have seen the bird seize a caterpillar which the ants had covered, and, flying to a tree, knock it from side to side to shake the ants off.

The peetooyoola is 7 inches long, with an $11\frac{1}{2}$-inch expanse of wings. The upper parts are reddish-brown; the crown of the head, breast, and throat a beautiful rosy red, the tips of the wings and thighs light gray, the belly light brown. The hen is smaller than the cock, reddish-brown above and light brown below. The nest, built in the fork of a tree, is like an armful of rubbish, but the entrance at the side leads to a smooth soft chamber. No precaution is taken against snakes, which I have found comfortably lodged in the deserted nests. The peetooyoola associates in little flocks of eight or ten, of which one or two only are cocks.

There are three other species of Formicivora, which are called by the Indians tarring yoola, pets of the 'marching army' ants. They are all polygamous, and have strange and pleasing notes.

When it is just beginning to be daylight, I always meet my friends the little wagtails. They are already up, and bounding from rock to rock in the twilight. Their yellow backs only are seen, as they inspect the mossy stones and pick up water-beetles. They associate in little parties, and are always busy and active on the rocks and tree-roots in shady creeks. Higher up this creek are places overhung by craggy rocks capped with a deep bed of red earth, and crowned with gnarled bushy 'flood bush-trees,' called sung-sung by the Indians. The face of the rock is clothed in beautiful mosses and small ferns, and below the stream ripples over beds of pebbles. Through the dense bush over-head the sunlight finds its way, and illuminates the water in trembling patches of light.

This is a favourite home of the wagtail, which may be seen in dozens flitting about the face of the cliff, clinging to the edges of the rock, probing everywhere for insects in the dripping moss. Their green bodies are scarcely distin-guishable, and the yellow of their backs makes them look like butterflies flitting about among the moss. At night they roost in pairs in the niches of the rock, or on bare stumps in the middle of the creek. This species is called tilba yoola, or pet of the tapir.

Many of the forest birds are kept as poultry by the spirits, and if molested something awful will happen. Thus, the warree, or peccary, are herded by a fierce little dwarf man called Warree Dawan (owner), who lives in the rocks of the interior, and at night walks through the bush to superintend the various droves of warree, to direct them to their feeding-grounds, and, if they are disturbed, to drive them to remote parts of the bush. He is attended by a drove of white warree, which are so fierce that they must not be approached.

No one living has ever seen him, but in the old times he has been seen, and those who saw him were always torn to pieces by the peccary. This little man keeps a pet bird called warree yoola, partly for his own amusement, and partly to bring him news as to the ripening of fruits which the warree feed on, so that he may drive the herds during the night to feed where the bird has reported. The Indians will not kill this bird, as the old man would be angry. It is a solitary bird, 10 inches long, with 17 inches expanse of wing. The upper parts are light brown, the under parts brownish fawn colour; under the wings is a beautiful straw colour. Its notes are a variety of shrill, piercing whistles, which you must on no account take notice of, or attempt to imitate, as the old man is listening to what the bird says, and it is none of your business. It is better to keep on good terms with the bird, which sometimes causes mischief.

Thus, in the old days a party of men, women, and children were camped up a forest creek while the men were hewing a large cedar-tree into a canoe. In this creek there was abundance of game, and fat warree were numerous. One day the men went hunting and killed a large number, besides bringing out of the bush two warree pigs alive, which they tied to the posts of the hut for the children to play with. The pigs cried piteously while the children teased them, and at night when all went to sleep they still kept constantly crying; but before dark a warree yoola sat on a tree over the camp, and looked at the women singeing and cutting up the warree, and heard the constant crying of the pigs. It flew away far into the interior, where are the great rocks with caverns in them, and told the Warree Dawan what it had seen.

In the night it came on to thunder and lighten, rain fell in torrents, and terrible squalls blew, breaking down great trees all round in the bush. The women lay close up to their husbands with their children clasped in their arms, for all knew that the spirits were angry that night. In the middle of the night a man woke and rose to stir the fire, when he heard the angry singing of the warree like distant thunder all round the bush. He called the people to wake up and save themselves, and, seizing their children, they killed the pigs and rushed headlong into the creek, where they huddled together in the deepest parts. Scarcely had they done so than the warree burst out of the bush, tore everything to pieces in the huts, and charged down to the waterside, while a portion of the drove crossed a shallow ford and appeared on the other bank, so that the people were hemmed in and surrounded. There was no means of escape, as the night was quite dark, and their canoes had been left a long way down the creek. A fierce little old man, illuminated with a faint blue light, was seen running about among the infuriated drove, urging them to charge into the water and tear the people to pieces. Some did swim out, but the men heard their splashing and killed them with machetes. For hours the people were kept in the water shivering with cold, while the mothers tried in vain to quiet the children, whose cries of fear and cold almost unnerved the men in their terrible position. The pitiful cries of the little warree pigs were now answered, and soon the people would be torn to pieces to avenge the slaughtered game.

But Blowfly was a great friend of the people. Many a time he had fed plentifully on the offal thrown out of the camp. So he flew up to the tops of the trees and away out to the main river. He found Alwaney (the thunder-god) paddling in his canoe of stone, ordering the thunder and the rain.

Then Blowfly said: 'Oh, Thunder, help! for they are killing the people up in the creek.'

But Thunder said : ' Let me alone ; I have work to-night.'

Then he met Leewa [the Water-spirit] riding on a water-spout, and Blowfly said : ' Oh, Leewa, help ! for they are killing the people up in the creek.'

But Leewa said : ' Cabo Oolusska [the Sea-spirit] has sent me to drive his waterspouts over the land ; I have no time to spare.'

So Blowfly was very sad as he flew up the river seeking for help. At last he saw Deewass (the land-wind) sleeping on a rock under a sung-sung tree.

He awoke him and said : ' Oh, Deewass, help ! for they are killing the people up in the creek.'

And Deewass said : ' Go ; I will come.'

Then a cold white mist came down the river filled with the smell of flowers, and the morning star glimmered through it. When Leewa felt the cold mist and smelt the flowers, he felt very sick, and he dived down to the bottom of the river, where he lives in the still deep pool. Alwaney, too, did not like the cold mist, so he mounted up to the clouds where he lives ; and the little old man felt very ill when the mist came over him, so he drove away his warree, and went to his home in the caverns of the rocks, and the people came out of the water and were saved.

This was the story told me by an old man one day when I shot one of these birds, and he added : ' The white man may shoot the bird, but we must not do so, because it is very patient, and allows us to kill a few of the old man's warree ; for it knows that our women and children are hungry.'

One day I had an alarming adventure, which I shall never forget. The men were felling and cutting up some trees about a mile from our camp. Not feeling very well, I left them at mid-day, and strolled home through the bush without any weapon in my hand, and as usual barefooted. The track crossed a small creek, with a very little water on a gravel bed, and with vertical cliffs of earth 5 feet high on

each side. As soon as I had scrambled down into the creek
I heard something drop on the gravel, and saw a large
poisonous snake instantly coiling itself to spring. I jumped
away, and it fell at the place where I had stood, and started
after me. I had no time to climb the banks, so I took to
my heels down the creek bed, hotly pursued by the enraged
snake, which I am sure I heard snapping its jaws behind me.
After running some distance the creek formed a deep pool,
into which I jumped, and dived to the bottom, where,
clinging to the stones, I kept under water as long as I could.
I then came to the surface very softly, and, putting my eyes
and nose above water, saw the snake at the far end of the
pool swimming backwards and forwards with frightful swiftness. After a while it went ashore, and slowly took its way
over the gravel back the way it had come.

I then swam back to the end of the pool, and arming
myself with a stone in each hand, I went after the snake. It
heard me coming, stopped, and turned round, when, by great
good luck, the first stone I threw crushed it. I then sat
down and had a bad turn. I felt frightened and depressed,
and feared to tread the bush again. I hallooed to the men,
but they were too far off. Nature, however, came to my
aid, and after sitting for a long time I recovered my nerve,
and went home.

Some time after this I had an amusing adventure, which I
can no more forget than the alarming one. There is a very
large snake, common in the bush, called pluppantaya, which,
I think, is the rock-snake of the West Indies. It is black,
with yellow spots on the belly, and grows from 10 to 11 feet
long, and as thick as a man's arm. Though not poisonous,
it kills and swallows some of the poison snakes. At some
seasons of the year it is very savage, and, if molested, will
pursue a person, twist round his body, and lash him with its
tail; at least, so the Indians say. I never saw it do so, and
as they mix so many myths with their accounts of the habits

15

of beasts, one is never sure where the truth lies. For instance, they say that this snake cannot abide a woman in the family way, but attacks her at once. Now, as we know that the spirits have a like repugnance, so that a *sookia*, or medicine-man, while communicating with spirits or preparing incantations, must on no account see a woman in such a condition, the inference is that this snake is connected with spirits.

As I was returning one evening from our work in a pitpan with some of our men, we saw a large snake of this species coiled on a branch of a tree about 10 feet above the water. I told the Indians to paddle under it so that I might kill it with a pole. They said I had better leave it alone, as it might attack us; but I persisted, and they let me have my own way. I passed forward to the bow, and with my pole made a blow at the snake, which uncoiled itself, raised its head, and waved it from side to side, darting out its tongue. The canoe had drifted directly underneath when I made the next blow, and the snake instantly slipped down into the bow of the boat. I threw away my pole, and, dodging past the men, got to the stern. The man in the bow struck at it with his paddle, but missed it and fell overboard. The snake raised its head and came furiously at the next man, who without further ado jumped overboard too. So did all the rest, and as I saw the snake meant business, I did the same. When I came to the surface I heard roars of laughter from the men swimming about. Though the snake had now possession of the canoe, that was evidently not what it wanted, and it slipped into the water, upon which we all dived, and on coming again to the surface I heard a yell from one of the men, who on coming up had lifted the snake on his shoulder; but it swam to the shore and we got into our canoe again.

On another occasion the men were rolling logs at the upper camp, which was a day's journey further up the creek, and at mid-day they sat by the side of the pass, having a pipe after finishing their business. I was also sitting some distance from them, smoking my pipe, with my back against a tree. Suddenly I heard a rustling on the ground, and, turning, saw a boa-constrictor, or rock-boa, about 10 feet long, close to my side. It lifted its head to the height of my face, and moved it slowly from side to side, slipping its forked tongue out and in from its closed mouth. While I was thinking what to do, it suddenly lowered its head and made off across the pass. I got up and pursued it, calling to the men to come and kill the wowla, but it escaped into the bush.

This rock-boa grows to about 15 feet, but the Indians say that, after getting big and old, it takes to the river and swamps, and there attains a great size. I believe, however, that the rock-boa is a species distinct from the great boas which are found in the swamps of South America, and are said to attain a length of 30 feet.

One Sunday some of the young men went up the creek fishing, but soon returned to ask for the loan of my gun, as they said there were some fearless quashes (coati) walking about in the bush. I went with them, and after poling up some distance we pushed the pitpan into a little creek where the beasts were said to be. On the bank close by was a large silk-cotton tree, covered with parasites, and vines hanging round the trunk and from the branches to the ground. The boys went ashore into the bush to look for the beasts, and I lay on my back in the canoe smoking. They had not been gone long, when I heard a cackling noise, and, looking up, saw the thick branches of the silk-cotton tree swarming with quashes. They were evidently searching for insects, lizards, and nests, and seeing me were afraid to come down. They were running about, apparently trying to hide, for every now and then they would raise themselves and gaze over the branches at me, and keep up a little barking or wheezy sort of cackle. At last they seemed to have made up their minds, for a very large one came on to the thickest vine and walked down it from a height of 60 or 80 feet as easily as if it were level ground, to be followed by all the rest in what appeared to be an endless train. I cannot tell how many there were, but I think they took ten minutes before the last had walked down.

This beast belongs to the raccoon species; it is about twice as big as a cat, is covered with a thick brown fur, and has a long bushy tail. It has a long, pointed, flexible nose, with the mouth far back underneath, stiff whiskers, and small piercing black eyes, hind-feet plantigrade, and claws like a little bear's. It is a very restless and destructive animal, which ravages nests both in trees and on the ground, and digs up the nests of alligators, tortoises, and iguanas buried in the sand. How with such a keen, active enemy the ground-birds ever rear their young is a mystery. The quash eats everything it can get—birds, lizards, grubs, fruit, berries, plantains, sugar-cane, and maize.

Not long after this the hunters brought me a young one they had caught, and as there were always men in the camp on sick leave, they petted and reared the little creature. I never in my life saw such an inquisitive, active, pertinacious, fearless, impudent, amiable, and quarrelsome little beast as this was. It trotted about the huts as if it had never been accustomed to anywhere else; jumped into your lap and curled up to sleep without the slightest hesitation. If you treated it well, it would be most loving, playing with your hand, poking its long nose up your sleeve or into your pockets, and running all over you as if you belonged to it; but if you attempted to put it away before it chose to go, it would quarrel at once, snarl and bite, and twist its nose from side to side with the most impudent defiance. It followed us like a puppy, but not for the same reason as a puppy, which loves and depends on its owner: not a bit of it—the little quash followed us to see what was doing and what was to be got. If the men set their food down it would take possession at once, and a fearful row would take place before it could be dispossessed. It was everywhere and into everything; singed its little toes by walking through the wood ashes, when, instead of running away, it shrieked with rage, and began to dig and scatter the ashes in its ungovernable anger; then it rushed up a man's back to sit on his shoulder and lick its sore toes. It would get into the barrel of salt pork and smear its paws and nose with grease, and in that condition jump on your face when you were sound asleep, and insist on lying down there. He would persist in coming at all hours of the night to have a nap, and nothing would satisfy him unless he crawled under the men's coverings and up against their naked skins, where he was by no means careful with his sharp little claws, but to get rid of him meant nothing less than a stand-up fight. Everyone was fond of him, and everyone voted him to be a most unmitigated nuisance.

We had a few dogs in the camp, which were taught not to molest the quash. He never made friends, but always kept away from them, running in among the legs of the men if they came near, twisting his nose with an upward curve, and moving it from side to side to show his excitement and fear He never thought of running away. One day I took him in my arms about half a mile into the bush, where, setting him down, I ran home as fast as I could get through the tangled thickets. When I arrived he was there already, busy upsetting pots and calabashes. He was taken out to the main river, and I gave him to an Indian girl, and when grown to his full size he was tamer than ever, and as great a pet.

The Indians call this beast wistitting, the Creoles bushdog. There are either two species of them, or else the older and larger ones separate from the rest. They are usually seen in small droves of ten or twenty, but solitary ones of twice the usual size are often met with in the bush.

CHAPTER XV.

Von Tempsky left alone—Up Wakna Creek—Bees—Hauling out logs—
Down creek—Left behind—Rescue and ' chaff'—*Sookia* doctor.

WHEN we had completed our work at the waterfall camp,
we shifted to another nearly a day's journey farther up the
creek, leaving our goods at the lower camp, and with them
Von Tempsky all alone. This was a dangerous thing to do,
but he could not be persuaded to keep a man with him.
Some men love danger and court its presence, and he was
such a man. He had a dog with him, but even thus accompanied I would not on any account sleep alone in this bush ;
for besides the danger from the stealthy attacks of jaguars
or pumas, or the remoter risk of being seized in your sleep
by a boa-constrictor, there is a weirdness about the forest at
night which reason fails to dispel. It is so exceedingly
dark, it is so impenetrable and unknown, there are so many
strange, unaccountable sounds heard which even the Indians
cannot explain, and it seems so vast in extent, although
really very restricted. If it were open country, one could
gallop from the sea-coast to the savannas of the Spanish
settlements in three days ; yet how great the distance seemed
to us in the bush ! It takes many days of laborious paddling
and poling up the larger rivers to reach the Spaniards, and
away from the rivers the forest is impenetrable, and no one
knows what is in it. There are reports of wild, untamable
tribes, who are never seen, but whose stealthy arrow is

certain death ; and there may be truth in these reports, for many years ago some Creoles of Pearl Key Lagoon were hunting up the Wawashan River, when they came suddenly upon seven little children wandering about gathering eboe-nuts, whom they caught and brought to the settlement as slaves. They belonged to the Cookra tribe, supposed to be now extinct, but it is said that the Prinzoo tribe still lives in the bush.

We poled up the beautiful creek, which is entirely arched over by the forest. At many places I had to get out over the gravel banks, while the Indians dragged the pitpan over the shallow rapids. In other places the creek was blocked with masses of drift logs and bamboos, which were impassable until a lane was cut through them with an axe. At one place there lay an enormous tree, about 6 feet in diameter, right across the creek, on to which we had to climb and pile the luggage, while the pitpans were sunk under water and passed through below. While cutting through the raft of drift logs and bamboos, we perceived a bad smell, and found hidden among the drift, and floating belly upwards, the body of a tapir. On turning it over we saw that its back and neck were fearfully torn by a jaguar. When a puma or jaguar leaps on the back of a tapir, it always rushes for the water, the only chance it has to get rid of its enemy. This poor beast had got rid of it, but at the cost of its life. This day I shot a number of curassows and two fat monkeys, and the men, perceiving the faintest whiff of the scent of warree, landed, armed with their bows and arrows, and taking my gun with them, while two or three stayed with me in the canoes. They were gone a long time, and we were getting very impatient, when they appeared, tired and covered with mud. They brought six warree, having chased the drove so far that we never heard the gun, which was fired several times.

About three o'clock we arrived at the foot of a long rapid,

where the banks are narrow and rocky, and the water rushes over boulders and sunken logs at a fearful speed. All our things were unloaded, and carried by a track in the bush to the head of the rapid, while the men hauled the boats up by withes made fast to them, a most laborious job. By sunset we arrived at the old camp, and having had a plentiful repast of monkeys, curassow, and plantains, some of the men cleared out the huts, and some cut up and barbecued the warree.

In this part of the creek the bush is thin; that is to say, large trees were scarce, and the country was covered with very tall reeds like small bamboos. The bra sirpey, or small reed, is about the size of a pencil, and covers the ground densely. The bra tara, or large reed, is $1\frac{3}{4}$ inch in diameter, and grows in clumps; the joints are $1\frac{1}{2}$ foot long in the small, and 3 feet long in the large species. The joints of the small reed are used by the Indian children as blow-pipes, through which they blow little balls of black wax, and kill wasps, butterflies, and small house lizards. The large reed is used to make flutes, which they play at their festivals and *mishla* drinks.

Our men found here great quantities of wild honey, which we ate until we made ourselves ill. I kept a large quantity sealed up in reed joints to drink with our coffee and chocolate, which, however, had been left at the lower camp. In this, as in many other parts of the bush, these bees are very troublesome. They swarm over everything, and their favourite resort is the bare perspiring skin of the Indians, where they alight in great numbers to suck the sweat, causing much irritation, although they do no other harm than to crawl over one's bare skin. They are very fond of coffee, and it is very difficult to drink a calabash of it without swallowing them by dozens. Although we call them bees, they belong to a species of fly called mellipona, and have no sting. They build invariably in hollow trees, the size of the nest generally depending on the size of the hollow they occupy. Having found a rotten hole, the bees first clean it of all loose rubbish, and remove all the rotten wood that they can; then they fill it with their cells. The cells containing grubs are placed at one end of the hole, the honey cells at the other, and the centre is filled with cells full of pollen. The cells for grubs are six-sided, built on circular plates of wax, placed one above the other, with columns of wax to keep them apart. The honey and pollen cells are round, and stuck together in heaps with very short stalks of wax to keep the spheres together. The knot-hole in the tree which forms the entrance is filled with solid wax, leaving a passage large enough for the bees to pass, and terminating on the outside in a spout on which the bees rest before entering the nest.

There are many species, of which the following are the most common :

1. The nasma tara (great bee) is about the size of an English bee, brown with whitish wings. The honey cells are more than an inch in diameter. Each contains more than a tablespoonful, and a large nest may yield a gallon and a half of thick pale-yellow, very sweet honey, with a delicate flavour.

2. The wuckihra, about the size of a bluebottle fly, of a yellow colour; the honey cells as large as a good-sized pistol-shot; the honey clear and very sweet.

3. The nasma siksa (black bee), same size as above, black with whitish wings; honey clear, thin, as sour as lime-juice, and very scanty.

4. The patera, somewhat smaller than the last two; honey very sweet, thick, and yellow. This bee defends its nest stoutly, pursues the aggressor, alights on the skin, and deposits a minute drop of milky fluid which soon begins to smart, and after a while festers, and may turn into a trouble-some sore. The honey is obtained by smoking the nest with

a fire of dry leaves, and running away until the bees have died or departed.

5. The sitsit, about the size of a flea, brown with transparent wings; honey cells the size of a large pea; honey as clear as spring water, very thin, but exceedingly sweet; seldom yields more than a quart.

6. The toolung, about the size of a flesh-fly, brownish-black, white wings; honey cells half an inch in diameter; honey a yellowish-green, thin and watery. This bee when disturbed fastens on to one's hair and clothes, and bites sharply.

7. The poonkaya, a small yellow bee; honey cell as large as a buckshot; honey thick and greenish-yellow, and the flavour more like that of English honey than any of the others.

The wax of all the above species is brown and soft.

8. The mangrove bee lives near the sea, and builds in hollows of the mangrove-trees; its honey is a deep blackish-blue, very sweet with an acid taste, slightly irritating to the throat. It can only be eaten sparingly, as it is purgative. The wax is black and very hard.

9. The slaha, or wasp bee, stings painfully. It builds a large paper nest from 3 to 6 feet long and 2 feet wide, generally attached to a forked branch, one of the forks passing through the nest. All the cells in this nest are six-sided, 1 inch long and $\frac{1}{4}$ inch wide; honey clear like water, and very sweet. In September a large nest may yield from 5 to 10 quarts of delicious honey, but as the nests are built on very high trees, most of the honey is lost when the tree is felled.

The Indians in walking through the bush always keep a sharp eye on the knots and cracks in trees, and practice enables them to detect the smallest bee issuing from a hole at a great height. It is singular that, although the bamboos offer such convenient accommodation when there is a hole through the exterior wood, the bees never build in them.

As our European bee is not domesticated in any sense of the word, and takes to the woods as naturally as any of those here described, I think it would be as easy to keep any of these stingless bees as it is to keep our European species, and it would be well worth trying the experiment in tropical countries. The advantages of having stingless bees, the honey cells of which hold more than a tablespoonful, are evident enough.

The mahogany-trees which we cut in this neighbourhood were not large, so in place of rolling them with handspikes we were able to haul them endways to the water. The pass required for this purpose may be very narrow, instead of being as wide as the length of the log, as it must be if the logs are to be rolled. The Indians are not good at, and do not like, the rolling process. The lifting with stout poles placed under the log and raised by the shoulders is very severe, and if long continued causes a permanent callosity on the shoulder, which, as they are almost always naked, except for the waistcloth, is ugly and disagreeable. Hauling the logs endways is much preferred, as the exertion is of that intermittent character which they like in all their work. The pass, having been cleared of all trees and stumps, is laid throughout its length with peeled poles placed across ; the mahogany log is then slewed into the proper direction, its bark is stripped off, the smaller end is rounded off, and a deep notch cut in it, to which six or eight stout withes are fastened ; two axes are driven into the butt of the log, and all is ready.

Eighteen or twenty men take hold of the withes, and two men keep a tight hold on the axes at the butt. The signal is given, and with the most appalling yells and shouts the men start off at a run, dragging the log over the peeled skids, while the two men at the axes guide the hind end. After running a short distance they stop and have a good rest, then start again. The shouting and yelling must add considerably to their exertion, yet they never cease it while thus working in parties. It is a peculiarity which I have not noticed among any other people.

In this place we cut a number of fine cedar-trees and hauled the logs out with the mahogany, but our men did not like working with the cedar, as the strong smell of onions which the inner bark has soon makes one sick at the stomach and produces headache. The cedar of Central America is a tree allied to the mahogany, and not a coniferous tree. It is, I believe, the same wood that cigar-boxes and pencils are made of, and has a delicious smell.

We got on finely with our work, which was satisfactory, as the rainy season was coming on. We had already frequent rains, and many of us got an occasional touch of fever.

At last we were ready, and started to go down the creek one afternoon, but were delayed by the mass of logs we had thrown into the creek having drifted down and obstructed it, so it was nearly sunset when we got to the head of the great rapid, and I was rather apprehensive of shooting it in our pitpans. In the still water at the top the Indians stopped to adjust their waistcloths, secure the luggage, and make room for their movements. Then, having talked over the probabilities of getting down safely, two good men with their long poles stood in the bow and two in the stern, while the rest of us sat in the middle. We waited until the other canoe had gone out of sight; then our polemen carefully brought the pitpan to the proper channel and let her go. The speed at which we rushed down the rapid must have been more than 15 miles an hour. The creek was slightly flooded, and the yellow water boiled and roared among the boulders, in some places leaping over rocks and making formidable waves. Rocks projecting above water made the channel very crooked, and in this dangerous passage I could not but admire the Indians for their consummate skill and cool courage. All were silent and watchful; not an exclama-

tion was heard, only the short sharp words of direction from
the bowmen to those in the stern, which, amid the confusing
noise of the water, were instantly heard and obeyed. By
long practice, inherited from countless generations, the accu-
racy and swiftness with which they placed the poles on the
points of rock and turned the canoe at the right instant, and
the steadiness with which they kept their balance in the
narrow rocking boat, were marvellous, and considering that
if we had bumped on a rock and upset we should probably
all have been killed, their coolness and composure were
admirable.

After getting down some distance there were fewer rocks
and less danger, so I dismissed the strain of apprehension
which had braced my nerves as tight as fiddle-strings. But
accidents occur when least expected, and this is what happened to me:

A flock of curassows sprang up off the rocks with sounding
wings and flew into some low trees. The man at the bow
as we flew past shouted ' Coosoo-be !' (Look at the curassows !) At his voice and the sound of the wings I stood up
suddenly and looked back. The next instant I heard the
warning shout, ' Aman kihs !' (Take care !) I was struck in
the pit of the stomach, and instinctively clasped in my arms
the horizontal branch of a tree ; the canoe shot from under
me, and soon was out of sight. I swung my legs over the
branch, and, crawling to the bank, recognised the very unpleasant position in which I was. It was just falling dark,
the out-track was on the other side, and it was impossible to
cross the creek. The bush was dense and impassable in the
dark, the banks were obstructed by boulders and tree-roots,
and occasionally low cliffs of solid rock stood in the water,
which in places foamed and boiled hard up against the
bank. I did not know how far off the foot of the rapid
was, and did not think that the men could come to me
through the dense bush in the dark. Something must be

done, so I walked cautiously along the banks at the edge of the water, climbing over boulders and great roots, sometimes up to my shoulders in water, till, after going some distance, I slipped off a rock into the boiling current, but by lucky chance caught a tree-root, and saved myself from being swept into the current and drowned. This accident took away all my remaining courage, so, regardless of snakes and tigers, I crept into the dark bush. At first I tried to make my way down by keeping close to the banks, but the exertion of struggling through tangled thickets, the frequent falls, and the fright I got by stepping over the cliff and saving myself by the bushes, completely discouraged me. I sat down and shouted till I was hoarse. Nothing was to be heard but the roaring of the creek, so I tried to reconcile my mind to sitting where I was till morning, and taking my chance of not being discovered by a tiger.

After about an hour I heard a faint sound which I gladly answered. The shouts gradually approached, and soon I saw with the greatest relief the glimmer of a torch in the bush. Four men had provided themselves with torches made of split reeds, and cut their way with machetes to where I was. Soon I got to the camping-place, where the sight of an immense fire, the cosy little clearing they had made in the bush close to the creek, and the little thatched lean-to provided for me in case of rain, dispelled all my woes, with the exception of the pain in my ribs from the blow I had received from my tree. The Indians, finding I was all right, discussed the adventure at endless length, roaring with laughter at my plight, and at the way the girls would take it when related to them.

'A white boy perched on a branch like a white-faced monkey' (roars of laughter).

'Talk about monkeys jumping from branch to branch, that is nothing. Young nanny Ingliska [our Englishman] can leap out of a canoe going like an arrow, and sit on a

branch laughing, and waving good-bye with his arm ' (roars
of laughter).

' Our old men called this fall Walpa Tarra [the Great Rocks],
but when we are white-headed our children will say, " What
is the name of this fall?" and we will say, " It is called ' Ingliss
pluppan ' [Englishman fled]. An English boy lived with us
and we loved him, but his heart was hard towards the poor
Indians; he said they did not give him any ripe plantains or
fat fish out of the river, and that the girls refused to tie the
black thread round his knee, so when the pitpan was flying
down the fall he leaped into a tree and fled away from us
into the bush like a wild beast " ' (roars of laughter). And so
on until I fell asleep.

On returning to the lower camp, I found Von Tempsky all
right, except that he had had a touch of fever. He had,
however, had no adventures, and was rather disappointed in
consequence.

Several of our men had also had attacks of fever, and they
began to fear that there were some evil spirits about the
neighbourhood. They knew that I discouraged the practice
of their *sookias*, or medicine-men, who charge heavily for
imaginary remedies; but as nothing will shake their own faith
in them, they, without letting me know, sent to the main
river to ask a celebrated *sookia* to come to the camp, and he
came as if on a visit. He was accompanied by two wives of
his own and another man with his wife, and brought me a
present of a basket of chocolate beans and two bundles of
plantains. The first night he slept in a little hut erected
beside the men's, and next morning pretended to ' smell a
rat.' He whispered about that he did not like the place,
there was something wrong about it. His dreams last night
were not as they should be, and there were strange noises in
the direction of the big rocks. Mentioning the thing to me,
I said he had better see into it, and went with my men up
the creek to work. When I returned in the evening I found

he had erected a small hut of leaves on the edge of the bank overlooking our big rocks. He had cut a quantity of firewood and planted in the ground several thin sticks from which the bark was removed in rings, painted alternately red and black, and to them he hung little gourds containing alligator and tiger teeth, snake skulls, pretty pebbles, and seeds of some kind I had never seen. He had also painted his face in formidable patterns of red and black.

Next morning he came to me in a very excited state, saying this was not a fit place for the people to live in, and last night five ferocious spirits had come out from the rocks. He had had a terrible struggle with them, and had succeeded in driving them away, but he advised me to leave the place, as the waterfall was their dwelling, and they would certainly return.

Our new *sookia* was well treated, and stayed with us a few days to cure our sick. He was a pleasant man with plenty of talk and fun, but had a way of putting on an abstracted air, and was fond of lecturing the young men. The women were friendly and chatty, and were quite an acquisition to our monotonous society. Our men sent them fish and game, and made them presents of beads and fishhooks.

I asked leave to attend while our *sookia* cured a man of rheumatism in the shoulder. The Indians call rheumatism keeaya, or prickles, believing it to be caused by thorns which evil spirits have stuck into the flesh. A little hut was made to windward of the camp, and in it a *creecree*, or raised bed of sticks covered with bark, was placed. He planted his painted sticks round this hut, and surrounded the bed with *toonoos*, or blankets made of the bark of the indiarubber. The patient having been placed on the bed, the *sookia* issued solemnly from his own hut, carrying in his hand a polished hardwood cane, from the top of which were hung the small gourds mentioned above. He got inside the curtains of the bed, and so did I. He then sat on the ground, covered himself with a native blanket, and, lighting his pipe, proceeded to blow the tobacco smoke through a small reed into a calabash of water, making a bubbling noise and muttering some unintelligible words, among which I detected the names of evil spirits. He then covered the patient with the *toonoo*, and burned indiarubber and copal gum under the bed, filling the place with resinous smoke. Having asked where the pain was, he kneaded and pinched the place, and finally, holding the flesh between his finger and thumb, took out a thorn and showed it to me, but would not let me have it. I saw plainly, however, that it was a small fish-bone. He took out half a dozen such bones and dismissed the patient. Several others were treated, and then he departed, carrying away the payment he had received in cloth, beads, fish-hooks, and a little powder and shot given him as my contribution.

.

CHAPTER XVI.

THE rainy season was now coming on, and the people were impatient to get away. Our Smoos and Twakas left first. The former lived farther up the Toongla River, and the latter up the Twaka River, and they were very anxious to get home before heavy floods should make the ascent of the rivers laborious, if not impracticable.

I had to go out to the main river to get more men and provisions. Our Smoos departed in their pitpans by way of the creek. I and two Toongla Indians were to take the track and walk to the main river, a distance of 15 miles. The day was dark and threatening when I rose in the morning, and heavy thunder was rumbling to the eastward. We embarked in a small cranky pitpan and poled up the creek, but had not gone far before a squall was heard coming. It passed over us with an appalling uproar in the tops of the trees, broken branches and leaves flying before it, and in all directions was heard the crash of falling trees. Then the rain came down in sheets of water, and at once all pretence of shelter or covering was given up, and we were drenched.

We soon reached the track, where we landed and hauled

up the canoe. For a mile or more we walked on dry ground, following the cut marks made by the Indians, who use this as a hunting pass. Then we descended to slightly lower ground, and found the whole forest under water. I was up to my knees, sometimes to my waist, in water all day on this dreadful journey. There was a dog with us, which we had to carry in our arms by turns, as it was impossible for it to swim in the dense bush. The rain fell in torrents and the thunder was awful. One peal was such an indescribably fearful crash that it seemed as if the world was torn open. Cowed and dumfounded I dropped my gun, and sank down on my hands and knees in the water until I was lifted up and encouraged by my Indians, who were not so much affected by the war of the elements. Many a time I had walked through this pass in fine weather, when the bush was relieved by shadows and bright patches of stray sunshine. Now it had the most dark and dismal aspect. The trees, bent with the pouring rain, presented a vista of dark mist without one cheerful ray. Occasionally the gloom was suffused with the blue unearthly glare of the lightning, followed by the crash of the thunder, which rolled and rumbled through the woods and came back and back again in explosions like signal-guns at sea. All the shady nooks overhung with palms and creeping plants, which I had looked at with delight in the sunny days, were now ponds of water full of croaking frogs. All the pleasant streams were roaring torrents. The songs of birds, the cheerful cries of animals, and the dreamy music of the insects were replaced by the roaring of the rain, the croaking and clamorous bleating of the frogs, and the occasional booming of the great bull-frog.

For hours I toiled on through the water, falling headlong into it many times, and occasionally swimming across depressions in the ground, where one's body was entangled among the trees and bushes, and one had to work oneself along by hauling at the branches. I was sorely tempted to

drop my faithful double-barrelled gun, which had fed me so
many times, but my Indians relieved me of it every now and
then.   I had had several attacks of ague, and was not too
strong for this work, so I consumed much time in rest, sitting
on roots up to my waist in water, while the Indians, shivering
and dripping, patiently waited for me.   In the afternoon the
rain descended more softly, but as night was closing we heard
the thunder again growling, and the rain and the wind came
on again as hard as ever.   Then we got on to rising ground
out of the water as it became dark.   We groped our way in
the dark, the Indians finding the track with wonderful skill.
At last there was an opening in front of us, and by the
lightning flashes I saw the river full to its brim, but flowing
with a silent current, carrying on its red water rafts of bamboo, trunks of trees, and islands of floating grass.

Shivering with cold, I threw myself down among the cutch
grass and rested my head on my knees, while one of the men
went down to the bank to look for the little canoe which was
usually kept tied to the bank.   It was not to be found.   The
men discussed what was to be done, and I heard them say,
'We could stay here all night, but the English boy will die
of cold.'

One of them said he would go to the village and bring a
canoe.   I was too cold and exhausted to think about what
they would do, but the one who was going borrowed the
waistcloth of the other, fastened it round his chest, and
saying, 'I am going,' walked down through the high grass
and plunged into the flooded river.   I jumped up to see what
would happen to him, and by the flashes of lightning I could
see his black head for some time in the river, and then he
was gone.   But for some time I could hear his cheering
shouts, which were at once answered by the man beside me.
He seemed stuck in one place at the other side of the river,
and I asked my man what he was doing.   By the constant
lightning he pointed out to me a thicket of bamboos on the

other side, submerged probably 12 feet in the water. He was among these, breaking down dry bamboos and tying them together into a little raft with the waistcloth he had borrowed. Stretched on this, he swam down the river four miles to the village in the darkness and the rain.

I have no idea how long I shivered and dozed, sitting among the high cutch grass. The rain and the lightning ceased, and a soft drizzle continued. Then the mosquitoes came, and there was no rest. I had eaten nothing but a morsel in the early morning, having expected to kill game and cook it on the way. We had flint and steel in a horn, but it was not possible to light a fire. My companion sat beside me and slapped his mosquitoes with sufficient composure, but I was so hungry, cold, and irritated by the mosquitoes as to be ready to jump out of my skin.

At last the man said, ' Listen ! I hear paddles,' and he gave a shout that started the echoes of the forest. Then we heard answering shouts, and soon a pitpan arrived with six men, and getting into it we paddled joyfully down the river.

When I got to the settlement, there was nothing to be had but plantains and chocolate without sugar, but I was happy to get even such meagre fare. I put a *toonoo* round me while the women dried my clothes; then, putting them on again, I slept soundly in a hammock of string covered by a *toonoo* of soft, warm indiarubber bark.

The flood rose during the night, and when I woke I hardly recognised the place. I had known the village as 60 feet above the river; now it was not more than 10 feet. On the opposite side the banks were low, and the river was now flowing through the tops of the trees. The water was the colour of clay, and was bearing along the most astonishing quantities of stuff. Among immense rafts of trees, grass, and bamboos we occasionally saw canoes, thatched roofs, and piles of banana-trees. Many snakes were seen swimming about the river, and dead deer and peccary floated past.

While the river kept up and the rain lasted, we were all
on short commons. The bush was too much flooded for
hunting, and the creeks for fishing. The Indians keep
fowls and a few muscovy ducks, but they seem never to eat
them, so that opossums, tiger-cats, and hawks have all the
profit. I could never imagine how the vegetarians of
England get on, because when we had a week of plantains
and maize and chili-pepper, often without salt, the craving
for fat or meat became unbearable ; and when to that was
added the taunts of the women and the pleading of the
children, no good man could stay at home, whatever might
be the discomfort of the hunting-path. I often pitied the
men who went out in the pouring rain and returned in the
evening wet, shivering and hungry, and bringing perhaps a
partridge, a tortoise or two the size of one's hand, and a
couple of agouti, from which it was impossible to distribute
a mouthful apiece among the villagers.

The rainy season here is like the winter in Europe. It
brings starvation to man and beast.

During the rainy season a small fish like a sardine, called
blim, comes up the river in great numbers, and, taking
advantage of every flood, pursues its way to the headwaters.
I have sat and watched them leaping up little waterfalls in
the creeks, and admired their perseverance and skill. They
approach a fall by the eddies, and, taking their stand some
distance from it, spring out of the water and strike the fall,
say, two-thirds up, and with amazing exertion swim up the
remaining height. They will also jump into a mere trickle
of water flowing over mossy rocks, and wriggle up the wet
moss to the top.

Tortoises also take advantage of the full creeks, to ascend
them for the purpose of exploring a new extent of feeding-
ground, and may be caught in numbers. During the hard
times of the rainy season the Indians patiently fish for the
little blim, scour the bush to capture the tortoises, and bring

home a frugal feast. Occasionally they surround the islands in the river while the flood is rising, and when the water has driven all the animals to the top they land and kill them, pursuing in canoes those that try to escape by swimming. This manœuvre produces a plentiful supply of agoutis, pacas, armadillos, and deer, but an island yields only one harvest in the year.

The Indians generally hunt with arrows. They vote the gun a failure for them, as they are always out of something necessary for it. When they have powder they are out of caps, or if they have caps, they are damp and miss fire. They are fully aware of the advantages of a gun, but declare that it is not an entire success. I often lent them my double-barrel, but they found fault with it; for although the man with the gun got more game than he would have done with bow and arrow, they complained that the noise of it put all the bush on the alert, and there was no getting near the game.

I got fever and ague every third day, and had to stay in the village when all were away except the women and children. I got into such a state that, but for the headache which followed it, I used rather to enjoy my fever. When the ague was on me I used to cover myself with every blanket I could get hold of, and lie on the ground full in the blazing sun. When the fever succeeded, I lay in a string hammock in the cool breeze that blew through the open house. My fever was just as if I were drunk, and I enjoyed it as topers are said to do their brandy. It is impossible to describe the tumultuous crowding of ideas through the brain, and the vividness and rapidity with which they were changed. I was a general, charging through the flying enemy with the wildest excitement, cheers and yells on every side. Then I was a sailor on the deck of a man-of-war; the fifes and fiddles played a brisk jig, and we were all dancing, hundreds of us, in mad fun and enjoyment. Then the air was filled with lovely music, and angels were seen floating about and singing. Then I was a poet, reciting blank verse, surrounded by a vast audience in rapt attention. And so on in endless succession. Gradually the fever subsided and I slept, to wake bathed in perspiration and with a splitting headache.

After a while I had an attack of intermittent malarial fever, in which I was delirious; but the Indians took such care of me as I could scarcely have hoped to receive in a civilized country. One woman sat on the ground for twenty-four hours with my head on her lap, putting young plantain leaves on my forehead, and changing them as they withered. The fever left me so weak that I could not walk, and the Indians carried me in their arms wherever I wanted to go. The process of recovery brought a most delightful feeling. It was as if I had just come into the world with all my senses brand-new. When I woke in my hammock at daylight, the cool land-wind was like a heavenly breeze. The sweet smell of the bush and the flowers, not perceived in health, was like the delicious scent of the land which one feels at sea in the early morning, when the land-wind first comes off. The cries and songs of the birds had a charm altogether new, and recalled an enthusiasm and love for nature which cannot be felt so strongly in good health. The craving for food was a serious trouble, because the appetite must be satisfied with an amount of caution which the convalescent cannot exercise, and as I had only ripe plantains and maize gruel, and there was no one to check my eating, I occasionally nearly died of indigestion. While I was in this state I wandered one day down to the river bank, and saw a pitpan which had just arrived from the coast. Everything had been taken out of it, and the people had gone up to the village. With the keen sense of a hungry dog I perceived the smell of turtle meat, and, looking into the canoe, saw a lump of raw fat lying trampled and filthy in the bottom. I seized and devoured it like a dog.

When I was well enough to walk about the bush, my first desire was to shoot some of the large green macaws (*Ara militaris*) that frequented the high trees near the village, in order that I might have the rich nourishing soup which these and all the parrot tribe furnish when cooked. Accordingly I used to hide under the trees, first to watch their gambols, and then to shoot at them ; but they kept at such a great height that I got very few, and the birds soon left for more distant parts.

This bird is not so well known as the gaudy red and yellow macaw, which is also common in this country, but is mostly found in the savannas.   The green macaw is about 3 feet long (the tail being 2 feet), and $2\frac{1}{2}$ feet across the wings.   When plucked the head appears enormous, being nearly half the size of the body.   It has a remarkably powerful beak, and it can crack the hardest seeds.   The flesh is dark and coarse, like beef.

They generally fly in pairs, and pass over the forest at a great height, uttering a caw like the English rook, but much louder.   In the heat of the day they sit on a high tree and amuse themselves by preening each other's head and neck, or playing at fighting, one hanging by its claws from a branch with its wings spread out, while another perched above it pretends to make formidable demonstrations of attack, both uttering the most deafening screams.   Some hobble along a branch with the toes turned inwards, and suddenly drop like a stone, but rise again like a boat on a wave, wheel in graceful curves round the top of the tree, and return to perch.   They are very tenacious of life, and when wounded and fallen to the ground they climb the trees with beak and claws, and are out of reach in no time.

It is singular how wilfully wasteful the parrot tribe is. They not only pick and throw to the ground ten times as much as they eat, but they 'put in their time' by picking or throwing down seeds that they do not eat ; and it is not unusual to find droves of peccary busily feeding on the seeds thrown down by the macaws. The eboe-nut is so hard that it is usually opened by striking it on the edge with an iron bar, while the nut is secured by placing it in a hollow cut in a stone. But the macaw with one bite scoops out a piece of the shell, and extracts the kernel through the hole.

The paroquets are the joy and pride of the bush, and the whole countryside would be dull without them. They seem to enjoy life more keenly than any other bird, and take care that all who have ears shall hear how happy they are. They are not often seen in the forest or up shady creeks, but the banks of the large rivers are their favourite haunts, and one never tires of listening to their cheerful scream. Every here and there one sees a colony of them enjoying the morning sunshine on some withered tree; or at noon you hear them chattering in the depths of a shady tree, or they are seen rushing in headlong flight across the river with joyous screams, keeping together in a compact body as if guided by a single impulse.

There are many species of paroquets, of which the commonest are the red-wing, the large green, and the orange-chin. Although associating in flocks, the paroquets live in pairs, male and female, and are faithful to each other till death parts them, which happens frequently enough. When parrots are flying high over the forest so slowly that one can count them, one may always see single birds in the flock, which no doubt are widowers.

The Indians are fond of bright-coloured feathers, just as the South Sea Islanders are fond of flowers, and the women have always little stores of such to work up into ornaments in their leisure time; but it must be observed that the men only are adorned. The women only decorate themselves by covering their bodies with a pale red paint, made from the seeds of the anatto, and by heavy masses of red and black beads worn round the neck.

I was lying in my hammock one very hot day, and the woman of this part of the house was sitting on a sheet of bark on the ground near me, busily spinning cotton-yarn with the spindle, clayball, and calabash, as is their custom. Beside her, hung from the rafters, was her baby, lashed to a piece of bark on which were hung shells, seeds, teeth, and claws, and from time to time she agitated the bark, baby and all, on the theory that the rattling of the shells, etc., would soothe it to sleep. Being tired of spinning, she unrolled a piece of *toonoo* (indiarubber bark cloth), in which she had a store of all kinds of beautiful feathers and pieces of white down. She produced a most gaudy and beautiful head-dress, made of a wide band of cloth, through the threads of which were fastened the long tail-feathers of the red macaw; below them a band of the beautiful yellow feathers of the yellow-tail, while the shafts of the longer feathers were covered in patterns with the short red feathers of the toucan's breast, black feathers of the tick-eating blackbird, and white down of the harpy eagle. I asked to look at it, and she handed it to me, but when I put it round my head she was displeased, and said, 'Do not do that; it is for a *seecro* [festival of the dead]. This head-dress must only be worn by the *sookia* on the occasion.'

The yellow-tails, of which she had so many feathers, had built a few of their hanging nests to the ends of the fronds of the prickly soopa palm, a cultivated palm always grown around the villages, the fruit of which is a delightful vegetable when boiled with salt. The birds build in this situation, confiding in the protection of man, and being thus betrayed, they had left the nests; but a little farther up the river a great colony of them had festooned a mountain-guava tree with their long hanging nests.

This is the most conspicuous and most elegant tree in the country. No thieving monkeys can reach its isolated branches, no snake wind its way up its smooth and slippery bark; and, secure from all but winged foes, the yellow-tails cover its outer branches with long hanging nests, and rear their noisy broods. These nests are a striking feature on the banks of the river, being so compact and strong that, although never used a second time, they swing in the wind for years before they rot away. They are 3 feet to 4 feet long, and 1 foot in diameter at the bottom, diminishing upwards until they terminate in the fibres firmly woven into the end of the branch by which they are suspended. These nests are closely woven of the long dry leaves of a grass, mixed with parasitical roots and dry pieces of withes. The inside is comfortably lined with leaves 3 inches thick. About a foot from the bottom is the entrance hole. Two eggs are laid in each nest, white, speckled with horn colour.

A mountain-guava tree, hung round with sixty or eighty nests, is a most interesting object. As it were a bird town with busy traffic, one sees an incessant stream of birds, from every point of the compass, going and coming, some disappearing head foremost into the nest, where they are received with shrill cries by the hungry young. The clucking of the hens on the nests, the gabble of the cocks perched on the highest branches, and the whining cry of the flying birds, make an incessant uproar, heard a long way off. The more industrious birds have already well-grown chickens, but others are still sitting, and the laziest birds are weaving nests. Birds are coming in with material streaming from their bills. They dive into the nest with it, and other birds fly past and pluck it away for their own use before the owner can get out to eject the thief.

Although the yellow-tails use such foresight in securing their nest from some enemies, they have to take their chance with others. The toucans plunder the nests occasionally, devouring eggs and very young birds. The large hawks are also a sore annoyance to the birds when nesting. A hawk will fly to a tree with nests; the birds sally out to repulse him. Sometimes they succeed ; his courage fails, and he retreats in great confusion, assailed by hundreds of birds. He buffets his assailants with his wings ; strikes at them with his claws, rolling over in the air to strike upwards or sideways. He is confused with the noise, wounded by the sharp bills, and altogether he is in a sad plight, and glad to tumble helter-skelter into the bush. Sometimes, however, he succeeds in perching on the tree, causing infinite alarm to the birds, which wheel round and round him with loud cries, but his threatening beak keeps them off until he sees his opportunity, when he suddenly rises in the air, darts upon a bird, buries his claws in its back, and both flutter to the ground, when the hawk, after a while, flies away with a satisfied and peaceful flight.

The cocks, of which there are three or four in a flock, have very singular notes. While the hens are feeding, the cock selects a conspicuous perch, and crows from time to time. In so doing, he throws himself forward, like an Asiatic making a profound salaam. Hanging by his feet, with his wings spread, he first utters a strange rustling sound, like shaking a leafy branch. This blends into a liquid gabble, ending in a high loud cry, like the word ' pwäick,' that can be heard a mile off. The Indians persisted that the rustling sound was produced by shaking the wings, but by careful observation I found that it is a vocal sound. One must be careful how one handles the bird when wounded, as it will, if it gets a chance, drive its bill half an inch into the hand.

The forehead of the yellow-tail is in the same line with the bill, which gives the bird a singular appearance.

After a long day of rain with thunder, lightning, and frequent squalls, towards sunset the turmoil of the elements subsides, the heavy rain-clouds no longer roll up from the east, the sky settles into a dull, leaden, streaked appearance, and allows the declining sun to burst through before setting. Then all the dripping, shivering animals hasten with cries of delight to snatch a few mouthfuls of food before night closes in.   The Indian travelling in his little pitpan, his skin blue with the cold and wet, ties his frail craft to a bush, wrings out his shirt, and, turning his bare back to the sun, lights his pipe for the first time that day, and prepares to cook his frugal meal.   Droves of monkeys, bounding from branch to branch, hasten to some well-known fruit-tree. Flocks of clamorous parrots crowd the trees that overhang the river.   The air is filled with swallows, day-bats and goatsuckers, capturing the winged females of the white ant, which rise in myriads as soon as the rain is passed.

This is the time when the toucans may be seen in flocks, flying to the branches of the highest trees that overlook the forest, where they have a general concert, tossing their heads upwards as they utter their pleasing and liquid notes, which may be heard for a great distance.

The river Indian when far away from home is often over-come with emotion and home-sickness at the well-known cry of this bird, which to him is as ' those evening bells ' to the sentimental poet, and recalls some bright sunny evening when he poled his pitpan over the clear, rippling rapids in sight of his little village, where the girls and children stood on the bank watching his arrival.   I too used to be touched with emotion and melancholy pleasure, as weak from fever I sat on my log in the evening, looking out over the quiet, shining river and the beautiful forest on the opposite side, and listened to the far-distant ' evening bells ' of the Central American bush.

The cry of the toucan is loud and in a high key, but plaintive, liquid, and musical.   It resembles the words ' peeakos-tulluk-tulluk.'   Consequently the Indians, who always give birds and animals their own names, call this bird ' peeakos.'   The toucans go in flocks of ten to fifteen. They are active and lively in hopping about the branches, but slow and heavy in flight.   During a long flight the body droops at short intervals from the weight of the head, and the bird flaps its wings to rise again to a higher level, giving an undulating path to the flight.

There are three species in these woods, distinguished as peeakos, ooruk, and pillis, the ooruk differing from the peeakos in the colours of its bill, which is light green at the end, yellow in the middle, and shaded into pink at the root. Its cry is like the loud croaking of a frog, resembling ' ooruk-ooruk' repeated for a long time.

The pillis is the smallest of the toucans in this country. It is very common, and no doubt most destructive among the nests of other birds. One day at Blewfields Bluff, while observing a colony of about forty yellow-tails which had hung their pendent nests to the branches of a tree growing in the middle of a plantation of cassava and sugar-cane, I was much surprised to see a pair of pillis fly straight out of the bush and alight each on the bottom of the nest, which they tore open most vigorously. One of them got at the eggs and swallowed them, but the other had not time to do so before the owners arrived, when the two thieves flew off in a great hurry. I wondered why these depredators did not enter the nest they intended to plunder through the proper entrance, and how they discovered that the owners were absent; but probably they have learned that it is dangerous to peep into a nest, as a stroke of the bill from the yellow-tail would disable them, whereas by tearing open the bottom they might get at the eggs from beneath the sitting bird, and have time to retreat if she made a sortie.

It is not pleasant, while contemplating the bright, free, and happy life of all living creatures on God's beautiful world, to think of the treachery, rapine, and cruelty that contribute to the life and pleasure of one part of animated nature, and of the suffering and constant state of alarm under which the rest lives. They can only enjoy their life under the condition that they forget the dangers that surround and await them. Injustice, selfishness, and brute force seem to be the basis of Nature's government; suffering and misery attend the administration. The animals enjoy Nature's gifts and forget her wrongs, and only reflective man looks on amazed alike at the incongruity and the success of the whole affair.

The pillis has so many oddly placed colours that it looks like a piece of living patchwork. Its bill differs from those of the other species by having nine notches, by being flat on the top, and by its great thickness and strength.

I do not know how our rivers would look without our little green swallows. Certainly we could not spare them, and fortunately they never think of leaving us. They put life into the river landscape, and relieve the solid stability of the surroundings, constantly skimming, darting, turning, twittering, chirping; what an ideal they are of freedom, lightness, motion, enjoyment! They seem to have no object in life, no fixed purpose in anything, except in the enjoyment of swift motion for its own sake. Here gravity is set at defiance, friction has no part to play, weariness is unknown. One gazes at them with amazement. Motion with us is such an effort; so many forces oppose it; exhaustion waits so closely upon it. Our ideal is rest, and to it we look forward with our fondest hopes. To enjoy motion we must employ forces not our own—a horse, a railway, a balloon; or we dream that we shall enjoy free motion when we shall have parted with this 'too solid flesh.' But this little creature has this gift in the flesh, and knows no weariness nor sighs for rest. Night comes, but only to give it new zest for to-morrow's flight. It devours space and is happy.

It is pleasant to be ill, if only to enjoy the recovery. You have nothing to do; your friends and your duty require that you shall take no care for the morrow. You seem to have shed a rough and thorny shell, and now are clad in a soft garment through which the breath of every pleasure reaches your soul with the least alloy. Your day-dreams are without self-reproach ; your idle wanderings are your most important business. Nature is kind and loving, for you have neither the will nor the strength to oppose her.

The Indians have no delicacies in the way of food, and to one weak with fever the coarse, ordinary diet of plantains, maize, and cassava is frequently repulsive. They have also little fruit except alligator pears, papaws, and mammee apples. The first is more like green butter than any fruit. The last two are luscious, but wanting in the acid so grateful in hot countries. Their oranges invariably turn bitter from being left to run wild. In fact, the people never remain long enough in one place to allow of the cultivation of fruit.

Sometimes they brought me a quantity of wild chocolate, which grows on rich damp soil in the shadiest parts of the bush. This plant is not quite like the cultivated chocolate. It grows to a height of 6 to 10 feet. The flower differs greatly from that of the cultivated kind. It is dark purple, and of a soft fleshy substance. The fruit is exactly like the cultivated chocolate, but very much smaller, being only $3\frac{1}{2}$ inches long, and grows all over the stem just as the chocolate does on its branches. The seeds inside the fruit are surrounded by white pulp, sweet, acid, and very refreshing. I tried to make chocolate from the seeds, but it was rough, bitter, and altogether undrinkable. The Indian name is 'tiger chocolate.'

Most of the men in this settlement were away with my brother-in-law in the Wakna Creek 'driving mahogany'— that is, taking every advantage of the frequent floods to drift the logs down the creek towards a boom in the main river, where they were collected. Now, it is not usual in these rivers for the men to be away at this time of year, and as I remained at the village getting over my fever, the women did not hesitate to tell me that, as I had taken their men away, they were 'meat hungry'; but all I could do was to accompany them every day to their respective cultivations, and while they did a little weeding I strolled round the edges of the bush to shoot anything that appeared, or one or two of them paddled me slowly and noiselessly up the river, when I seldom failed to shoot a few iguanas, quams, curassows, and sometimes a monkey. Many a pleasant picnic we had, when we would land on a sandbank, light a fire, and devour our game instead of taking it to the village.

Once when I accompanied the women to one of their plantations, I partly climbed, partly walked, up a thick sloping tree at the edge of the bush, intending to sit on a branch and enjoy the view and the breeze. Coming to a great rotten hole in a fork of the branches, surrounded with vines and parasites, I saw a black hairy beast lying curled up asleep. This gave me such a start that I slipped and fell out of the tree, and might have been hurt had I not broken my fall by clutching at the withes that surrounded it. I hastened to the women to tell my adventure, and they burned with curiosity to know what it could be, so they sent to another plantation and summoned a young man, who came and joined in the interesting discussion. At last, encouraged and urged by the women, he stuck a machete into his waistcloth, and ascended the tree with much misgiving, and prepared for immediate flight. Peeping very cautiously into the hole, he did not fly with terror, as we were prepared to see, but took out his cutlass and stabbed the beast, holding it for awhile pinned to the tree, while all we could hear was a great scuffle and scratching. Then he drew out his machete, and lifted by the tail a great horsetail ant-eater, which he threw to the ground amid much laughter and exclamations of wonder, for this species is rare, and seldom seen in this part of the country. We took it home to show the children, who were immensely excited over it. It is singular this beast should be so rare that I have only seen it thrice in fifteen years, yet in Brazil it is common enough.

One day at the mahogany works I was walking through the bush with ten or twelve men, going to our work in the morning, when they saw some fresh tracks made in soft ground, after studying which intently they declared themselves ignorant what animal had made them. As usual, they at once began to terrify themselves with superstitious fancies. Some thought it must be a young *wihwin*, a fabulous spirit that lives in the sea, and sometimes roams through the bush at night to devour all it encounters. Others thought it must be the little dwarf man, the owner of the peccary, who, as is well known, has terrible claws on his hands and feet, with which he can tear people to pieces. So terrified were they at this explanation, which they all agreed was the correct one, that they positively refused to go into the bush, and, returning to camp, I had to provide other work for the day. Next day I brought an old Smoo Indian to the place, and he said it was the track of the great ant-eater, on which they laughed heartily at their terror of the day before.

The only defence which the ant-eater can make is to lie on its back with its legs displayed, and if an enemy seizes it, instantly to clasp it in its arms, burying its powerful claws in its body. From such a hug it is said that even the jaguar cannot extricate itself. At Blewfields I remember the negroes bringing in one which had been attacked on the ground by their dogs. It clasped one in this manner, and it took several men to release the dog, which howled in the most helpless condition. The great and the small ant-eater, as well as the sloth, defend themselves in this way. I have seen a sloth lying on its back, and every time it was touched on the breast with a stick it clasped its legs in the most violent manner, just as men buffet themselves in frosty weather to warm their fingers.

CHAPTER XVII.

Industrious women—Family life—Women left alone—Egg harvest—
Alligators as playthings—Trade and commerce—Race differences—
Daily occupations.

THE women in this village were always busy, although they never worked hard. In the middle of the day the noise made by the hammering of *toonoos* sounded like a small factory. The *toonoo* is the universally worn native cloth. Women at their ordinary work wear it round their loins, and they are in full dress when they don a wrapper of print or gray shirting. The men wear it as ordinary waistcloths, and all blankets and pillows are made of it.

The elderly women are spinning cotton-yarn in every spare moment, a few bushes to supply the cotton being always planted among the maize and cassava. They weave cotton cloths 15 inches wide and 9 feet long, as waistcloths for the men, only to be worn on important occasions, or as a change when they repose in the bosom of the family after a severe day's wetting in the bush. Some of these are beautifully ornamented with patterns in black, red, and white, in which is mixed the snowy down of the muscovy duck, forming a soft fringe all round the selvage and ends.

The women have their infants fastened to a strip of bark, suspended by a string, and hung round with strings of shells, claws, and seeds, the rattling of which is intended to soothe the baby to sleep. Older babies are carried on the back, secured by a waistcloth wrapped round the child and the woman's body, and fastened below the breasts. In this manner the woman can pursue her avocations unencumbered, just as the monkey can with its infant clasping its back. Unlike the negroes and Creoles, the Indians never let their children go about naked, but as soon as they can walk they are clothed in thin little waistcloths. Their ideas of decency are just as strict as among Europeans. A woman must never expose her thighs or loins; a man is never seen without his waistcloth, and little children are not more exposed than grown-up people. Among the negroes, on the contrary, girls of ten and boys of twelve go about in their birthday dress.

Families and married people live on elevated stages just under the eaves. Unmarried girls and boys sleep anywhere, usually in hammocks. On lower stages, made of round poles, and covered with a large sheet of bark, the little children sleep, with an elder sister with them to take care they do not fall off.

The Indians do not sleep like Europeans, going to bed at a fixed hour, and not rising till morning. They take their sleep in snatches like a dog, rising once or twice in the night to smoke and stroll around looking at the stars, or even to change their bed. On fine warm nights they frequently sleep on the ground out of doors, regardless of the moonlight or the dew.

As is usual among all people living this simple life, there are very rarely unmarried girls. If there are any spare girls, the principal men take two or more wives, so that the supply is never in excess of the requirements, and all are happy.

It results from the women being scarce that they are so much the more prized, and as either man or woman can leave each other at choice, there is no friction in married life. Habit weaves their wants and feelings together. Children form a common tie, with the result that the con-

stancy of married life with them is about on a par with that
of any other people, Europeans included. When sober,
a man seldom or never beats or ill-uses his wife, as he
would incur the risk of fighting her relations, or she might
go off with a kinder man, and the chiefs justify her separa-
tion. As wives are hard to find, unless one marries an infant
and waits many years for her to grow up, such a contingency
is not to be risked lightly. To be without a wife is not only
an ignominious, but a most distressing plight for an Indian.
The women are allowed complete freedom, and infidelity is
common enough. If it is discovered, the injured husband is
usually contented with the payment of the customary fine.
Sometimes the co-respondent fails to pay, then quarrels
occur, and, indeed, it is the faults of the women which give
rise to nine-tenths of the quarrels.

Notwithstanding the looseness of the tie which binds them,
the Indians are as kind to their wives as the average of
civilized people. They are exceedingly fond of their children,
instruct them carefully in the small range of their duties and
in all the arts of life; but they never correct or beat them,
leaving them to grow up just as nature made them. Accordingly, they are wilful to a degree, and one would expect
to see the result in confusion and demoralization. This,
however, does not take place. They grow up fond and
loving to their parents and to each other; I might almost
venture to say more so than is found among the lower classes
in civilized life.

We call these people savages, but it is impossible to deny
that they lead a happier life than nine-tenths of all civilized
men. There is among them a remarkable absence of crime;
they are cheerful and merry, sympathetic and kind to each
other.

In the dry season all the Mosquito Indians of the coast,
as well as the Toonglas of this river, who are a colony of
Mosquito Indians living a riverine life, go to sea to engage

in turtle-fishing, and do not return until the rainy season. There remain in the villages the women and children and old men.

The women, left to themselves, pass the time in ease and enjoyment. Embarking in their pitpans with their children and dogs, they wander over the bright sunny river, or into dark lonely creeks, fishing as they go, and with the help of the young lads and the dogs killing agoutis, pacas, iguanas, tortoises, and such easily captured game. Without a care or thought of the future they paddle lazily along, the dogs barking in the bows of their pitpans, the children squatting on the bottom, and tame parrots, curassows, ducks and hens perched on the gunwales. When the sun is hot, they land on the sandbanks and bathe in the river, swimming, diving, and playing for hours, teaching their children to swim at the earliest ages. I have seen a number of women standing on the river bank throw their infants into the water, 12 feet deep, then dive after them and swim ashore.

In April the egg harvest has to be gathered, and the women are away sometimes for weeks, visiting every sandbank in the main river, paddling and poling up the creeks, and ransacking all the deposits of silt and sand. The quantity of eggs they get is astonishing. I have seen them return to their homes with the canoes heavily loaded with alligators' eggs ; and this was only the surplus left over, for they consume as they find them most of the more palatable eggs of river-tortoise and iguana. The alligator eggs they expose to the sun for a week, then pack them in baskets and hang them in the smoke, to be eaten when hard times come in the rainy season.

It is an odd sight to see a bevy of women and children searching an extensive sandbank for eggs. They are all walking on their heels, each carrying a sharpened stick. When anyone feels her heels sink unusually, she tries the ground by thrusting the sharp stick several times into the sand, and at once perceives whether an egg has been pierced. The alligator lays from thirty-eight to forty-five eggs, never more than fifty in one nest; but it is possible that it may make two nests in the season, as the sea-turtle does. The egg is 4 inches by 2, perfectly elliptical, with a very thick shell, and under it a skin so tough that the egg is not broken even if dropped from a height. It has exceedingly little white, and a large pale yellow yolk. It is excellent eating, if a slight musky smell be disregarded.

The iguana burrows a very deep hole, nearly horizontal, in the sloping side of a bank of earth or sand. The tortoise lays in sand, silt, or even in stiff earth, with the clods barely covering the eggs. Both lay from eighteen to twenty-four eggs in a nest. The eggs are round, enclosed in a tough calcareous parchment. The egg of the iguana is nearly 2 inches, that of the tortoise $1\frac{1}{2}$ inch, in diameter. The iguana makes many investigations into the nature of the soil, and lies sunning herself beside her nest, to dry her eggs, as the Indians say, before laying them.

In the middle of May the eggs hatch, and the young alligators and tortoises make for the water. No sooner do the little creatures see the light than they are assailed by many enemies—the little iguanas and tortoises by hawks, cormorants, man-o'-war birds, fishes, and four-footed enemies of all sorts; the alligators by their own species, which lie in wait at the edge of the water and snap them up as they come down from the sandbanks. I have slept on a sandbank, and in the morning found that the sand had been ploughed up in every direction during the night by alligators, as the Indians told me, digging up their own eggs to eat them before they hatch. I have often seen many alligators cruising at night round the sandbanks about the time when their eggs are expected to hatch, and the Indians, by imitating the squeaking noise of the young, attracted from all directions the parents waiting to devour their progeny.

It seems incredible that such an instinct should exist in any animal as that of habitually devouring its young, but although I have not seen it, the Indians assure me that the alligator does so, and what I have observed of its habits inclines me to believe them.

The Indian children catch numbers of little alligators to play with, so that sometimes the village is full of them, and you can hardly walk without treading on one, and having your toes snapped at. Dozens may be seen tethered to the house-posts, rolling over each other and hopelessly entangled. The children feed them with flies, worms, and scraps of meat. They are entirely uninteresting, and show no attachment, but the most virulent hostility. On being touched they wheel round and snap at the fingers, uttering a peculiar squeak, but their bite is quite harmless. They are very active in catching flies, at which they snap with incredible rapidity. When newly hatched they are about 6 inches long, but they grow quickly, and then it is time for the children to knock them on the head, which they do accordingly.

The Indian women spend much time wandering in parties with their children and dogs in the bush, gathering seeds of the eboe, yarey, and keesoo, from which they make oil to barter with the coast Indians, to anoint their long black hair, or to mix with anatto paint for the purpose of smearing over their bodies. These women are not more expert with the bow, the lance, or the gun than the average Englishwoman is with our weapons, yet they wander fearlessly through the bush when the men are away. I have frequently met parties of them camped at the heads of dark lonely creeks, and accidents from the attacks of 'tigers' or from snake-bites are not so frequent as to deter them.

The men of the river Indians—that is, the Smoos and Twakas—never go to sea for the turtle-fishing, but in the dry season camp with their families at the heads of the creeks, and stay two months or more cutting down large cedar-trees, from which they cut out canoes in the rough to barter with the coast Indians, who trim or finish them off with great skill and neatness. The sea-canoes are beautiful models and fast sailers, but very crank. They are of all sizes up to 6 feet beam and 40 feet long, cut out of the solid without any addition. The pitpans, or river-canoes, are very long and narrow, square-ended like a scow, but with a flat platform at each end, large enough for a man to stand on. The river Indians also prepare stools, benches, platters, wooden troughs, and great slabs hewn out of mahogany or cedar; and their women prepare quantities of *toonoo* (or indiarubber bark) blankets, also large clay jars to hold drink for their festive occasions.

The river Indians collect a little indiarubber in thick circular cakes, which in my time they used only to burn in order to make black paint from the melted gum. They collect a white gum with a very pleasant smell, called *pantipee;* also the fragrant roots of a rush, both much liked by the Indian women to perfume their persons, and ' make the young men love them.'

These articles, with tiger and deer skins, a little chocolate, maize, and plantains, form their export trade, in return for which they receive from the coast Indians cutlery, cloth, beads, iron pots, salt, fish-hooks, hoop iron, files to make arrow-heads, and flints and steel for kindling fires. This minute trade is carried on with little labour and no competition. The value of the articles is fixed by custom, and no cheating or adulteration is possible or thought of. So much confidence have they in the honesty of transactions, that I have frequently seen at the mouths of rivers a peeled and painted stick planted in a conspicuous position, and on landing have found hanging to the trees bunches of plantains, baskets of maize, rolls of *toonoo* cloth and skins, and attached to each article a sample of what was wanted in return, such as a fish-hook to one, a few beads to another, a pinch of salt to the next, and so on. These were placed there in the expectation that the coast Indians passing by on the main river would make the required barter. After a while, if they are found to remain untouched, the river Indians bring the articles to the coast villages. Even these savages (as we choose to call them) are restrained by honour and fair dealing if trusted.

The village I am staying at now is a Toongla village, and the Toonglas are a sort of nondescript people. They claim to be the same as the Mosquito Indians, but although they speak the Mosquito language, they do not quite resemble the Mosquito men. But neither do they resemble the interior and riverine tribes, such as Smoos, Twakas, Ramas, etc. The Mosquito men are prone to domineer over the Toonglas in much the same manner as they do over the Indians of the interior. The Toonglas account for the differences which distinguish them from the Mosquito men by the circumstance of their living on the rivers and not on the sea-coast; but they do not know how they came to live up the rivers, as no Mosquito Indian can live far from the sea. The Toonglas have in smaller measure the adventurous daring character of the Mosquito men, the same fondness for undertaking long voyages in their canoes, and the same frank, independent bearing towards the whites or other strangers; but whereas the Mosquito Indians are prone to quarrelling and fond of fighting with the fist, the Toonglas, like the interior Indians, are much more peaceable, and partake of the stolid endurance so characteristic of the Smoos, Twakas, and the other interior tribes.

Let me describe one of our usual days, such as we passed with unvarying monotony for weeks. Just as day dawns sufficiently for you to see your way about, the elder women descend from their elevated beds, called *creecrees*, and, seating themselves beside the embers, proceed to blow up the fire, which is built between a few large stones on the earthen floor of the hut. The housewife then peels and roasts some plantains, either ripe or green, and when roasted she crushes them up with her hands in a calabash of cold water, making a sort of gruel. A calabash of this is handed to her husband, who by this time has also descended, and is sitting in a string hammock. The children and others of the family are served with a portion of the same mess. Instead of crushed roast plantain the women may prepare a potful of *bishbaya*, which is maize buried in the ground until it ferments, then thoroughly dried and preserved in baskets in the smoke. Two or three calabashfuls of this are put into a pot and boiled with water, when a thick soup is formed with an offensive smell; but disregarding the smell, it is very nice and very nourishing.

After this light breakfast the people go down to the river, wash their mouths and faces, and then disperse for the work of the day, which is mostly regulated by their fancy or inclination. The small and scattered patches of cultivation are visited by the family to whom they belong, a little weeding is done, and if a bunch of plantains or bananas is found to be ripe, it is cut down; a root or two of cassava and a yam or two are dug up, and an armful of sugar-cane is cut. All are stowed in the pitpan, and then a little domestic hunting and fishing is carried on for some hours, the wife paddling along and turning into every likely creek, while the husband shoots fish or iguanas, dives for tortoises, hunts in the shallows for crayfish or fresh-water crabs, or by the help of his dog pursues a paca to its hole at the edge of the water and digs it out. He is in luck if he should come across a troop of monkeys, or a small drove of peccaries browsing on the convolvulus vines at the edge of the forest, and it sometimes happens that he sees a deer or a bush antelope half hidden in the tall cutch grass, and stupidly gazing at the canoe.

During the powerful heat of mid-day they land at some shady sandbank; the wife makes a fire and roasts a plantain or two, and with this and a broiled fish they make a frugal meal. They then shove off, tie the pitpan to a bough overhanging the water, and, lying down in the bottom, have a good sleep.

As evening begins to fall, they gather some firewood, and slowly paddle home.

The less responsible members of families have in the meantime put in the day according to their fancy. The women with young children have stayed in the village, beating out bark cloth, spinning cotton, weaving waistcloths, making bead bracelets or necklaces, dyeing yarn, making oil of seeds, or concocting perfumery and cosmetics, weeding the yards, sweeping out the huts, and splitting firewood. During the heat of mid-day relaxation is sought by bathing and swimming in the river, in which the little children join the women, and are taught by them, until at a very early age they acquire perfect confidence in the water.

The young women and girls generally keep together, and either wander in the bush or stray up or down the river in their small pitpans. They find something to do either in gathering withes to make baskets, stripping the leaves of silk grass, and washing and combing the beautiful white fibre, from which they make fishing-lines; or they strip and wash the inner bark of the moho-tree, and make it up into balls of coarse twine, from which are made the netted string hammocks in which all recline at their leisure or sleep at night. They also know where certain trees are ripening their fruit, and parties of them resort to such places to gather nuts, generally for the purpose of extracting the oil.

I have said that the Indian women are not more skilled with their weapons than our women are with our guns and revolvers. There is always some little risk in wandering in the woods, consequently parties of girls generally get a

young man to go with them if one is to be had, for the
feeling of security that a bow and arrow, or a lance wielded
by a man's arm, gives to their helplessness. The women
are very clever at fishing, and can use the axe fairly well;
but I do not remember ever seeing one use the bow or spear,
much less the gun, and although their eyes and ears are as
keen as those of the men at detecting the presence of game,
they have to rely on the young lads, in the absence of the
grown-up men, to furnish any game which their own feminine
skill cannot capture.

When the sun declines over the forest and evening sets in,
one by one the wanderers begin to return. As the sound
of the paddles is heard on the river, the children rush down
the bank to the landing-place, eager to see what has been
caught or killed for their dinner, and soon they are seen
returning with little loads of fish or game, or with some
choice wild fruits which the parents have gathered for their
darlings, for the thought of the children is never absent from
the mind of the Indian parent.

Now the glad fires are all lighted, and while the children
crowd round to see the game or fish cut up and cooked, and
to pick up and roast little stray fragments that their mothers
give them, the young women carry up the heavier provisions,
the firewood, and the necessary bamboos of water, while the
men recline in hammocks and tell the news of the day to
the stay-at-homes. Dinner is a ceremonious feast after a
fashion, for there is usually a mutual interchange of dishes.
This family has only boiled fish and the soup of it thickened
with *bishbaya*, so small portions of fish on waha leaves and
calabashes of the soup are sent round to the other families.
In the same hut, at the far end, a family is cooking monkeys
and iguanas, in the soup of which a quantity of green
bananas is boiled to a pulpy mass seasoned with red peppers,
and complimentary portions of this are exchanged for a taste
of the others' messes. The poor old man and his wife in

the adjoining hut have only a few crayfish and two small tortoises as big as the back of a hair-brush, but their daughter's husband has had luck, for his wife is boiling two curassows and roasting a great lean male iguana nearly 6 feet long, and the old people will have a taste of both.

When dinner is done there is still some daylight left, and the boys now amuse themselves shooting arrows at a target made from a block of soft wood, or throwing spears at a cocoanut husk. The men sit by the fire and mend their broken arrows, or straighten and prepare bundles of canes for new ones, or give an hour's work to filing a small piece of bar iron to make a fish harpoon, or filing arrow-heads out of iron hoop, or looking over their little store of material, which consists of balls of black beeswax for preparing the joints of arrows or spears, twine for wrapping the same, half a dozen arrow-points of hardwood still in the rough, bundles of selected canes for the arrows, all cut into lengths and carefully straightened in the fire, a slat of lignum vitæ or soopa palm wood, from which is being made a new bow, which will perhaps be finished next year.

The wretchedly thin dogs have licked all the calabashes and pots; the women wash them up, then split some firewood for the night, then lie down on a strip of bark upon the floor and have a talk and a smoke—that is, if there is any tobacco to be had, which is not always the case. Night has set in, and now is the time for the boys and the girls, who almost invariably resort to an outhouse, where round a fire they tell stories, laugh and sing, play reed flutes or jew's-harps, and have a good tousle and romp. Towards nine o'clock the women and girls climb up to their *creecrees*, and the lads seek repose in their string hammocks, swinging from the posts of the house.

Nothing can be imagined more temperate and more innocent than this sylvan life, and such it is for the greater part of the year. It must not be taken for granted, however, that this temperance and frugality is a virtue, for it is only the result of the conditions of their life. No people in the world are so helplessly intemperate if they have the means to be so. But these people have found favour at the hands of God, who loves to look upon their innocent simplicity, and has forbidden that they should find the means to be intemperate and wicked. They seldom have the means to buy rum from the white people, and to make their own intoxicating *mishla* drinks requires more cassava than they can spare; consequently drinking orgies are few and far between, and are enjoyed with a relish proportionate to their rarity. Their sins are almost entirely confined to intrigues with other men's wives. That is their form of dissipation, and as it is far less hurtful to them than drinking habits are to European nations, we may conclude that the whites exceed the Indians in wickedness by their drinking alone, besides the enormous catalogue of other crimes of which the Indians are entirely ignorant.

CHAPTER XVIII.

The King and I grow up—We visit his relations—Keys—Turtle-fishing—
Pleasant hours on coral keys — Duckwarra — *Oopla smalkaya* —
Sermon of the teacher—Its application—Love for mothers.

IN due course of time the King and I were nearly grown up, and the cares of State were now borne by him.   On the occasion now going to be related, he had to go to the north on business matters, and to see his relations, who lived up the Wanx River.   He asked me to come with him, and his three sisters were to go with us.

He had a fine boat, which was called a ' craft ' on the coast, being a very large cedar canoe, raised, built up, and decked over so as to afford the shelter of its hold and a very small cabin aft.   Carrying two masts with shoulder-of-mutton sails and a large jib, it was a fast sailer, and much admired as a craft fit for a King.

The little cabin was given to the three girls, and in the large hold the rest slept on top of the stone ballast.   Our crew consisted of one man, who was the King's *quatmus*, or quartermaster, two mulatto youths, the King, and myself. The cabin had a little companion-way closed by a sliding top ; the hold had a hatch.   In rough weather all was closed, but the flush deck had stanchions and a stout rope all round to prevent our being washed overboard, and a pair of sweeps enabled the boat to be propelled when there was no wind.

We set sail from Blewfields with the land-wind, about nine

18

in the evening, and by daylight we anchored on the west or lee side of the largest of the Pearl Keys. We landed and made a fire, at which the girls cooked our breakfast of roast plantains, boiled turtle, and coffee. Then, while the girls walked about the island and bathed in the clear sandy pools surrounded with coral, we had a sleep under the shade of the beach grape-trees.

At noon, with a fresh breeze, we sailed through the reefs of coral, gained the open sea, and made for King Keys, which we reached by night, and slept there, though our sleep was much disturbed by soldier crabs, which crawled over us, nipping our toes, fingers and ears.

Long before daylight we departed with the land-wind, and by 10 a.m. reached Maroon Key and had breakfast, after which we set sail for Duckwarra on the mainland.

The principal time for turtle-fishing is the month of May, during the calm sunny days of which they delight to float asleep on the surface of the sea. At this time frequently a hundred canoes assemble on the Man-o'-War and King Keys, where the Indians encamp under the grape-trees, surrounded by an enclosure of live turtle, turned on their backs, whose silent sufferings are unnoticed, and their life only evident by their discharging the air from their lungs and taking a deep breath every twenty minutes. Poor creatures! their eyes are covered with flies, and no one thinks of throwing water on them to cool their shell, intensely heated by the sun.

The Indians are in the height of enjoyment, for this season is a continual feast. Some are roasting fins, or calipees, some mending their harpoons, others sleeping on the sand. Along the beach, between the grape-trees, lines are stretched, which are covered with turtle-meat drying in the sun. The whole island is strewn with fragments of meat, and the smell of the green fat fills the air and is smelt miles to leeward. Here one sees the wastefulness of the Indians displayed in

GEORGE AUGUSTUS FREDERICK, KING OF MOSQUITO.

the most wanton manner. The seashore is littered with half-eaten turtle ; fins, heads, and chunks of meat are everywhere. Often the Indians kill a turtle, and, finding it not so fat as they expected, throw it into the sea.

In the morning all set out for the turtle-banks, which are 8 to 10 miles off, and it is a beautiful sight to see them returning in the evening. The sea to windward is covered with sails winding in and out among the coral banks. Every now and then they seem engulfed among the snow-white breakers, then appear in the deep blue of the channels. On reaching the banks, which are discovered by the number of turtle rising to blow, the sail is taken down, and they keep a lookout for blowing turtle. A stormy day is preferred, as the noise of the waves drowns that which may be made by the paddles. The turtle rising to blow generally floats on the surface for a few minutes, and the Indians endeavour to approach either behind or directly in front of it, as the turtle does not see well straight ahead. When within 20 or 30 yards, the man in the bow rises cautiously, and throws his long heavy staff, so that it falls nearly vertically on the turtle's back; the little bulbed weapon sinks into the shell, and the turtle dives to the bottom, dragging out the long line to which the staff and a bob of light wood is attached. It must rise to blow every twenty minutes, and is soon exhausted, and hauled into the canoe. Often the Indians so overload the canoe with turtle that it is unseaworthy, and is swamped by the waves time after time ; but the turtle are tied by the fins to the canoe, and by constant baling the Indians at last reach the keys with their loads. The harpoon is so short that the turtle is not injured by the wound, but it takes great violence to pull it out of the shell, as the middle is swelled like a boy's tip-cat.

The Indians also fish by night, when they resort to the shoals among the coral reefs, where the turtle are seen by the line of phosphorescent light they make in the water; but there are disadvantages about night-fishing, as they often harpoon a shark or a sawfish, which gives much trouble.

Schooners from the Cayman Islands come regularly to the coast to buy or net the turtle. The nets for this purpose are 80 to 100 fathoms long, and 6 feet wide; the lower edge weighted with lead, and the upper floated with corks. Near the nets decoys are placed, which are great pieces of wood, shaped like a turtle in the act of blowing. The turtle when they rise to blow always look about over the surface, and seeing the decoys, they approach and get entangled in the net.

Large enclosures, called *kraals*, are made in the shallow water, and the turtle are kept in them until a shipload is secured. The hawksbill turtle, which furnishes the shell of commerce, is much smaller than the green turtle. None of them are found about these coral banks; they frequent the southern coasts. These are never netted or captured by any but the Indians and Creoles, who spear them or take them when laying their eggs on the beach. Tortoise-shell is worth 6 dollars a pound, and a good shell weighs 4 pounds. The shell adheres to the bony calipash in large plates or scales.

The Indians dig up great quantities of the eggs of both green and hawksbill turtle, and nothing has ever been done to stop this ruinous practice. Turtle never lay on the coral islands, but always on the beach of the mainland; also it is observed that not every beach pleases them, but certain tracts of beach are selected on which they always return to lay. The she-turtle select the darkest nights to come on shore and lay their eggs in June and July.

I have spent many pleasant hours on these pretty coral keys, where, after a weary sail in a cramped canoe, one jumps ashore on the glittering sand to stretch one's legs and enjoy the rising sun. While the Indians are cooking breakfast under the grape-trees, I wander round to the windward side of the island to study the life of the keys. Far to windward the swell of the sea roars and boils on the reefs, inside of

which it is smooth as a millpond. Walls of dead coral en-
close large basins of blue water, in which multitudes of fish
seek shelter from the restless sea; shoals of sprats, chased
by barracouta, every now and then leap out of water, and
fall again like a cartload of pebbles; porpoises puff and blow,
sending up tall jets of steam and spray, sometimes jumping
out of water bellowing like calves. Now and then the fin of
a ground shark is seen slowly making the round of the bay.
Flocks of pelicans, with their great bills resting on their
breasts, as if in grave meditation, swim in stately procession,
while every now and then one rises on the wing a short distance and dives head - foremost into a school of sprats.
Clamouring flocks of snow-white *kricums* (kittiwakes) line
the walls of coral, drying their wings in the sun, fighting
and pecking one another, then rising to make excursions to
neighbouring reefs, and returning with loud screams. The
graceful man-o'-war bird soars over all, watching with keen
eye the rising sprats, or pursuing and plundering the terrified
gull which has caught a fish. Nothing can exceed the grace
and swiftness of this unscrupulous bird. In vain the gull,
with loud outcry, dives down, or soars on high, or turns
sharp round in zigzag flight. The man-o'-war bird presses
hard on it without flapping a wing, following it round and
round as if tied to its tail. Suddenly the gull drops its fish,
when, with a graceful swoop, the plunderer catches it before
it reaches the water, and sails off to look for another bird to
rob. This singular bird has no power to fish for itself, but
lives entirely by plundering others. The man-o'-war or
frigate-bird is the most noticeable bird we have, because
whenever we look up at the sky one is sure to be seen at a
vast height, soaring and wheeling on motionless wings.
From this height he watches everything that is going on,
and if he sees a commotion among the gulls many miles off,
he makes for that spot at a speed which some observers have
given at 100 miles an hour.

The negroes, or Creoles, as they prefer to be called, have stories of treasure buried here by the buccaneers. Maroon Key has an ominous name, and may have some ghastly record now lost. For hundreds of years the Spaniards cruised among these islands and reefs, and the names they gave them are significant of their experience: Viciosa (Vicious), Quita Suena (Wake-up), Roncador (The Snorer), Alargate (Keep off).

Late in the evening we reached Duckwarra, and put up at the house of a chief, which was the largest in the place. As soon as we had eaten, the women came and carried off the King's sisters to have a good talk, and the old men gathered in our hut to hear the news. Hearing much noise outside, I went to see what it was, and found that our *quatmus* was going to *oopla smalkaya* (or teach people) in the name of the King. A clear moonlight with a soft balmy sea-breeze was just the sort of weather in which to inculcate morality and good behaviour to the unruly youths and maidens of Duckwarra.

Our *quatmus* had a stout upright post to which the culprits were made fast by a rope tied to their wrists. There did not seem to be any order or ceremony in the selection of culprits to be admonished, but one powerful Sambo and a lot of playful youths captured people promiscuously, and dragged them to the ordeal.

At first, one after another, young men were brought to the pole, and their wrists tied up with *moho*, or bark cord. A *toonoo*, or indiarubber-bark blanket, was then thrown over their backs, and the King's quartermaster stood ready with a manatee strap to teach law and order. Before and during the operation he made a speech to the surrounding audience, who listened with respectful attention while the—I will not say culprit—but rather example, meekly stood with his wrists above his head and his feet on the ground.

'People, the King is here; he is in that house talking

with your old men. Why has the King come to Duck-warra ? Why have I, his *quatmus*, come with him in his *krap* [craft] ? The oosoos [vulture] smells the rotten meat as he flies high in the air. He can see where the dead game lies in the bush. Your King smelled a bad smell. He said, "What is this ?" They told him it was you people of Duckwarra, for you had no law in your hearts, and the stink of your wilfulness filled the country. Then the King said to his old men and to his *quatmusnanny* [quarter-masters], "Let us go to the people of Duckwarra ; let us put law in their hearts, that they may listen to their head-men and not be *coopias* any more." [*Coopias* means wilful, heartless, rash, or brave, according to the context.] This youth is very proud '—whack !

' Oh, mother ! oh, don't whip me—oh !'

' He laughs at the old men when they teach him ; all night he prowls after men's wives '—whack !

' Oh, mother !' etc.

' But his own wife has no cloth on her back ; his women-kind are sick with meat hunger. The little children look at his hands to see if he brings them fat turtle or sweet game meat from the forest, but his hands are empty '—whack, whack !

' Oh, mother !' etc.

This culprit is then released and runs off laughing, and another is tied up in his place.

Sermon continued : ' Yes, his hands are empty. Where-fore shall the women and the little children look after him, longing for meat ? He has no meat '—whack !

' Oh, mother ! oh, it hurts dreadfully ! Oh, mother !'

' How shall his wife hide her shame ? She has no cloth to cover her loins ; she has no beads to hang round her neck '—whack !

' Oh, mother !' etc.

Culprit released, and another tied up.

Sermon continued : ' How shall he give good things to his womenkind, and feed his little ones with sweet fat meat ? All day long he is drunk with the strong drink of the whites, or with *mishla*. He quarrels and fights, but he will not work. He passes the night hunting after men's wives, and he is covered with the debts which he owes to their husbands '—whack, whack !

' Oh, mother !' etc.

Culprit released, and another tied up, and so on with all the unruly youth of Duckwarra.

The girls and women meanwhile have been laughing and jeering at the sufferers, making unmerciful fun at each one's expense ; but as soon as they perceive that the supply of young men is running short, they begin to look serious, and before the last has had his dose of whacks they bolt for the bush. But the youths have their eye on them, and one by one or in batches they are captured and dragged to the post, filling the calm night with piercing screams, answered by shouts of laughter from the boys. Soon one is tied up by the wrists, but old women are at hand to see that two-ply *toonoos* are thrown over her back.

Sermon continued : ' Why is the King's heart troubled ? Why does he groan all night, and cannot sleep ? It is because the young women of Duckwarra are very foolish and very wicked '—whack, whack !

' Oh, mother, mother, they are killing me !' — loud screams, etc.

Culprit released, goes off laughing, and another, screaming fearfully, is tied up.

Sermon continued : ' Yes, old men with their hearts full of law, and white men who read books, came to our King and said, " What shall you do to the women of Duckwarra, for their badness is talked about in the lands beyond the sea " ' —whack, whack !

' Oh, mother !' etc.

Culprit released, and another tied up.

Sermon continued : ' The young women care only to wear fine beads, to paint their bodies with *tmaaring* [anatto paint], and to hang the sweet-smelling rush round their necks. They rub their breasts with sweet-smelling oils, and put bracelets of beadwork on their arms.   Then they walk along the sea-beach, and beckon to the young men to come and play with them '—whack, whack !

' Oh, mother, it hurts !   Oh, let me go !   Oh, mother !' etc.

Released, laughing, and another tied up.

Continued : ' They laugh and play, but their hearts are hard.   They love their sweethearts, and mock at their husbands before the young men.   They tell all the secrets of other women, and tell lies about their husbands' other wives.   Then the men fight about the lies that the women tell, and every man is in debt for the blood that is spilled.'

This continued until most of the young women had been whipped.   No elderly men or women were touched.   When this part of the sentence of the court was concluded, the quartermaster and some other men dragged to the post a strong, dissipated-looking Sambo, who was accused of beating his wife continually and cruelly.   He was tied up and well flogged without anything on his back.   He took the punishment with great fortitude, concerned only at the jeering of the boys, to whom he said, ' You may laugh, but if it was you, you would cry like babies.'

This practice of publicly whipping the youths and young women by the King's quartermasters on their annual journeys round the coast has been in vogue for a great many years, probably for centuries.   It answers the purpose of our sermons in the churches to inculcate principles of good conduct and morality.   The quartermasters also try cases of crime, and summarily administer the punishments.

I was once present when a man was accused before the quartermaster of taking his cousin as a wife, and was condemned to be hanged because, as the quartermaster said, 'only dogs do such a thing.' However, the English residents represented that the English do not hang men for marrying cousins, and on the strength of this the man was flogged and condemned to pay a fine of a canoe, and the woman was taken from him.

It will be observed that during the whipping the culprits always invoked their mother, and this the Indians do upon every occasion when we should invoke God. Their invocation of their mother is quite as comforting and consoling to them as it is to us to invoke God. I never saw anything so touching as a young Indian, who died from a wound in the stomach, crying with his last breath, 'Oh, mother, mother!' His mother had been dead several years.

CHAPTER XIX.

INLAND from Duckwarra is all savannas and pitch-pine ridges, with groves of live oak and papta palms—very pretty country, where the forest is seen only along the courses of the creeks and rivers. The place is surrounded with lagoons, in which fish abound. Duckwarra in Mosquito means an island (the literal meaning is, 'cut off'), and Lee Duckwarra means water island, or a lake. I never ascertained why it was called island.

These savannas abound in deer, antelopes, and armadillos, but I noticed that the bush game, though dearly loving the sunshine, is very shy of coming out into the open, never venturing out of easy reach of cover. But at the edge of the forest, which grows at the riversides and in patches on good soil, all sorts of game come out in the early morning or evening. Warree, peccary, agouti, paca, curassows, quail, and partridges take great pleasure in coming out of the bush. I do not doubt that they have the same feeling we have of exhilaration and delight at getting out of the sombre shade and looking at the sky and sun. Monkeys and tapirs view the savannas with great suspicion, and will have nothing to do with open country, though they also love sunshine ; but the narrow strip of cutch grass along the river banks, with forest at the back, is where they prefer to take the air of mornings and evenings.

I have seen raccoons, singly or in pairs, bustling about in the savannas, where they are much taken aback at being discovered, and make for the banks of creeks or the groves of papta palms with all convenient speed. I like the raccoon, for he has many good points. He will suffer no one to interfere with him; he sticks to his own business, and never interferes with other people. He never goes pottering about your fowl-house at night like the opossum, and he leaves your ripe plantains, mammee apples, and soopa-nuts alone, which is more than can be said of his cousin, the quash. Crabs are his standing dish, but he likes mice, and drops on to a bird now and then as she sits on her nest on the ground.

I was once wandering in the bush, making a short cut to where our men were working, when I saw a wide open place, and, creeping cautiously forward, peeped over a bank on to the dry bed of a large pond. There I saw a raccoon very busy digging. I watched to see what he was going to dig out, when he gave a start, and looked attentively at the sky. I did the same, and saw a large kooskoospeeram, or crested eagle, cruising about over the top of the forest. The raccoon then went on with his digging. Presently there was a rushing sound; the raccoon jumped away about 4 feet, and tumbled over on his back, hissing and squealing fiercely, while the hawk brushed past him like a shot out of a gun, and disappeared over the bush. He got up and looked anxiously all round, then resumed his digging. I threw a stick at him, when he hastened under a bush, and continued there a long time gazing fixedly at me, but would not move from his place, so I left him alone.

On this north part of the coast the flies in the daytime are intolerable to a newcomer, and annoying to those most used to their attacks. There is a large sulphur-coloured horsefly, who when he bites will not fail to make you jump off your seat or roll out of your hammock. There is a still larger dusky brown one, of whom you had better beware, for his bite is like a spiteful child poking a pin into you. But the most numerous and most annoying is a small black fly with transparent wings tipped with crape — a most remorseless biter, but sly and cautious in his attacks. He is not so simple as to fly about your face or the exposed back of your hand; he knows well enough which part of your own person you can see. His favourite place of attack is up the leg of your trousers (no one wears shoes or stockings), or up your sleeve, or perhaps where your shirt is sticking out of your trousers a small bit at the back, or wherever your shirt or trousers touch your skin close and you are not looking.

There are in the bush great numbers of a fly three times the size of a flea, black in the chest part, and of a dark bottle green in the posterior part, the Creole name of which is a little indelicate. This fly does not venture out of the bush, but it is very annoying there, biting every exposed part of you, and with a bite that itches, which, fortunately, the bites of the previously mentioned flies do not. Sand-flies along the beach only come out when it is calm, but then they are a terror to both men and horses.

As if to belie its name, the Mosquito Coast is freer from mosquitoes than most tropical countries. They are troublesome along the low marshy parts of the rivers, but there are few or none in the higher interior, and I never was troubled with them in Blewfields or any of the Creole or Indian settlements along the coast.

The natural history of the mosquito offers many paradoxes for which I do not know how to account. In Australia, the driest country in the world, mosquitoes are very troublesome. They swarm in thousands of millions in the forests of Canada and the bleak tundras of Siberia, nor are frequent hurricanes capable of sweeping them away from the isolated islands of the West Indies or Pacific.

Some mosquitoes attack always in the daytime; most of them, however, are nocturnal. Some are exceedingly shy and wary; other tribes are heedlessly blundering and stupid. Some itch and irritate intolerably; with others the bite produces no bad effects. Mosquitoes have been accused of inoculating into the human blood the germs of intermittent fever, which live in the soil of hot damp places, and, if this is true, it must be allowed that the iniquity of the mosquito surpasses that of any living creature.

Ticks, which are such a nuisance in Brazil, the West Indian Islands, and Queensland, are found here, but they are not very numerous. They generally lie in a cluster the size of a small walnut. The cluster contains some thousands clinging all together, attached to the under side of a leaf. If you should brush by, the cluster attaches to your clothes, and immediately the ticks disperse all over your body. In such a condition the irritation to your skin, covered with ticks the size of a pin's head, is intolerable. You are impelled to tear your clothes off and rush into the water. This, however, will not remove such as have taken hold of your skin, for which purpose it is best to rub them over with chewed tobacco. Generally when you come home in the evening you find a dozen or so fast to the tenderest parts of your body, their heads buried under the skin, and their abdomens just beginning to fill with blood. You should not pull them off, or the head may remain, causing sores; but tobacco will make them let go.

Jiggers are common enough on the coast, but there are few in the interior. This is a very small flea, which lives in the sand or dust. It cannot jump, but runs very quickly. The female burrows into the skin, generally of the toes, and getting down just as far as the quick, without hurting you, there it gestates its eggs. Soon its abdomen increases, until it is some hundred times the size of the body, and looks like a small pea with a little brown speck on it, the speck being the mother's body. It is easily and painlessly removed by the old women, and when this has been done, the gaping hole in your toe is filled with tobacco ashes, and there is no more trouble. Sometimes, however, they cause sores, probably when the person's blood is in bad condition. If the jigger is not taken out, the thousands of eggs hatch in the mother's abdomen and are born. The mother dies and leaves her body in your toe, while the young ones leave the egg-shells, with the result that microbes assemble and cause bad sores.

After staying a few days at Duckwarra and being well feasted on all the good things procurable, we set out with the land-wind at 8 p.m., and made as much offing as possible. Towards 2 a.m. we got among the coral-banks, and could see the bottom, now shining white over patches of sand, now black over banks of coral. Soon a squall came up from the south-east, which turned into a fresh squally sea-breeze, at which we bore away for Cape Gracias à Dios with the wind astern.

Soon we got out of the shoal water, and then found the sea running very high. Immediately we shut down close the companion doors leading to the little cabin where the girls were, closed and secured the main hatch, and stood on the bare deck with only a rope all round to keep us from being washed overboard. We had to haul down the jib, but while everyone called out ' Stow the jib !' no one would venture to do it. Ashamed at our want of discipline, I said I would stow it, and cautiously proceeded forward for that purpose. It was pitch dark, and the canoe was yawing wildly over the waves as her stern was lifted in the air. I got on the bowsprit and crawled out, when suddenly I went under water about 5 feet deep, and if I had not wrapped legs and arms round the bowsprit, I should have been washed off and lost, for they could never have picked me up in that sea. I was very frightened, and kept still for a while, but several more duckings made me recover courage, and I managed to stow the jib and make it fast. When I got back on deck, the girls were hammering and screaming to us to open the door and give them air; so I was set to watch the door and open it when I saw a chance. The girls insisted on coming on deck, but the King would not allow them, and pushed them in again with all his force. Meanwhile the wind and sea were rising, masses of water came over the decks, and the driving spray blinded us. The wild yawing of the boat became dangerous, but the King, who always got excited on such occasions, cried out, 'Carry on, boys! let her have it!' The eldest of the Creole boys, a cool-headed fellow, was steering with the utmost difficulty, and uttering warning grunts, when the boat yawed violently and threatened to run under. At last he called out, 'Better take in sail before we capsize,' and the King was just turning to abuse him for his fears, when our stern was lifted very high, the boat rushed ahead, and, running her bow under water up to the foremast, slewed round and fell on her side. In a moment the other Creole boy let go the halyards, the steersman left the tiller, and, diving into the water, let go the sail sheet. Down came the sail, and the boat righted just in time to save us from sinking.

The girls screamed so much that we became demoralized and frightened, and for a while the boat swashed violently in the trough of the sea, with her sail dragging in the water. I opened the door to comfort the girls, but they yelled and screamed, 'Oh, we will be drowned! let us out!' So I let them out, but the poor things were received with roars of 'Look out!' 'Hold on!' 'You'll be washed overboard!' 'Go below, quick!' So at last, entreating their brother not to put up sail, they went below again, and I shut their door. As I had stowed the jib, I was asked to go and loose it, and, with my heart in my mouth, I crawled out to do so. Instead of being dipped head over heels in the sea, I was violently swayed from side to side this time by the rolling of the vessel, and had great difficulty in keeping my hold; but with one hand and my teeth I managed to loosen the sail, which was then hoisted, and, gathering in our mainsail, we bore off on our course.

The day was now breaking, and sea and sky looked wild and threatening. Black clouds with squalls and driving rain were rolling up from the south-east, and the cold gray sea was covered with breaking waves and clouds of spray. No land was in sight, and we had no compass, but we knew our course in a general sort of way by the run of the waves, which we knew was east-south-east. We dragged along under jib only until day was clear, when we set a close-reefed mainsail, under which we got along well, though still yawing wildly as we ran before the sea; but our oldest Creole boy was a first-rate hand at steering, and not at all apt to get alarmed.

Towards mid-day, finding we were quite safe, we opened the girls' door and let them out, giving them a rope to hold on by. We then cautiously opened the main hatch, and brought out a pot of boiled cassava and turtle meat, prepared for us the day before by the Duckwarra women. We made a comfortable breakfast, and sailing on till 2 p.m., we saw through the rain the trees to the north of the Cape. We therefore hauled our wind and bore to the southward, and soon saw the ghastly line of breakers surrounding the entrance to the harbour. We did not like the look of the surf on the bar, so we brought up head to wind, and considered the subject, and in this state of suspense we made two tacks out and in again. We then saw a canoe with a strong crew, dancing on the crest of the breakers at one moment, and disappearing out of sight the next. Before long we saw that the canoe was outside the breakers and

19

rapidly approaching, driven by the paddles of eight men.
When they came alongside we saw that the crew of strong
Mosquito men, with nothing on but shirts of calico and loin-
cloths of *toonoo*, were wet through, and panting with the
exertion of paddling against wind and sea. They said they
had been sent by Mr. —— Haly, an old resident and magis-
trate of the Cape settlement, to show us the way in. We
asked them what they thought of it, but all they would
say was, 'Siapia ooyasi' (There are heavy breakers). We
asked could they get back in again in the canoe. 'Yes,'
they said, 'we can get in all right.' We then asked them
to take the King's sisters ashore and we would follow them
in the craft. So we transferred the girls, who certainly
seemed to show more confidence in eight stalwart Mosquito
men and a big empty canoe than in our stylish but cranky
yacht.

As soon as the canoe was gone, we took a turn or two,
approaching the breakers and then standing out, all the time
watching the canoe, which when close to the surf rested a
while, looking out for the smallest seas. Then we saw them
make for the breakers and disappear among the seething
waters. Presently we saw them high on the top of a roller,
but between them and us we saw an immense toppling wave
which immediately burst into a white mass. The King
looked on, speechless with fear, while our old *quatmus* exclaimed, 'Alai yaptum!' (Oh, mother!). It seemed to us that
they were upset, it was so long before we could see them.
At last we saw them rise on a breaker a long way in, and
knew they were safe.

We had now to decide what we should do. The King
wanted to set full sail and run in; but wiser counsels prevailed. Our cool-headed Creole boy urged that we could not
sail in, as she would not steer with her stern in the air, and
if she broached to she would certainly roll over; and as to

pulling in with the sweeps, it was not to be thought of. She would take a run with the breaker and broach to, and it would be all up with us. So we reluctantly put to sea close hauled, and passed a weary night beating about, plunging bows under, and all wet to the skin. The wind and sea rapidly subsided, and next day we sailed in comfortably.

CHAPTER XX.

Gracias à Dios—Turtle-tax hunting—The King's second sister—Up the Wanx River.

IN the time of Columbus, and for 250 years afterwards, the harbour of Cape Gracias à Dios was a fine lagoon, enclosed by a sandspit from all winds, and with water enough for the largest ships. About 1740 the English settlers, with their slaves, had brought much of the land under cultivation, and there was a large trade in sugar and other productions. The cultivated land was on the banks of the Wanx River, which flowed into the sea 6 or 8 miles north of the harbour, and the sugar had to be brought in lighters out of the river, round by the sea, and into the harbour. To avoid the delays and inconvenience of such a transit, the settlers, assisted by the Government of Jamaica, cut a canal from the river to the harbour. The river gradually worked its way through the canal, and very soon the whole of it was flowing into the harbour, which was entirely silted up, and a shallow bar formed across the former deep entrance.

One may have an idea of the perplexities which beset the engineer who studies nature in his efforts to make artificial harbours, from the fact that about 1866 the harbour of Greytown did exactly the opposite to that at the Cape. It was formerly a fine deep lagoon, enclosed by a sand spit from all winds, with the San Juan River, which drains Lake Nicaragua, running into it. A small creek, called the

Colorado, flowed out of the river to the sea about 12 miles south of the harbour. In 1856 this creek showed signs of enlarging, and in 1866 the whole San Juan flowed down the Colorado, and the harbour of Greytown was entirely silted up.

The Indian village of the Cape is built at the head of the harbour, with a view over the lagoon and out to sea. The country all round is level and mostly savanna, with clumps of pitch-pine, live oak, and papta palms, while to the north the forest is seen which lines the banks of the Wanx River. The inhabitants are half Sambos, half pure Indians, and this was formerly a powerful and warlike town, which at a moment's notice could raise 1,000 armed men; but now the whole settlement does not number over 500 people, the pestilential breath of civilization having killed them off.

Here a fine house belonging to Mr. —— was assigned to us. It had raised boarded floors, and walls wattled with papta laths, the doors and wooden shutters to the windows and roofs being thatched with silico palm leaves. The owner's Indian wife occupied one room, the King's sisters another, and we slept in hammocks in the big room. We never cooked or ate in our house, either cooking on board the yacht, or dropping in to take pot-luck at any house we chose to enter. The King's sisters were taken possession of by the Indian girls, and never came home till night.

The Cape had long been the home of several white men—English, German, and French—who, disgusted with civilized life, had sought peace and rest among the Indians. We therefore found here many fine half-caste girls, some nearly as white as I am, but wearing nothing but wrappers, and speaking nothing but Mosquito. Although an Indian girl looks perfectly well and suitably dressed in a wrapper, one is taken aback at seeing a white girl in one; but it cannot be denied that for the tropics it is the most beautiful of all female costumes. We also saw some very handsome Sambo girls, whose tall, lithe figures, glossy dark bay skins, and curly heads were quite a contrast to the true copper-coloured Indians.

I have mentioned above how the Sambos came to inhabit the part of the coast from Duckwarra to the Cape. In Brazil the cross between the Red Indian and the negro is looked on as a very bad breed—idle, vicious, violent, prone to all crimes and incapable of settled industry. There is very little crime of any kind on the Mosquito coast, but I remember that, of the little there was, most was among the Sambos. There is some amount of shooting, and fighting with machetes, and one case occurred of what was called 'piracy'—that is, a ship wrecked near Duckwarra was plundered; but this sort of crime is common to every civilized country. However, the Sambos of this coast are good hunters and fishers; they do some work at the mahogany cutting, and are good and faithful servants of the King.

While we enjoyed ourselves at the Cape, receiving all the attention and hospitality which the people always offer to the King and his retinue, the King had occasion to go with Mr. Skelton, a mahogany-cutter, to the Patook River, and he left me in charge of his sisters and his craft.

But first I was instructed to take the quartermaster and twelve men, and go with the craft and a large canoe to the turtle banks, 20 miles to the south-east of the Cape. I was to deliver the King's letter to the captains of two turtling schooners, demanding payment of the tax on the turtle captured, and, failing receipt of the money, to seize all the turtle.

We sailed with the land-wind in the morning, and reached the banks by mid-day. We found one schooner anchored a long way off the banks, and, leaving the craft anchored in smooth shallow water, we had a hard paddle against the sea-breeze to reach the schooner. I made the quartermaster present the letter to the captain, who said he was a free and independent British subject, and he would be d——d if he would pay tax to any *waika*, King or no King. *Waika* in Mosquito means brother-in-law or friend, and is the nick-name given by the English Creoles of Belize to all Mosquito men. We then re-embarked, and, taking the Mosquito men in the canoe, we sailed away for the turtle kraals, about 5 miles to the southward.

Here we found two large kraals full of turtle. The kraals were made of mangrove posts driven into the sand, and lashed together by withes, in about 4 feet of water. In one kraal were about 300 turtle, in the other about 100. The Indians first harpooned six or eight she ones, and secured them to the posts; then they took down the posts in different places and drove the turtle out. Before this was half done we saw the boat from the schooner sailing towards us. When it came up to us the captain, in a furious rage, handled his fowling-piece, and threatened to shoot someone. But the quartermaster and Indians were not to be bullied, and drawing the canoe up to the boat—the quartermaster and several others armed with guns and the rest with machetes—they kept hold of it until the rest of the turtle were out, when they let the captain and crew go, telling him that we would pull down every kraal as fast as it was built unless the tax was paid. We then loaded four of the turtle and returned to the yacht, and in the evening fetched the other four and sailed back to the Cape, where we feasted the village on good fat turtle.

Whilst preparing to go up the Wanx River to visit the King's relations, I noticed that a fine, tall, handsome Indian was always following and hanging about the King's second sister, and that she seemed not at all displeased to see him. I was in charge of the girls, but this was a case I had not contemplated, and I did not know what to do. So I called the attention of the eldest sister, Agnes, to the goings on, and warned her to see that no improprieties were indulged

in.   This courtship was delayed until I had left the country,
but resulted happily at last, and the present King, Clarence,
is the legitimate result.

Having secured the yacht by taking the masts down and
covering the whole deck with sails to keep the sun from
warping the timber, we set out in two canoes for the Wanx
River.   We had a crew of Cape youths, among whom was
our lover; and two half-caste girls, Miss Julia Haly and
Miss Rebecca Warman, accompanied the King's sisters as
playmates.

The river runs through country which is savanna in places,
but generally the banks are lined with forests of black, red,
and white mangroves.   The red is that well-known tree
which grows at the waterside with interwoven roots, the
tree being supported on these at a height of 8 feet or so
above the mud.   The white and black are tall forest trees,
which only grow in boggy land where the salt water reaches.
Any quantity of palms, such as hone, silico, papta, and
others, line the banks where the mud is not too soft.

In the evening we arrived at the settlement where we
were to pass the night.   This village, on the left bank, is
situated nearly two miles back from the river on the rising
savanna.   On passing by a muddy track through a belt of
forest, we found before us a vast meadow covered with
water, and dotted with clumps of pitch-pine and live oak on
the isolated spots which were dry.   The whole meadow was
covered with horses and cattle, grazing on rich grass, over
their knees in water.   As the girls could not wade through
this water, we left them in care of an Indian, and went on
towards the village.   I do not remember ever having such
a wade as this.   We stumbled along over the knees, and
sometimes up to the waist in water, making for the dry
spots to rest at, till at last, utterly exhausted and wet
through, we reached the settlement, where we got some boys
to catch horses and go back for our girls.

This was a village of pure Indians, and all the men were away at the northern mahogany works, only women and boys remaining. Everything I had was wet, as I had tumbled headlong many times into the wet savanna. There was no change to be had, not even a shirt could be found; so I had to put on a man's waistcloth till my clothes were dried. All young men are vain, and I never had my vanity so severely rebuked, or felt so much ashamed, as sitting among these astonished women in a waistcloth. At first they were struck dumb at seeing a white man in their native garb, but presently they shrieked with laughter. The more sedate and elder ones attempted to condole, saying, ' Poor white boy, he is so cold, and his clothes are all wet !' but they could not keep from laughing at times, and I heard the remarks, ' His skin is like a scraped pig !' ' And his yellow hair —why, it's just like a red monkey !' However, the women were very good to me, made a roaring fire, and fed me with ripe plantains, *mishla*, boiled soopa-nuts, cassava, and turtle-oil. As their men were away, they had no meat ; but the Indians of the coast generally have bottles of turtle-oil, which keeps fresh a long time, and is eaten with cassava, plantains, etc.

Towards night the girls arrived on horseback, and then we had a consultation about food. There were plenty of cattle, but no one volunteered to let us have one. However, we inquired whether the headman had cattle, and decided to take one of theirs in the name of the King. In a moment lots of boys volunteered to kill one, so we sent off a number of them with one of our men, and very soon the whole village was gorging fresh beef. The cattle of this village graze in the flooded meadows, which are never dry even in the dry season. They sleep on the rises and hillocks, but in feeding time are always up to their knees in water, consequently their hoofs are very soft, and often drop off, when the animal has to be killed.

Next day we went back to our canoes on horseback without saddles, while a pack-horse carried bundles of sugarcane, baskets of cassava, bunches of plantains, and several chunks of pitch-pine for light at night. These were the presents which the women gave to the King's sisters.

As we paddled up the Wanx River, I noticed the difference between this river and the rivers of the south. The savanna shows up in many places along the banks; the river is shallow, with gravelly banks, in which are cornelians, agates, and other beautiful stones. Fan-palms and willows are much more common, and only on the alluvial bends is there any forest. The savannas are shown by the overhanging banks to be composed of stiff red, white, and mottled clays, with layers of quartz gravel, the surface being covered with a peaty soil, while in places are seen vast patches of the white quartz gravel. These savannas present the appearance of a beautiful park, the ground here level, there rising in undulations and gentle hills clothed in long coarse grass. The clumps of papta or fan-palm dotted here and there are lovely; there are groves of lofty pitch-pines, and in places there are bits of quite European verdure—in dells overgrown with live-oak, willows, and banks of long fern.

At the higher parts of the river the savannas give place to forest, but from here to Brewer's Lagoon the whole country is savanna for 50 or 60 miles in from the coast, and from Brewer's Lagoon to Roman River the country is half forest, half savanna. The Indians have great herds of horses and cattle on these fine pastures. The country is exceedingly beautiful and very healthy, and affords the advantage to settlers of living on the lovely breezy savannas, and cultivating the adjacent rich soil in the bush.

This is the country taken possession of and occupied by the English 200 years ago, but given up in 1856.

Paddling and sailing up the river with a fine sea-breeze following us, we stopped occasionally to shoot the muscovy ducks which we saw on the sandbanks. The drakes are very quarrelsome, fighting furiously on the water, in which occupation they are so absorbed that they may be approached and killed with a stick. At mid-day we landed on a large gravel-bank and had dinner, and then slept under the shade of the sung-sung trees for an hour or two. In the cool of the evening we proceeded up the river, and camped at 8 p.m. on a gravel-bank at a place where a lofty forest clothed both banks. As we lay on the gravel, we listened to the strange cries in the bush—the hooting of the wowya owl, the plaintive cry of the sun-down partridge (tinamu), the occasional screams of parrots, and many strange sounds which came from no one knew what beast or bird. For some hours we heard in a large tree a beast uttering its little warning cry at the sight of our fires, ' queeo, queeo, queeo,' repeated continually at intervals. This is a very rare animal, and I have never seen it in this country, but it is commoner in the far south. It is about twice the size of a guinea-pig, of a golden-brown colour, with the finest fur imaginable. It never ventures out in the daylight. In the books it is called kinkajou.

Towards morning one of the boys woke us up, and we heard the rustling of a tapir in the grass of the river-bank, and its plaintive, whistling cry. We listened for awhile, for it was too dark to do anything; then we shouted, and it rushed into the river. Then we debated whether we should go to sleep again. The morning mists were closing down on us. At a great distance we heard the deep resounding roar of the howling monkey. In the bush the sleepy ' cheep, cheep' of the tarring yoola (formicivora) announced that day was coming, and the snake-hawk was just commencing his melancholy call, ' waaka, waaka,' which can be heard for miles; so we resolved to begin the day at once. Soon we had a steaming pot of coffee, with roast plantains and a piece of beef roasted on the embers, and, having packed our blankets and *toonoos* in the canoes, we set out up the river.

Among the willows of the river-banks are seen flocks of the beautiful cooliling. All along the Wanx River, where the sea-breeze sighs through miles of willows, or rustles through the cutch grass of the banks, and the sun shines upon reach after reach of pebbly banks, one hears the sweet tinkling note of this bird, resembling 'cooliling-ling-ling.' At times large flocks of them are seen migrating to other parts, but they do not all leave the country. As they fly past at night on their migrations, one might imagine that one heard the higher notes of a hundred pianos struck, or that a hundred triangles were tinkling. It lays in June, making a nest in a tuft of grass, and while the hen sits the cock perches close by, warbling very sweetly. The cooliling is 5 inches long, with an expanse of wings of 9 inches; both male and female are quite black, but the former has a patch of red on each shoulder like epaulets.

This day we had a hard fight with the current, but using by turns the paddle, the pole, and the sail, by about 5 p.m. we approached the settlement on the left bank, where the King's mother and others of his relations lived. We fired off guns, which drew all the Indians to the edge of the high bank, and when they made us out we were received with volleys of guns. Then men, women, and children ran down to the landing-place to welcome us. Their cousins and aunts took the girls by the shoulders and smelt their cheeks, which is their fashion of kissing, and the men shook hands heartily. We did not see the King's mother, for she was waiting in her house to give a proper official greeting to her daughters and her step-daughter, for the mother of the youngest, Matilda, was dead long ago. We then all went up the steep bank to the settlement.

CHAPTER XXI.

Reception by Queen-Dowager — Cattle hunting — Fording river — Fly-catchers—Swifts—Bathing—Jaguars—Farewell.

ALREADY the Queen-Dowager was crying, or rather singing, a dirge, and as soon as her daughters came she fell on their necks, and made them sit down. Then she covered herself and them, and, laying a hand on each of their heads, poured forth her dirge, in which, as she was well practised in grief and had a good voice, she performed beautifully.

THE MOTHER'S DIRGE.

' Oh, my children, you have come back to me ;
I was lonely without you.
Other women had their children. I saw them,
And my heart was sore with longing for my daughters.
In the night I thought of my dead boys ;
They called me, " Mother !"
I thought I was alone, and had no children.
I remembered my daughters,
But they were far away among the white people.
My children have come back.
My heart is like the young plantain-leaf,
That shoots out when the sun shines.'

Then, laying her hand on Matilda's head, she sang or cried :

' My girl, your mother is dead ; you will never see her again.
I am your mother now.
Do not cry for your mother ; think of me. I am your mother.

My heart was sore for you when I thought of your dead mother.
When we were young we galloped over the savanna with your
    father.
They are all dead, but you, my girl, are here.'

Then, seeing me looking on at the door, she drew me in,
put her hands on my shoulders, pressed me to a seat, and
threw her cloth over herself and me, and cried to this effect :

'Tookta Saaley [Child Charley] has a white skin ;
He is the playmate of my son.
He grew up with my children.
When I thought of my children among the white people,
I said, "Tookta Saaley is with them ; they will not be lonely."
Often when the sea-breeze blew up the river
I looked for the canoe with my children.
I said, "Tookta Saaley will bring my children to me ;
The white boy will come with them." '

This impressive ceremony over, we were all happy, and
telling the news of the coast to the people who crowded
round. Crowds of women and girls came to see the King's
sisters and their guests, the girls from the Cape. In no time
there were boys yelling, dogs barking, and fowls shrieking,
which was a good sign for supper. The men and boys of
our crew quartered themselves wherever they liked, and I
occupied a string hammock in the house of a man I knew at
the mahogany works. I was at once served by the women
with three boiled alligator-eggs, and roast plantains with salt
ground up with chili-peppers ; but the old Queen sent me a
calabash of boiled fowl and cassava, with another calabash
of chicken-broth. The headman announced that there was
to be a cattle-hunt next day, and we should have a grand
feast of beef.

Early next morning a number of boys went after the horses
and soon drove in about thirty. These were caught with the
lasso and bridled, that is, a small rope was tied loosely
round the lower jaw, leaving two ends for reins. Then each
man, with a lasso and a machete at his waist, mounted

bareback. I was given a horse that did not look up to much, but was said to be quiet, and we all set out for the ford, about half a mile up the river.

The ford was a very wide gravel bank which sloped gradually under the water. On the far side for 200 feet the river was deep, and flowed under clay banks overhanging the water, about 10 feet high; but just above was a gravel beach sloping up the bank.

One by one the men rode into the river some distance above the gravel beach, so that the drift of the current should just land the horse on it. Each man, as his horse got out of its depth, slipped off its back at the up side, and holding on by the horse's mane, swam beside it, to mount again when the horse touched bottom. I was uneasy as to whether I could swim my horse in this manner, and an Indian offered to swim it for me if I would swim over without it; but I thought I should be laughed at by the girls, and the boys would give me a nickname which would stick to me; so I made bold to swim my horse. Accordingly, I rode into the river last of all, and when the horse threw up his head and began to swim I slipped off. But I must have foolishly kept hold of the reins, for the horse turned his breast to the current, which brought him into an upright position, with his fore-hoofs pawing the air. The current swept me into his breast, and he struck the top of my head with his hoof.

I went down under water senseless, but came to the surface near the high clay-banks, and the Indians running along the bank as I drifted past, at last managed to catch me in the noose of a lasso, and dragged me ashore. After disgorging a gallon of water, I recovered sufficiently to mount my horse, which had turned back to the far side, but was captured and brought over again.

For about half a mile we rode through thick forest, and then came on a beautiful savanna with groves of oaks, pines, and fan-palms dotted all over it, with a sea of waving grass, over which the shadows of the clouds chased each other, as they drove before the strong trade wind.

I soon tired of riding over the endless undulating grass, driving herds of cattle before us, so I rode about to amuse myself, keeping near the path so as to know when the men would return. I came upon large coveys of the pilgaro fly-catcher buried in deep grass, probably feeding on the seeds. Occasionally they would rise in the air and be drifted about by the strong wind, with their long tails bent under or over their bodies in a most uncomfortable manner, till they again found refuge in the grass. I once saw one of these birds perched on a twig near a heap of ashes from a large fire which had gone out. Presently it darted into the middle of the heap and flapped its wings vigorously, covering itself with a cloud of dust, stood among the ashes for a minute or two, then returned to its perch. This it repeated twenty or thirty times, till it had dispersed the ashes, and then flew away. This bird is 12 inches long, of which the tail alone is 7 inches

I saw also pairs of the battledoor flycatcher perched on burnt trees, and patiently hawking for flies. They constantly call to each other in a peevish tone, 'Mees, mees,' from which the Indians call it mees. This is a very elegant bird, 5 inches long with 8 inches expanse of wings. It is all black, with the crown of the head gray, and a streak of gray passes from the head down the neck and back. The tail is short and square, but the two outer feathers, narrow and flexible, are three times the length of the tail.

The large gray swift, called by the Indians pleeplee (the javelin or throwing spear), from the amazing velocity with which it flies past, is here seen coursing over the savanna, sometimes rising over the high trees, then skimming the grass, wheeling and circling all over the country in pursuit of flies. These birds are migratory. They come to us in February, whence they are hailed by the Indians as a sign of the dry season, when bush may be burnt for plantations. I have seen them in November, assembling in great flocks and flying off towards the north-west.

As we waited a long time for the King to come from Mr. Skelton's mahogany works at Black River, we had fine times hunting and fishing, but we took the greatest delight in bathing in the river. About a mile above the settlement there was a lovely gravel bank sloping into deep water. The water was clear as glass, and there were no alligators about. The whole of the young men and boys, and all the girls and young women, would go down to bathe together, in number about 200. The girls went round the turn of the beach to take their wrappers off, and soon were seen in shoals swimming, diving, and playing at water games, such as they practise, while the men and boys, separated from them by a hundred yards or so, pursued their water sports on their own ground. How beautiful and happy they all looked as they swam about like fish, and what a contrast to the solemn misery of Europeans bathing in their elaborate costumes, with oilskin caps to keep the hair dry! Yet these Indian men and women are just as modest as we are, and more innocent, and happier.

While we waited here some Indians from farther up the river brought the skin of a black jaguar as a present for the King. It measured 7 feet from the nose to the root of the tail. This beast during the past four months had killed twenty cattle, nearly as many horses, and all the calves in the neighbourhood.

The black jaguar is more frequently found in the northern parts of this country, but is so rare that I never saw one alive. Although all the leopard tribe have their black variety—the Indian, African, and American—I think that ours is only a 'sport,' that is, that the spotted jaguar occasionally gives birth to the black kind. In the districts

20

of Black River and Truxillo they are somewhat numerous, and people are often killed by them.

I met an Indian once who was fearfully disfigured. Both his ears were gone, and one cheek had only some stretched skin adhering to the bone. His left breast was entirely gone, and only a thin skin attached to the ribs. There were large holes on his shoulders and neck. The flesh was torn off his ribs in several places, and his belly, thighs, and legs showed great scars. He told me that he and his companions were hunting, when they came on a drove of warree, and separated to surround it. He was making his way through the bush, when he came face to face with a black jaguar. He wished to avoid it for fear that the noise might frighten the game he was after. So he turned off another way, but he soon met the beast facing him again. As he could not get away peaceably, he let fly an arrow at it. The arrow touched a twig, and passed through the thigh of the 'tiger' instead of its heart as intended. Instantly it sprang at him and dashed him against a tree, sending his arrows flying out of his hand. For a minute he defended himself with his bow, but that soon broke to pieces, and his back slipping off the tree, he fell to the ground with the 'tiger' on top of him. In this position he received the wounds of which the scars were such shocking evidence. A minute or two more would have decided the contest, but the drove of warree having escaped, his companions now heard his cries, and one of them transfixed the 'tiger' with an arrow. At that moment its hind claws were buried in the man's thighs, and as it sprang into the air at its death-wound, it tore his thighs down to the shin-bones of his legs.

Probably no white man would have survived such wounds, much less with the unskilful treatment and rough food which this patient had; but the Indians recover in a marvellous manner from the most desperate wounds; and the same

thing is noticed in the blacks of Australia, who easily recover from wounds that would be fatal to Europeans.

It is now a great many years since I left the Mosquito
Coast. Since then I have seen all the great civilized communities of Europe, America, and the Colonies. I am
therefore able to judge the results of the various schemes of
life under which the nations live, and, judging by results,
one cannot resist the conviction that our scheme of civilization is a failure in securing to the peoples the happiness
which constitutes the sole object of life. We see that all
the triumphs of civilization, which are its pride and boast,
must necessarily be confined to one-tenth of the people, while
nine-tenths are doomed to live a life compared with which
that of these Indians is an earthly paradise. We see these
Indians, though far inferior to us whites in mental ability,
yet possessing a more intimate knowledge of nature, and
even of all their surrounding world; with a keener and more
wholesome interest in all the phenomena of nature, and of
the sayings and doings of the people around them, than
nine-tenths of the vast multitudes of the civilized world
possess. They are more sympathetic and more loving to
each other, fonder of children, parents, and relations, and
more gentle and more longsuffering to each other's failings
than civilized people are.

They are singularly free from crimes of all kinds, especially
the gentle, tractable Indians of the interior; and in all my
long sojourn among them I was treated with a kindness and
disinterested affection such as I could hardly expect to receive
from white people in similar circumstances.

Living the precarious life of hunters, they suffer all the
vicissitudes of hunger and plenty, hard work and complete
relaxation. They have neither religion, nor laws, nor
police, yet they are orderly, well-conducted, cheerful, and
happy, and when it comes to the last they die with dignity
and composure, very different from the death of appre-

hension and fear which I have so often seen among my Christian fellow-countrymen and women.

The only miseries these people have to endure arise from their contact with civilization, which is slowly exterminating them. They are afflicted with the continual importation of new diseases, engendered amid civilized life, which spread among them with frightful virulence. Chief among these is our common catarrh, or cold, which spreads periodically from the coast among the tribes of the interior, assuming a virulent development unknown to us, and most fatal to young children, who generally die of some affection like pneumonia.

Of course I know that it is impossible for a civilized and Christian people to look upon any savages and heathens without aversion and contempt, and regarding them, as we do the animals, 'as the beasts that perish.' Nevertheless, one has only to learn their language and live among them as one of themselves, to find that they have all the faculties, affections, emotions, loves, hates, and fears, just the same as ourselves, to which their innate simplicity and unsophistication lend a peculiar charm.

Even after 200 years of contact with the most debauched and vicious of Europeans who live among them, the Mosquito Indians still preserve much of their original frank, honest, courageous, and open-hearted nature.

Their end, however, is at hand now. Delivered over by the English to their hereditary enemies, already they are worried to death by proselytizing monks and priests ; and every pretext is sought to infringe upon their liberty, to bring them under taxation, and force them to live in industrial communities ; and we know that such radical change of habits is fatal to all free and wild people, just as it would be fatal to a stag to yoke it to a cart.

APPENDIX A.

LANGUAGE.

THE language of the Mosquito Indians is supposed to be a dialect of the original Caribs of the Antilles, and is different from those of the other tribes in the country, although many words are by long contact common to the Woolwas, or Smoos, and the Mosquitoes. It has the well-known peculiarities of construction and of grammar which distinguish the languages of the American Indians. The grammar is precise and somewhat complicated, but probably less involved than the grammár of French or German; and it seems strange to find among an uncultivated and uncivilized race rules of grammar as precise and well known as are used by the most cultivated nations of Europe. The Indian, who has no literature, no written or defined rules, uses the grammar of his language with uniformity and without confusion. How is this to be explained? Let me give an example.

Every verb in the Mosquito language ends in ' ahya '— ' ihsoobahya,' to be born; 'prooahya,' to die; 'balahya,' to come; 'wahya,' to go; 'dowkahya,' to make; 'bihkahya,' to break.

Many verbs are irregular; most are regular. Thus a regular verb is 'wahya,' to go; 'wun,' gone.

Indicative present.

yung (I) wahya, I am going.
man (thou) wahya, thou art going.
wittin (he) wahya, he is going.

Plural and singular are the same in the verb, the pronouns being ' yungnanny,' we; ' mananny,' you; ' wittinanny,' they.

Indicative imperfect.	*Indicative future.*
watney, I went.	wahmney, I shall go.
watma, thou wentest.	wahma, thou shalt go.
wata, he went.	wahbia, he shall go.

Imperative.	*Interrogative.*
wahs, go thou.	wahtna ? did I go ?
wahpey, let us go.	wahmna ? shall I go ?

An irregular verb is 'yahya,' to give ; 'yun,' gave.

Indicative present.	*Indicative imperfect.*
yung issney, I give.	yung issatney, I gave.
man issma, thou givest.	man issatma, thou gavest.
wittin issa, he gives.	wittin issata, he gave.

Future.	*Imperative.*
yahmney, I shall give.	yahs, give thou.
yahma, thou shalt give.	yahpey, let us give.
yahbia, he shall give.	

Interrogative.

issatna ? did I give ?

yahmna ? shall I give ?

Of course there are more tenses than the above, compounded with prefixes as in European languages.

The language is remarkably complete and full in all terms which the Indians are likely to use ; in some respects even more so than English. It is, however, poor in terms to express abstract thoughts. Such abstract terms as they use are adopted from simpler words in precisely the same way as in European languages, only they have not carried the process so far as we have. Thus there is no proper word for 'love,' but 'lahtwan' is made to do for it. 'Sowra lumptwun ih dowkisa' (I love you very much) literally means, 'Pain for you affects me badly '; or, 'Your pain affects me badly.'

All nouns have inflections; thus 'wahtla,' house ; 'wumtla,' your house ; 'wytla,' my house ; 'wahtla,' his house ; and one must beware of the irregularities which occur here. Thus 'yool,' dog ; 'yoolum,' your dog ; 'yooley,' my dog ; 'yoola,' his dog ; 'ruckboos,' a gun ; 'ruckboos-kum,' your gun ; 'ruckboos-key,' my gun ; 'ruckboos-ka,' his gun.

The most singular thing about this language is one common, it is said, to all the American languages. In a sentence some of the words are cut in pieces, and the pieces stuck into the sentence in different places.   Thus 'kitty oompmapara eews ih tihbisma nicka,' means 'sit over a little; you are squeezing me.'   Here 'kitteewahya,' the verb 'to move,' has imperative 'kitteews,' ('move you'), which is cut in two; a 'y' is added to the first half, and the other half, 'eews,' is stuck in elsewhere.

With all this the Mosquito language is easily learned, and the pronunciation is simple.   The Mosquito Indians handle their language with skill and facility; but, like all American Indians, they make extensive use of gestures by hands, eyes, and head. They are lively, talkative, and, like all healthy people in whom the nerves are not cultivated at the expense of the body, they are cheerful and good-tempered.

APPENDIX B.

I.

(1) Keeka mihren tumnia-nanny teelara towkee
Awala beela mookoos eewee-can
Moona weena owas keea bihwee-can,
Yoo coom youngra lookeemooney
' Mahma palley watma-key
Alai mahma yawan kihkatna-key
Yawan palley beelam bihkra walatna-weesmaba,
Alai, alai, alai !'

(2) Keeka mihren sarcum sowra Ih dowkeysa
Tum ia-keea palley lookisney
Lameea poora lihla prawi Ih dowkeysa
Coona nahara Doos moona bowisney
Keeihmara Cabo bin man walisney
Seeapeea lattara tilwee coona
Beelam-bihkra sip walruss-key
Alai, alai, alai !*

II.

Alai Yaptey-yaptey oompeera
Alai yaptey ansara warum ?
Sarkum atia loopiam-nanny innee bungweeba
Nowala yowanwul ihseekata coona nānara bārra prahwisma.
Alai yaptey teela weena coopiam bihwey owmakey
Lumptwan apia katnaki ?
Lattera miham ih macoopey eeweeba
Nahara mihrin any ih weeta srookey eeweebung-weeba
Sahrkum atia seeka.
Bun bacoona ih loolkisiwarum
Alai mawan klee kihkamn' apia-ba
Klee beelam bihkra walamn' apia-ba.†

* English version on p. 89.
† English version on p. 91.

APPENDIX C.

PROCLAMATION.

' KNOW all men by these presents, that We, George Augustus Frederic, by the Grace of God, Hereditary King of Mosquito and its Insular Dependencies, being now of more than full legal age to entitle Us, according to the Laws and Usages of other Nations and to those of this our Kingdom of Mosquito in particular, to assume, in our own person, the supreme power in all matters connected with the government of this our Kingdom of Mosquito, which power has hitherto, during our minority and since its expiration, been exercised by the Consuls of our beneficent Ally and Protectrix, Her Britannic Majesty, as acting on our behalf, We have deemed it expedient, for the benefit of our said Kingdom and the more regular and satisfactory administration of its affairs, to assume the said supreme power in all administrative matters ;

' We therefore Proclaim and Declare it to be our will and our determination to assume the said supreme power accordingly, and that every official Commission, Warrant and other writing, connected with the administration of this our said Kingdom of Mosquito and its Insular Dependencies, issued henceforth, must, in order to give it legal validity, possess our signature and seal, or the signature of the individual to whom, in each Department of Government, We may see fit to delegate the power and authority connected with each such Department, and that henceforth all Customs, Dues and Taxes appertaining to the general revenue of this our Kingdom of Mosquito and its Insular Dependencies must be paid or remitted into the hands of the functionary or functionaries whom We shall empower to receive them, and who shall be empowered to grant competent discharges.

' Given under our hand and seal, at Blewfields, this fourth day of March in the year of Grace one thousand eight hundred and fifty-four, and of our reign the twelfth.

' By His Majesty's Commands.

' JAS. STANISLAUS BELL,

' His Mosquito Majesty's Principal Secretary.'

APPENDIX D.

(Copy of letter to James S. Bell.)

BLEWFIELDS, *June* 20, 1854.

' MY DEAR SIR,

' I received your note respecting the people who robbed your goods at Prinzapalka. I have also to say that it was my intention to have called at Prinzapalka on my way down, but could not on account of bad weather. I will, however, take the first opportunity of inquiring into it.

' Will you be good enough to let me know what arrangements were made between Mr. Green and yourself regarding your mahogany-cutting location, as I do not see any record of it in the book of grants Mr. Geddes brought up here with him.

' With regard to the Rama you allude to, I heard from another Rama that he was shot by accident and not intendly, but perhaps you have heard more about it, so I should like to hear the truth.

' An answer will oblige

' Yours truly,

' GEORGE R.'

(Copy of letter to C. Napier Bell.)

PATOOK RIVER,
April 4th, 1855.

' MY DEAR CHARLEY,

' I am sorry to say that Mr. Skelton was still absent when I arrived here, and I am told that he will be up the river about three weeks, so I have made up my mind to take a trip up to his works, as my business will not allow me to return without seeing him. I leave this morning, and hope to be down again in about ten days. I shall make all the haste I can to be here at the fixed time. If you have succeeded in getting turtles, please to tell Nicholas to take them down to Blewfields ; he must also get a crawl made to put them in, but he must try and get the loan of Christopher's crawl until he finishes the one I wish him to make.

' Remember that my sisters are to accompany you as you have to go down in the largest boat. Please to see the other boat pulled up under the cocoanut-trees and the sails properly dried and put away before you leave.

' If you get turtles pick a good one for yourself, when you get to Blewfields.

' Yours faithfully,
' GEORGE A. FREDERICK.'

INDEX.

THE END.